No Fear Guide for
First Time Parents

FOCUS
ON THE
FAMILY®

NO FEAR GUIDE FOR

First Time Parents

THE
FOCUS ON
THE FAMILY
PHYSICIANS RESOURCE
COUNCIL, U.S.A.

PRIMARY AUTHOR
Paul C. Reisser, M.D.

MANAGING EDITOR
Melissa R. Cox

EDITORS
Vinita Hampton Wright, Lisa A. Jackson

Tyndale House Publishers, Inc.
WHEATON, ILLINOIS

The information contained in this book provides a general overview of many health-related topics. It is not intended to substitute for advice you might receive from your child's physician, whether by telephone or during a direct medical evaluation. Furthermore, health-care practices are continually updated as a result of medical research and advances in technology. You should therefore check with your child's doctor if there is any question about current recommendations for a specific problem. No book can substitute for a direct assessment of your child by a qualified health-care professional.

Visit Tyndale's exciting Web site at www.tyndale.com

The Focus on the Family No Fear Guide for First Time Parents, first printing, 2002. Excerpted and adapted from The Focus on the Family Complete Book of Baby and Child Care, ©1997 by Focus on the Family. All rights reserved. International copyright secured.

Focus on the Family is a registered trademark of Focus on the Family, Colorado Springs, Colorado.

Scripture quotations are taken from the Holy Bible, New International Version®. NIV®. Copyright © 1973, 1978, 1984 by International Bible Society. Used by permission of Zondervan Publishing House. All rights reserved.

Cover photographs copyright © 2001 by Michael Hudson. All rights reserved.

Edited by Vinita Hampton Wright and Lisa A. Jackson.

Designed by Kelly Bennema

Printed in the United States

ISBN 0-8423-5614-2

08 07 06 05 04 03 02
7   6   5   4   3   2   1

Table of Contents

Introduction

Why call a book about caring for a tiny, helpless infant a "No Fear" guide? If you are about to have your first baby, or you've just brought your firstborn son or daughter home from the hospital, you no doubt have an idea why this is an appropriate title. It's one thing to admire a smiling cherub in a magazine ad, or to coo and cuddle with someone else's baby, or even to serve a tour of duty baby-sitting for an evening. It's quite another to have twenty-four-hour responsibility for your own infant, who for the next few months can do nothing whatsoever to take care of himself (except to let everyone know, in no uncertain terms, when he isn't happy).

The questions that may be looming in your mind can be very unsettling: *What will it be like to have someone need me around the clock? Am I ready for this? What if I make a mistake? Aren't newborns awfully fragile? And what about* my *life? Will it ever be the same again?* These concerns will be magnified, and may even seem overwhelming, if the circumstances surrounding the arrival of a new baby are less than ideal. A troubled marriage (or no marriage at all), a pregnancy that was unexpected or a full-blown crisis, financial hardship, conflicts with relatives, and a host of other problems may make the thought of caring for a newborn a source of flat-out, gut-wrenching fear.

The good news is this: You are not the first parent to have felt some anxiety (or near panic) about the prospect of adding a newborn to your family. And there's even better news: Generations of parents have gone before you—not to mention physicians, researchers, and a host of other professionals—and have blazed very well-marked trails for you to follow. The best news is that the Creator of every newborn already knows and loves your baby, and you as well. For those who seek Him, He is a "refuge and strength, an ever present help in trouble. Therefore we will not fear" (Psalm 46:1-2). It is our prayer that this book will help allay your fears by serving as a parent-friendly guide to the first few months with your new son or daughter, and by encouraging you to trust God, the perfect (and always available) Parent, for daily wisdom and encouragement.

The *No Fear Guide for First Time Parents* is an updated edition of several chapters and relevant sections of *The Focus on the Family Complete Book of Baby and Child Care*. It includes a detailed chronological tour of your baby's life from conception through the first three months after birth, including:

- Details about physical and behavioral development
- Specific preparations—physical, emotional, and spiritual—that parents can and should make prior to the arrival of their firstborn
- Practical information about basic topics such as feeding, sleep, safety, and signs of possible problems during the newborn months
- Particular chapters dealing with important topics such as adoption, birth defects, and "baby blues"
- Encouragement for strengthening your marriage, meeting the special challenges of single parenting, avoiding burnout, and in general surviving and thriving during this unique period of your family's life.

As you begin to read this book, or refer back to it in the future, it is important that you keep a few cautionary points in mind. First, this book is intended to serve as a road map to help orient and guide you through the first few months of your baby's life. It does not provide detailed directions for every conceivable situation you might encounter along the way, nor is the advice it contains cast in concrete. The basic principles set forth in this book must be molded and adjusted to best fit you and your baby.

Second, this book is not intended to serve as a substitute for specific input that you will receive from your baby's physician. You will be encouraged many times throughout these pages to contact a doctor or (if the situation is urgent) to take your newborn directly to a medical facility. *No book can substitute for a direct assessment of your baby by a qualified healthcare professional.*

Finally, despite our ongoing efforts to include the most current information, the "current wisdom" in the field of health care changes continuously, especially in areas such as immunization guidelines. What was hot news when this book went to press may be outdated in a matter of months. This is another reason to check with your baby's doctor if you have any questions about particular situations you might encounter.

For the physicians who serve on the Focus on the Family Physicians Resource Council, the *Complete Book of Baby and Child Care* and its various special editions and updates have been an ongoing labor of love. It is our heartfelt desire that this particular resource will greatly enhance the first months of your parenting journey.

Paul C. Reisser, M.D.

Foreword

by Dr. James Dobson

If you've picked up this book, it is likely that you are a parent, soon to be one, or know someone who is. Maybe you and your spouse are expecting your first child. Pregnancy has been an experience more precious and indescribable than you could ever have imagined. Ultrasound photos, despite their blurry resolution, provide incontrovertible evidence of your baby's developing hands and feet, the shape of his or her head, the not-yet-seeing eyes. As this fragile life takes shape, you can't help being filled with wonder at the intricate, unfolding miracle of God's handiwork.

Perhaps your scenario is not so idyllic. Maybe you are not yet out of high school. The father of your baby conveniently excused himself when he learned of your condition. You've lived at home with your mom and dad throughout your pregnancy, or perhaps in a halfway house with other girls in crisis pregnancies.

Or your grown daughter has rejected her own baby, and now you're being asked to bring up your grandchild. Or you're a single dad trying to find your way in a world that fails to recognize that sometimes daddies have to be mommies as well. This book was written with you in mind as well.

Under the best of circumstances, becoming a parent for the first time is a challenging assignment. As your child grows up—and perhaps other children are added to your family— you will be called on to don a variety of hats, among them teacher, doctor, psychologist, friend, and pharmacist. As you contemplate the challenges ahead, you may feel overwhelmed by the responsibility. How will you nurture healthy self-esteem in your children? How will you teach them to protect themselves from unhealthy ideas, attitudes, habits, and associations? How will you build within them discernment and self-discipline? How will you develop in them, day by day, the values that are so basic to their well-being? And—one of the toughest questions of all—how will you guide them into independence until they themselves are walking with God in wisdom and truth, rather than simply following you?

The most discerning, vigilant, and competent parents ultimately find themselves feeling inadequate to accomplish these important tasks. A parent must have support, guidance, and encouragement—from other parents, from friends and family, from physicians and pastors. And we believe that, ultimately, each child must be entrusted to the care, love, and protection of Jesus Christ. I urge you not to shortchange your children by underestimating the importance of biblical precepts—either in the values you teach or in the way you conduct your own life. The stakes are simply too high.

Here at Focus on the Family, we recognize that parenting a child involves the care and nurture of the whole person—body, mind, and soul. That's why I'm particularly excited to be able to introduce to you this wonderful new offering from Tyndale House Publishers, *The Focus on the Family No Fear Guide for First Time Parents.* This comprehensive, well-researched volume offers detailed advice from many of the country's most highly respected physicians and medical authorities. Some have appeared as guests on the *Focus on the Family* radio broadcast, and many are members of Focus's prestigious Physicians Resource Council. This book is full of practical, specific guidance on every aspect of one of the most challenging and exciting times in your life: those first few months of parenting.

And what truly sets this book apart is the spiritual guidance and encouragement woven throughout its pages. You will find bits of wisdom straight from Scripture to not only encourage you as a parent, but also to help you begin thinking about ways to instill in your little ones the timeless truths of the Bible—and the foundation of faith upon which rest our ultimate hope and salvation.

You yourself may have gotten a rough start in life. You may not have received the nurturing and encouragement you deserved as a child. Maybe you've struggled with issues of low self-esteem and feelings of rejection from your own parents. If that's your story, I have good news for you: Starting here, you can do better by your own child. It begins with dedicating yourself and your baby to the care of the only truly perfect parent—the Lord Jesus Christ.

Whatever your parenting situation—be it by choice or by chance, whether the circumstances are ideal or heartbreaking, whether yours is a background of poverty or privilege—it matters not. What does matter is that you have been charged by God with a profound and sacred trust: that of shaping and nurturing a human life. Handle it with care. God bless you!

James Dobson

Acknowledgments

In many ways, the preparation of this book has resembled the process of parenting a child from infancy to adulthood. Our "baby" was born in enthusiastic brainstorming sessions, during which exciting and formidable proposals were set in motion. During the book's infancy, as the first chapters and reference topics were written, we slowly began to appreciate the amount of time, effort, and patience that would be required before our "young adult" would be ready to meet the world.

But there was no turning back. We eventually hit our stride over a period of months as more chapters and topics were written, reviewed, debated, revised, and reviewed again—often as many as nine or ten times over the course of several months. Our "child" grew and matured and received ongoing prayer, loving attention, and correction until another rite of passage arrived: an "adolescence" of sorts, when hundreds of pages of manuscript were presented to Tyndale House Publishers. More questions, suggestions, and insights from Tyndale's team led to further refinements, sometimes after spirited (but inevitably fruitful) discussions.

Finally graduation day has arrived, and our offspring is now vacating the nest and beginning an independent life, one that we pray will enhance and assist your family.

This project is the result of a diligent and cooperative effort of many talented individuals over a period of nearly three years. To all of them we are deeply indebted. While we cannot fully acknowledge the full length and breadth of their contributions, the following is our attempt to give credit where it is most certainly due.

First of all, a standing ovation is due to the members of the Physicians Resource Council review team, who spent endless hours in conference calls and many days in sometimes cramped quarters reviewing literally every letter of the manuscript. We thank you for your dedication, perseverance, patience, professionalism, and commitment.

THE FOCUS ON THE FAMILY PHYSICIANS RESOURCE COUNCIL REVIEW TEAM AND CONTRIBUTING EDITORS

Marilyn Maxwell Billingsly, M.D.
Internal Medicine/Pediatrics—ST. LOUIS, MISSOURI

Douglas O. W. Eaton, M.D.
Internal Medicine—ATHENS, ALABAMA

J. Thomas Fitch, M.D.
Pediatrics—SAN ANTONIO, TEXAS

Patricia O. Francis, M.D.
Pediatrics—MORAGA, CALIFORNIA

Gaylen M. Kelton, M.D.
Family Medicine—INDIANAPOLIS, INDIANA

Richard D. Kiovsky, M.D.
Family Medicine—INDIANAPOLIS, INDIANA

Robert W. Mann, M.D.
Pediatrics—ARLINGTON, TEXAS

Paul Meier, M.D.
Psychiatry—RICHARDSON, TEXAS

Mary Anne Nelson, M.D.
Family Medicine—CEDAR RAPIDS, IOWA

The remaining members of the Focus on the Family Physicians Resource Council, in both the United States and Canada, also contributed to this project in a variety of ways.

UNITED STATES

John P. Livoni, M.D. (chair)
Radiology—SACRAMENTO, CALIFORNIA

Peter F. Armstrong, M.D.
Orthopedics—SALT LAKE CITY, UTAH

Reed Bell, M.D.
Pediatrics—GULF BREEZE, FLORIDA

Robb Blackwood, M.D.
Family Medicine—CHESAPEAKE, VIRGINIA

Eugene Diamond, M.D.
Pediatrics—CHICAGO, ILLINOIS

Thomas E. Elkins, M.D.
Obstetrics/Gynecology—BALTIMORE, MARYLAND

W. David Hager, M.D.
Obstetrics/Gynecology—LEXINGTON, KENTUCKY

Walter Larimore, M.D.
Family Medicine—KISSIMMEE, FLORIDA

Alan A. Nelson, M.D.
Psychiatry—REDSTONE, COLORADO

Claudia Nelson, M.D.
Pediatrics—REDSTONE, COLORADO

Donald Nelson, M.D.
Family Medicine—CEDAR RAPIDS, IOWA

Jeffrey B. Satinover, M.D.
Psychiatry—WESTON, CONNECTICUT

Curtis Stine, M.D.
Family Medicine—DENVER, COLORADO

Morton Woolley, M.D.
General Surgeon—LOS ANGELES, CALIFORNIA

CANADA

Margaret Cottle, M.D. (chair)
Palliative Care—VANCOUVER, BRITISH COLUMBIA

Ron Calderisi, M.D.
General Surgeon—VANCOUVER, BRITISH COLUMBIA

Stephen Genuis, M.D.
Obstetrics/Gynecology—EDMONTON, ALBERTA

Jim Gilbert, M.D.
General Surgeon—PEMBROKE, ONTARIO

Rosemarie Gilbert, M.D.
Family Medicine—PEMBROKE, ONTARIO

Ron Jarvis, M.D.
Family Medicine—DUNCAN, BRITISH COLUMBIA

Tim Kelton, M.D.
Family Medicine—NORTH YORK, ONTARIO

Peter Nieman, M.D.
Pediatrics—CALGARY, ALBERTA

Dickson Vinden, M.D.
Family Medicine—CANNINGTON, ONTARIO

Peter Webster, M.D.
Respiratory Medicine—TORONTO, ONTARIO

In addition to the members of the Physicians Resource Council, we would like to thank the many contributors who provided research, written material, and reviews of topics in their field of expertise:

Jane Anderson, M.D.
Pediatrics—SAN FRANCISCO, CALIFORNIA

Karl Anderson, M.D.
Urology—SAN FRANCISCO, CALIFORNIA

Brian L. Burke Jr., M.D.
Pediatrics—GRAND RAPIDS, MICHIGAN

Robin Cottle, M.D.
Ophthalmology—VANCOUVER, BRITISH COLUMBIA

Sarah Chandler, M.D.
Family Medicine—LUBBOCK, TEXAS

M. C. Culbertson Jr., M.D.
Pediatric Otolaryngology—DALLAS, TEXAS

William G. Culver, M.D.
Allergy-Immunology—LOVELAND, COLORADO

Joyce Fischer, M.D.
Pediatrics—BLUFFTON, INDIANA

Russell Engevik, M.D.
Emergency Medicine—JULIAN, CALIFORNIA

Linda Flower, M.D.
Family Medicine—TOMBALL, TEXAS

Lawrence P. Frick, M.D.
Family Medicine—CHILLICOTHE, OHIO

Stanley Hand, M.D.
Ophthalmology—ORLANDO, FLORIDA

John Hartman, M.D.
Family Medicine—KISSIMMEE, FLORIDA

Gerald Hough, M.D.
Pediatrics—BRANDON, FLORIDA

Duke Johnson, M.D.
Family Medicine—TUSTIN, CALIFORNIA

W. Kip Johnson, M.D.
Family Medicine—IRVINE, CALIFORNIA

Ronald Jones, M.D.
Pediatrics—SPRINGFIELD, MISSOURI

Paul Liu, M.D.
Pediatrics—PHOENIX, ARIZONA

Margaret Meeker, M.D.
Pediatrics—TRAVERSE CITY, MICHIGAN

Carl Meyer, D.O.
Pediatrics—GREENVILLE, PENNSYLVANIA

Michael C. Misko, M.D.
Family Medicine—HOLDEN, MISSOURI

D. Brett Mitchell, M.D.
Family Medicine—DENISON, TEXAS

John Moyer, M.D.
Pediatrics—DENVER, COLORADO

Steve Parnell, M.D.
Family Medicine—FAIRMONT, MINNESOTA

Jan Payne, M.D.
Pathology—ST. PAUL, ALASKA

John C. Rhodes, M.D.
Family Medicine—LAS VEGAS, NEVADA

David Sadowitz, M.D.
Pediatric Hematology/Oncology—CAMINUS, NEW YORK

Bodo Treu, M.D.
Family Medicine—OMAHA, NEBRASKA

G. Scott Voorman, M.D.
Otolaryngology—THOUSAND OAKS, CALIFORNIA

James C. Wilkes, M.D.
Pediatrics/Pediatric Nephrology—LEXINGTON, KENTUCKY

Franklin D. Wilson, M.D.
Orthopedics—INDIANAPOLIS, INDIANA

Gentry Yeatman, M.D.
Adolescent Medicine—TACOMA, WASHINGTON

*We would like to thank the following individuals for reviewing
segments of the completed manuscript for accuracy:*

Mary Beth Adam, M.D.
Adolescent Medicine—TUCSON, ARIZONA

Stephen Apaliski, M.D.
Pediatric Allergy—FORT WORTH, TEXAS

Sarah Blumenschein, M.D.
Pediatric Cardiology—FORT WORTH, TEXAS

Paul Bowman, M.D.
Pediatric Hematology/Oncology—FORT WORTH, TEXAS

Preston W. Campbell, M.D.
Pediatric Pulmonology—NASHVILLE, TENNESSEE

James Cunningham, M.D.
Pediatric Pulmonology—FORT WORTH, TEXAS

Mary Davenport, M.D.
Obstetrics/Gynecology—BERKELEY, CALIFORNIA

Mary A. Eyanson, M.D.
Pediatrics—CEDAR RAPIDS, IOWA

David Michael Foulds, M.D.
Pediatrics—SAN ANTONIO, TEXAS

Roni Grad, M.D.
Pediatric Pulmonology—SAN ANTONIO, TEXAS

W. Wayne Grant, M.D.
Pediatrics—SAN ANTONIO, TEXAS

David Gregory, D.Ph.
Pharmacology—NASHVILLE, TENNESSEE

Lyn Hunt, M.D.
Pediatric Gastroenterology—FORT WORTH, TEXAS

Vernon L. James, M.D.
Developmental Medicine—SAN ANTONIO, TEXAS

Cheryl Kissling, R.N.
Lactation Consultant—CEDAR RAPIDS, IOWA

Mary Kukolich, M.D.
Genetics—FORT WORTH, TEXAS

Risé L. Lyman, D.D.S.
General Dentistry—SAN ANTONIO, TEXAS

Everett Moody, M.D.
Pediatric Ophthalmology—ARLINGTON, TEXAS

Britt Nelson, M.D.
Pediatric Intensive Care—ARLINGTON, TEXAS

Amil Ortiz, M.D.
Neonatology—SAN ANTONIO, TEXAS

Steve Phillips, M.D.
Pediatric Neurology—SACRAMENTO, CALIFORNIA

Judith L. Pugh, M.D.
Pediatric Nephrology—SAN ANTONIO, TEXAS

S. DuBose Ravenel, M.D.
Pediatrics—HIGH POINT, NORTH CAROLINA

Brian Riedel, M.D.
Pediatric Gastroenterology—NASHVILLE, TENNESSEE

James Roach, M.D.
Pediatric Orthopedics—FORT WORTH, TEXAS

Mark Shelton, M.D.
Infectious Diseases—FORT WORTH, TEXAS

Glaze Vaughn, M.D.
Pediatric Surgery/Urology—FORT WORTH, TEXAS

Teri Walter
Physical Therapy—ARLINGTON, TEXAS

Paul Warren, M.D.
Behavioral Pediatrics—PLANO, TEXAS

Rick Weiser, M.D.
Adolescent Medicine—PLEASANTON, CALIFORNIA

Also, this project would not have been possible without the immeasurable support of our loving spouses, Alan Cox and Teri Reisser. Your love, patience, and endurance literally kept us going. This project is not only ours but yours. We appreciate and love you!—Melissa R. Cox, Paul C. Reisser, M.D.

Editorial Staff

PRIMARY AUTHOR: Paul C. Reisser, M.D.
MANAGING EDITOR: Melissa R. Cox
TYNDALE EDITORS: Vinita Hampton Wright, Lisa A. Jackson

Focus on the Family

Bradley G. Beck, M.D., MEDICAL ISSUES ADVISOR
Lianne Belote, ADMINISTRATIVE ASSISTANT
Lisa D. Brock, RESEARCH EDITOR
Bob Chuvala, RESEARCH EDITOR
Kathleen M. Gowler, ADMINISTRATIVE SUPPORT
Karen Sagahon, ADMINISTRATIVE SUPPORT
Keith Wall, RESEARCH EDITOR

Special thanks to:

Glenn Bethany
Kurt Bruner
Charmé Fletcher
Anita Fuglaar
Al Janssen
Mark Maddox
Dean Merrill
Craig Osten
Mike Yorkey
Rolf Zettersten

CHAPTER 1

Preparing for Parenthood

Whether you are beginning to think about starting a family

... or have just learned that you are going to be a mother or a father in a few months

... or are a day or two away from a trip to the delivery room

... or are planning an adoption,

this book is dedicated to enhancing the journey you have started.

Parenting is an adventure, a source of incredible fulfillment, and a unique privilege. It's a voyage of discovery, a humbling responsibility, and a learning curve. On many occasions, it brings both laughter and tears. It is, above all, a gift from God—one that deserves to be received with joy and treated with the utmost respect.

Many people enter parenthood unexpectedly, at times even suddenly, often in a state of panic. Nearly everyone who accepts the assignment develops qualms at some point. You may have already progressed from "Am I really ready for all the responsibility of bringing up a child?" to "What am I going to do if _____ happens?" to "How in the world did I get into this?"

If any of those questions have passed through your mind, take heart, and remember some fundamental truths of parenting:

- You're not alone. Many millions have traveled the path before you.

- You probably know a lot more than you think.
- It's never too late to learn, to mold your attitudes and refine your skills.

Whether you're aware of it or not, the process of becoming a mother or a father actually begins well before the doctor announces, "It's a boy!" or "It's a girl!" It begins before conception. In fact, it begins before the physical intimacy that sets the biological marvel of reproduction in motion.

And for an event of this importance, it's nice, as much as is humanly possible, to be prepared. This chapter is all about getting ready, but it's worth reading even if a lot of water has already passed under your parental bridge.

FEARFULLY AND WONDERFULLY MADE: HOW A BABY DEVELOPS

Many authors and poets, after hearing the cry and seeing the first flailing movements of tiny arms and legs at the moment of birth, have declared that the process of coming into the world is a miracle.

But while childbirth is truly awe-inspiring, the real miracles began long before this transition of the baby from one environment to another. If you are expecting an arrival in the near future, be assured that wondrous and marvelous events have already taken place in the warm sanctuary of the womb. For it was there that a tiny cluster of 64 to 128 cells embedded in the thickened lining of the uterus, just six days after this new human life began with the meeting of egg and sperm. Within seventy-two hours of establishing a temporary residence, he or she sent a powerful hormonal signal to override the mother's monthly cycle, preventing the shedding of her uterine lining.

Then began the astonishing process of differentiation, as new cells took on particular shapes, sizes, and functions, aligning themselves into tissues and organs, eyes and ears, arms and legs. Each of these cells contained all of the information needed to make any of the multitudes of cell types in the body. Yet during the process of constructing and organizing, integrating and communicating with one another, individual cells began to express unique qualities in very short order, but in a seamless and orderly pattern. The intricacy and timing of these events are nothing less than masterpieces of planning and engineering.

Before the end of the first six weeks of life, your child's heart has started to beat, eyes are developing, the central nervous system is under construction, most internal organs are forming, and small buds representing future arms and legs have sprouted. One cell created by the union of egg and sperm has now become millions, and your new daughter or son has reached the length of one-quarter of an inch.

By the end of eight weeks, the fingers and toes have been formed. Heart, lungs, and major blood vessels have become well developed. Taste buds and the apparatus needed for the sense of smell have appeared. Tiny muscles have generated body movements, which at this point a mother cannot feel.

When twelve weeks of growth have ended, your baby has reached a length of three inches. The heartbeat can be heard using an electronic listening device. All of the organs and tissues—including heart, lungs, brain, digestive system, kidneys, and reproductive organs—have been formed and are in place. The only necessary remaining ingredient is time: six more months for growth and maturation.

Sixteen weeks after conception, eyebrows and hair are growing. Your baby, now measuring six to seven inches and weighing nearly as many ounces, kicks, swallows, hiccups, wakes, and sleeps. Soon the mother can begin feeling movement inside, an important milestone still referred to as "quickening."

Four weeks later, with weight now approaching one pound, your baby can hear and react to sounds, including Mom's heartbeat and stomach rumblings, as well as noise, music, and conversations outside the uterus. (Whether any of these sounds are recognized or become part of early memories is uncertain.)

At twenty-six weeks of life, breathing movements are present, although there is no air to be inhaled. Depending on their weight, babies born prematurely at this time have a 50 to 75 percent chance of survival with expert care, although complications are common. With each additional week that passes within the mother's womb, the baby's likelihood of surviving a premature delivery improves, the risk of long-term complications declines, and the medical care needed after birth usually becomes less complex.

The final fourteen weeks are the homestretch, during which your baby grows and gains weight very rapidly. By the end of *thirty-two weeks,* the bones are hardening, the eyes are opening and closing, the thumb has found its way into the mouth, and the arms and legs are stretching and kicking regularly. Your baby is twelve to sixteen inches long and weighs about three pounds. Over the next four weeks, the weight nearly doubles, and you will feel all sorts of kicks, prods, and pokes much more strongly. A baby born at this age will need some assistance with feeding and keeping warm and could still develop more complicated medical problems as well. However, the vast majority of those born a month or so ahead of schedule do very well.

Finally, after a few more weeks of rapid weight gain (about half a pound per week during the last six weeks of gestation), your baby is fully developed and ready to meet you.

Every mother and father awaits the birth of a child with a mixture of anticipation, excitement, and anxiety. Who will this new person be? Will this be a son or a daughter (or more than one)? Will she have her mother's eyes? Will he have his father's chin? Will everything be in the right place? Could there have been any problems that occurred silently during the passage from conception to birth?

No one can answer all these questions until the moment of birth. Furthermore, a baby may have some initial problems that clear up quickly and easily, while a more serious disturbance may not be apparent until a number of days, weeks, or even months have passed. Obviously, everyone involved in the debut of a new life is hoping, praying, and working toward the safe arrival of a healthy baby to a healthy mother. While no one can guarantee this happy outcome, there are many positive steps and basic precautions that can dramatically increase the likelihood of a joyful "special delivery."

PLANNING AHEAD: LIFESTYLE AND HEALTH QUESTIONS FOR THE MOTHER- (AND FATHER-) TO-BE

In a very real and practical sense, parenting begins well before the news arrives that a new family member is on the way. The state of the union of the parents-to-be and particularly the health of the mother before pregnancy strongly affect her health during pregnancy, which in turn plays a vital role in the baby's well-being both before and after delivery.

If you are planning to begin a family, or even if your pregnancy is well under way, you would be wise to review the following list of self-assessment questions. Much of what follows is directed toward the mother, but the ongoing health and habits of both parents are very important. (Expectant fathers, please read on.)

> *One important note:* This book is not intended to be a comprehensive resource on pregnancy and childbirth. The information given in this and the next chapter is intentionally limited to parenting before the delivery room—matters that specifically affect the health of the baby to be born. This is not to imply that a mother's

health is any less important, or that her well-being and her child's are not intimately connected. Nevertheless, the length, breadth, and depth of pregnancy care are beyond the scope of this book. If you are pregnant (or may be soon), it is very important that you find a physician who will not only guide you through pregnancy but also recommend books and other materials from which you can learn more about this miraculous process.

How well are you taking care of your (one and only) body? Imagine what would happen if a strict law were passed declaring that you could buy only one automobile in your lifetime. Suppose the law also included a stiff penalty for riding in anyone else's vehicle. If your car ever became seriously damaged or fell apart, you would have to walk—everywhere. How well would you take care of your one and only car if the only alternative would be a pair of very sore feet? Would you fill its tank with the cheapest grade of no-name gas or find the best premium fuel on the market? Would you get the oil changed, engine tuned, and wheels aligned on a regular basis or wait for rumbles, rattles, and warning lights to appear before heading for the service station? When you weren't using it, would you keep the car snug in the garage or let the elements beat on it mercilessly day and night?

The analogy to your one and only body should be obvious: If it deteriorates and malfunctions, you can't borrow anyone else's. *And neither can your baby.* Poor nutrition, smoking, and the use of alcohol and drugs can have a serious impact on your baby's development, especially during the first eight weeks when the vital organs are under construction. But your pregnancy may not even be confirmed until this period has already passed. Therefore, *the habits you develop well before you even think about having a child are very important.*

So how are you treating yourself? Specifically:

How's your nutrition?

Contrary to what talk shows and tabloids say, good nutrition does not involve magic formulas, rigid restrictions, or tackle boxes full of vitamins and supplements. In fact, you are probably familiar with the basic principles of healthful eating that continue to be reinforced by research and consensus: variety, moderation, and proportion in selecting from the primary food groups. The U.S. Department of Agriculture and the Department of Health and Human Services have developed the Food Guide Pyramid to illustrate these concepts, updating the traditional idea of the "basic four" food groups.

The pyramid illustrates guidelines for the relative number of servings of various types of foods (the amounts should be adjusted for pregnancy). Remember that the concept of a serving is a simple tool that you can use to help track your general intake. It will vary depending on the type of food being considered.

The goal is not to become obsessed with meticulous counts of servings or calories but to understand which foods should be emphasized on an ongoing basis. If the "four food groups" in your current diet are burgers, soft drinks, doughnuts, and chips, you need to do some serious revision—primarily shifting to the lower-fat, higher-quality grain, vegetable, and fruit groups. Also, because an adequate amount of protein is critical for the development of a baby's brain and muscle tissue, you should try to consume 80 to 100 grams of protein daily during your pregnancy.

If you are a vegetarian, you should be able to continue through an entire pregnancy without difficulty, provided that you include a wide variety of foods. If you eat absolutely no animal products, such as milk, eggs, or cheese, you may become shortchanged on protein and calories, as well as on iron, calcium, vitamin B12, and zinc. Vitamin and mineral supplementation would be advisable, as would some consultation with a dietitian.

Theoretically, a woman who eats a variety of fresh, high-quality foods in the rough proportions of the pyramid should not need to take supplemental vitamins and minerals. But certain substances are so critical to a healthy pregnancy that most physicians will prescribe **prenatal vitamins** to make up for any deficiencies in the mother's diet. Remember, however, that *supplements do not make up for careless eating habits.*

There is evidence that taking supplemental **folic acid** will reduce the likelihood that the newborn will have one of several types of major problems known as **neural tube defects**. Within the first month after conception, a tubelike structure forms from which the brain and spinal cord develop. If the tube does not close properly, serious abnormalities of these vital structures can result. Unfortunately, neural tube defects may occur before you know you are pregnant. Therefore, the U.S. Public Health Service now recommends that *all women of childbearing age take 0.4 mg of folic acid daily* to reduce the risk of a neural tube defect occurring in an unexpected pregnancy. If you have already had a child with a neural tube defect, a higher dose of folic acid—4 mg per day—is recommended for a month prior to the time you plan to become pregnant and should be continued through the first three months. (This amount of folic acid requires a doctor's prescription.) You can, of course, obtain folic acid through foods such as dark leafy vegetables, cereals, whole grain breads, citrus fruits, bananas, and tomatoes. However, in light of the research favoring supplementation, you should check with your physician about the amount of folic acid recommended for your pregnancy.

A pregnant woman needs additional **iron**, both for her increased blood volume as well as for the growing tissues and iron stores within her baby. Iron is necessary for the formation of **hemoglobin**, the protein within red blood cells that binds to oxygen, thus allowing red cells to deliver oxygen to every cell in the body. If the supply of iron in a mother's food is inadequate to meet this increased need, iron deficiency anemia will eventually result. This can cause her to feel extremely tired—more so than she would normally expect from the pregnancy itself.

An intake of about 30 mg of elemental iron per day will meet the need of most pregnant women. (Those who are already iron deficient may require 60 mg or more to correct this problem.) Since a typical diet provides only 5 or 6 mg of elemental iron per one thousand calories of food, and because consuming five thousand calories per day would be both unwise and impractical, iron should be included in your prenatal vitamin regimen. Absorption of iron is improved when foods containing vitamin C are eaten at the same time.

A woman's daily **calcium** intake normally should be 1,000 mg per day during the childbearing years, but should increase to 1,200 to 1,500 mg per day during pregnancy because of the new skeleton under construction inside her uterus. Dairy products are a rich source of calcium—300 mg are available in a cup of milk and 450 mg in a cup of nonfat yogurt—so this added requirement is usually readily obtained from foods. If you can't tolerate dairy products, your doctor may recommend that you take calcium supplements, since prenatal vitamins alone typically do not include the full amount. Calcium carbonate or calcium citrate are the forms that are most easily absorbed.

Do you weigh enough or too much?
Obesity is a health hazard for many reasons, all of which are heightened during pregnancy. Excessive weight during pregnancy is a risk factor for **high blood pressure** and **diabetes**, both of which can lead to significant problems for mother and baby. The aches and pains (especially in the lower back) that are so common during the later stages of pregnancy can

become intolerable when there is already an extra burden of several pounds on muscles and joints. Recent evidence suggests that overweight pregnant women are more likely to have babies with neural tube defects, regardless of folic acid intake.

But being underweight before or during pregnancy is no great advantage either because the nutritional needs of the baby may be compromised. This can result in a baby of low birth weight who is at risk for a variety of problems, including difficulty maintaining normal temperature or blood-sugar level after birth.

If you have had a history of erratic nutrition habits or even a full-blown eating disorder (such as **anorexia** or **bulimia**), you and your baby will benefit greatly from ongoing counseling and coaching from a dietitian before, during, and after pregnancy. Similarly, if you are struggling with excessive weight, a gradual process of reduction (ideally under the guidance of a dietitian) prior to becoming pregnant would be wise. Attaining a stable weight prior to pregnancy will help prevent rapid regaining of weight after pregnancy begins. If you are already pregnant, however, a weight-loss program is not a good idea because the nutritional needs of both you and your baby could be jeopardized. Pregnancy would be a good time, however, to modify eating habits toward healthy patterns that will serve you well for the rest of your life.

Are you exercising your muscles, heart, and lungs?

A sedentary lifestyle—that is, one without deliberate exercise—has been specifically identified as a health risk for both women and men. Unfortunately, despite the numerous and well-publicized benefits of regular exercise, a majority of Americans still do not take part in any form of planned physical activity. But a regular habit of exercise established now will serve as an investment in long-term health and also improve the way you feel throughout pregnancy.

Several normal changes during pregnancy put new physical demands on your body. Aside from a normal weight gain of twenty-five to thirty-five pounds, your heart will be dealing with a 50 percent increase in blood volume. Muscles and ligaments in the back and pelvis will be stretched and subjected to new tensions and strains. Unless you have a scheduled cesarean section, you will also go through the rigors of labor—which is aptly named—and the birth itself. These are physically challenging events, and those who are well conditioned will usually fare better. In fact, their labor may even be shortened.

The increased stamina and muscle tone resulting from regular exercise will also increase your energy level, improve sleep, reduce swelling of the legs, and probably reduce aches and pains in the lower back. If you are on your feet all day, it may seem ridiculous to spend precious time for additional muscle motion. But unless you are a professional athlete, it is unlikely that your daily activities, no matter how exhausting, will specifically condition your heart and lungs. The good news is that you don't need to become a marathon runner to see some benefit in your health.

If you are not used to exercising, a goal of thirty minutes three or four times per week is reasonable. It is always better to do light or moderate exercise on a regular basis than heavy exercise intermittently. While stretching and muscle strengthening are worthwhile, aerobic conditioning—in which increased oxygen is consumed continuously for a prolonged period of time—has the greatest overall benefit.

The most straightforward and least costly aerobic activity is walking, ideally at a brisk pace of twelve to fifteen minutes per mile. No fancy equipment, health-club membership, or special gear (other than a pair of comfortable, supportive shoes) is needed. Pleasant and safe surroundings, a flat surface, and agreeable weather are advisable, however, as well as a companion. Another person (whether your husband, an older child, a relative, a friend, or another pregnant woman) will add accountability to the process, and the conversation can be enjoyable and help the time pass quickly. Gentle stretching for a few minutes before and after is a good idea, in order to warm up and then cool down leg and back muscles.

Alternatives to walking include:

- A home treadmill. Advantages: No concerns about weather, aggressive dogs, or finding someone to watch your children. You can be flexible about the time of day to use it. Disadvantages: Cost, size, and noise.
- An exercise video or book geared to pregnant women. Advantages: Same as above, with less cost. Disadvantage: Repetition could become boring.
- A prenatal fitness class at a local hospital or health club. Advantage: Interaction with instructor and other women can be helpful and motivating. Disadvantages: Cost. Also, scheduling and child-care needs may be complicated.
- Swimming. Advantage: Good aerobic conditioning involving many muscle groups, with no added strain on sore muscles and joints of the lower back and pelvis. Disadvantage: You need access to a pool.
- Stationary cycling. Advantage: Good aerobic conditioning and (depending on your anatomy) probably less strain on your lower back than from walking. Disadvantage: Many women become increasingly uncomfortable on this equipment as pregnancy progresses.

If you are already well conditioned, you should be able to continue using your specific exercise routine. If you are already a confirmed jogger or an accomplished tennis player, you can probably continue these activities through the early months of pregnancy. However, some obstetricians recommend shifting from high-impact to low-impact exercise through the entire nine months. Snow skiing, surfing, waterskiing, and horseback riding all pose specific risks during pregnancy because of the possibility of falls—especially as your center of gravity shifts and your balance becomes less reliable as the uterus enlarges. All of these activities should be reviewed with your physician throughout the course of your pregnancy. Note: Scuba diving is not recommended at any time during pregnancy.

A few special precautions about exercise during pregnancy:

- Pregnancy is not a good time to take on a new, intense form of exercise, especially if it involves jumping, jerking, high-impact motion, or sudden changes in direction.
- Exercise should not be so vigorous or prolonged as to cause exhaustion, overheating, or dehydration. During pregnancy your heart rate should stay below 140, regardless of the type of exercise you are doing.
- After the twentieth week of pregnancy, you should avoid exercises that require you to lie on your back.
- Exercise should not continue if any of the following pregnancy-related problems develop: preterm rupture of membranes; poor growth of the baby (**intrauterine growth restriction**); vaginal bleeding; high blood pressure; preterm labor; and **cervical incompetence**, a condition in which the cervix or "neck" of the uterus isn't strong enough to prevent a premature delivery. Exercise may also be limited if you are pregnant with more than one baby.
- If you have specific health problems such as heart disease, high blood pressure, irregular heart rate, epilepsy, fainting episodes, asthma, arthritis, or anemia,

review any exercise plans with your physician, whether
or not you are pregnant.

In addition to aerobic activity, a variety of gentle stretching
and muscle-conditioning activities can help prepare your
body for the changes of late pregnancy and labor. Your doctor
and/or childbirth class instructor will have a number of suggestions for such exercises.

Are you taking or inhaling any substances that might harm you or your baby?

As a result of widespread public-health announcements,
most people are aware that smoking cigarettes, drinking excessive amounts of alcohol, and using illicit drugs are risky
and destructive, especially during pregnancy. Yet it's often
difficult to believe that "this could happen to me"—that we
might actually suffer the bad effects we hear about. Furthermore, even if one is convinced of the dangers of these substances, gaining freedom from their grip can be a real uphill
battle. If you need any additional reasons to separate yourself
from cigarettes, alcohol, or illegal drugs, or some extra resolve to remain free of these unhealthy habits, consider carefully the following facts:

Cigarette smoking. This is a form of legalized drug addiction
that is harmful to the smoker, those around the smoker, and
especially the baby growing inside the smoker. Thousands of
chemicals in cigarette smoke flow directly from the mother's
lungs into her bloodstream and then directly into the baby.
Nicotine specifically causes constriction of blood vessels
in both the placenta and the baby, thus reducing the baby's
supply of vital blood and oxygen. Carbon monoxide in
smoke binds tightly to red blood cells and displaces oxygen.
The overall effect is a recurrent choking of the baby's oxygen
supply, resulting in smaller (by an average of half a pound)

and shorter babies. Unfortunately, these infants (whom doctors refer to as "small-for-dates") are more likely than their counterparts to have a variety of medical problems after birth.

The smoker's baby is more likely to be born prematurely or to be stillborn. The tragedy of **sudden infant death syndrome (SIDS)** occurs twice as frequently when the child's mother has smoked throughout pregnancy, and the risk increases drastically if there is continuing exposure to secondhand smoke after birth. According to a study published by researchers at the University of California, infants exposed to smoke from ten or fewer cigarettes per day are more than twice as likely to die of SIDS than babies in smoke-free environments. When the exposure involves more than twenty cigarettes per day, the risk soars to more than twenty times that of infants not exposed.[1]

Exposure to cigarette smoke after birth is linked to colds, ear infections, and asthma. And the child who sees Mom and Dad smoke is also much more likely to pick up the habit than are his peers who live in homes where there are no smokers.

Let's not forget smoking's effect on the mother. Aside from the long-term risks of chronic lung disease, heart disease, ulcers, and diseased blood vessels, she is more likely to have unexpected vaginal bleeding during her pregnancy.

The only good news about smoking is that *quitting early in pregnancy reduces the baby's risk of problems essentially to the level of a child born to a nonsmoker.* For many women, the emotional impact of a threat to the baby is powerful enough to override the compulsion to light up, and a pregnancy usually lasts long enough to help temporary abstinence become a smoke-free life.

But cigarettes are so powerfully addictive that additional support may be necessary to kick the habit. If you are a smoker, it's never too late—or too early—to stop. A success-ful decision to quit usually requires:

- A well-defined list of reasons that have some emotional power. ("I don't want to starve my baby of oxygen" or "I want to live long enough to see my kids grow up.") Since resistance to quitting often hinges on an emotional attachment to cigarettes, your reasons for giving up smoking should likewise motivate you on an emotional level.
- A specified quitting date that is announced to family, friends, and coworkers. Some gentle peer pressure can be a powerful motivator.
- Participation in a stop-smoking class. These are available in most communities through nearby hospitals or local chapters of national organizations (American Lung Association, American Heart Association, American Cancer Society).
- A firm declaration that your home, car, and workplace are smoke-free zones. Nobody, but nobody—spouse, in-laws, guests, visiting heads of state—lights up in your airspace.
- If you are not yet pregnant, you may wish to consider using nicotine patches or chewing gum to assist you through the withdrawal process. These are now available on both a prescription and nonprescription (or over-the-counter) basis. If you have any questions or concerns about their proper use, you may want to discuss them with your physician. You should not smoke while using nicotine patches or gum, and you cannot use them during pregnancy.

Alcoholic beverages. Daily consumption of alcohol during pregnancy, with or without binge drinking, may lead to a com-plex of problems in the baby known as **fetal alcohol syndrome**.

Babies with this disorder may have a variety of abnormalities of the head, face, heart, joints, and limbs. In addition, the central nervous system can be affected, causing mental retardation, hyperactivity, and behavioral problems. The damage appears to be directly related to the amount of alcohol consumed, especially during the early months of pregnancy.

A woman who enjoys an occasional drink may wonder how much alcohol might be safe during pregnancy. Some studies suggest that even two drinks a week may lead to a mild withdrawal syndrome in the newborn, with increased irritability and stomach disturbances. The simplest and safest course is to abstain from alcohol altogether during pregnancy. You would be wise to abstain or consume no more than two alcoholic drinks per week if you are not yet pregnant but might become so in the near future. If drinking is not an ingrained habit, this should not be difficult. But if you find it hard to stay away from alcohol or control how much you drink at any given time, total avoidance is even more important. It is likely that you will need outside help to do so, whether in a group setting such as a church support group or Alcoholics Anonymous, or individually with a professional counselor.

Illegal drugs. The use of illegal drugs continues to be a fearsome epidemic in our culture. The popular term *recreational drug use* is a contradiction because the word *recreation* implies an activity that has a positive, restoring, re-creating effect on mind and body. These substances, however, have just the opposite effect, draining away the resources, health, and, ultimately, life from their users. When the user is a pregnant woman, two lives (at least) are being damaged.

Regular **marijuana** users may deliver prematurely and even at term are more likely to have smaller babies. **Cocaine** use can cause not only major problems during pregnancy—including miscarriage, premature labor, and placental abruption (a sudden and dangerous separation of the placenta from the wall of the uterus)—but also the eventual delivery of a small, irritable baby who may have serious, lifelong problems. Aside from any difficulties that might arise from premature delivery, cocaine itself can damage the infant's central nervous system, urinary tract, and limbs by constricting their blood supply. Increased irritability during the newborn period, developmental delays, and difficulty with learning and interacting with others may also be attributable to cocaine use by the mother. (Frequently other substances such as alcohol and tobacco have been used as well, complicating the question of identifying specific consequences of cocaine.)

A mother's use of narcotics such as **heroin** or **methadone** throughout her pregnancy may subject the baby to a difficult withdrawal after birth. Symptoms, which usually begin during the first day or two after birth, can include increased irritability, tremors, a high-pitched cry, constant hunger, sweating, and sneezing. In severe cases, seizures, vomiting, diarrhea, and difficulty with breathing can occur. Furthermore, if these drugs are taken intravenously (that is, injected into the veins), there is an additional risk of acquiring HIV, which eventually causes **AIDS**. This will not only shorten the mother's life drastically, but could infect her baby as well.

As serious as all these health concerns are, they do not encompass the vast waste of resources and the chaotic lifestyle that so often accompany the use of illegal drugs. Chronic drug abusers are usually unable to deal consistently with the daily demands of child care. Food preparation, safety in the home, and basic health practices are likely to be compromised. Run-ins with the law and difficulty maintaining steady employment are not uncommon. Healthy relationships with friends and family members may be in short supply. The disturbances and distractions of chronic drug use seriously compromise a parent's ability to bring up healthy children.

Whether or not you are pregnant, the time to stop using any of these toxic substances is *now*, and seeking help to do so should be an immediate priority.

Caffeine. This stimulant abounds in everyday beverages such as coffee, tea, and soft drinks, as well as some headache remedies and pain relievers. A daily intake of up to 200 mg (the amount in one or two five-ounce cups of coffee) is widely considered safe during pregnancy. Larger amounts (over 500 mg per day) will keep both you and your baby awake, and his or her increased activity levels before birth may lead to a lower birth weight. If you consume coffee by the potful or sodas by the six-pack, you should begin cutting back to the 200 mg limit (see table) before you become pregnant or reduce immediately if you are already expecting. Decreasing the brewing time for coffee or tea will also cut caffeine content.

CAFFEINE CONTENT OF FOODS AND BEVERAGES

Food Source	Amount	Caffeine Content
Regular coffee	8 oz.	100-500 mg
Instant coffee	8 oz.	80-100 mg
Decaf coffee	8 oz.	3-5 mg
Tea	8 oz.	60-65 mg
*Regular cola	6 oz.	36 mg
Diet cola	6 oz.	18 mg
Chocolate bar	1 oz.	20 mg

*Read labels to determine the presence of caffeine in specific soft drinks, such as Mountain Dew, Dr. Pepper, etc.

Prescription and over-the-counter (OTC) drugs. In general, you should try to avoid using any type of medication that isn't specifically prescribed or approved by your physician. *Always be sure to inform any physician who treats you that you are or might be pregnant, since this could have a significant impact on medication(s) he or she might recommend.*

The fact that you can buy a drug off the shelf at the supermarket doesn't necessarily mean that it is wise to use it during pregnancy. Pain relievers, cold tablets, laxatives, and other medications, as well as vitamin, herb, and food supplements, may seem harmless merely because they are easily accessible or advertised as "natural." A number of these are, in fact, quite safe during pregnancy, but you should consult your physician, who is familiar with your medical history and the details of your pregnancy, before using any of them. Common examples of OTC medications include the following:

Pain relievers. Acetaminophen (Tylenol, Panadol, and various others) is generally recognized as safe for both mother and baby during pregnancy when used in the recommended dosage, but it can be toxic to the liver in an overdose. This drug reduces aches, pains, headaches, and fever. Both aspirin and the various brands of the anti-inflammatory drugs ibuprofen (Advil, Motrin, Nuprin, and others), naproxen (Aleve), and ketoprofen (Orudis KT and others) may increase the risk of bleeding in both mother and baby, especially around the time of birth. Anti-inflammatory medications taken late in pregnancy also may inhibit the onset of labor. Furthermore, they can cause a structure in the infant's heart known as the **ductus arteriosus** to close, resulting in potential circulatory problems after birth. While such complications are very unusual, you should avoid these medications during pregnancy (especially during the final weeks) unless they are recommended for a specific purpose by your physician.

Cold tablets. Decongestants, antihistamines, cough syrups, and nasal sprays are sold in a bewildering array of combinations and preparations. All are intended to relieve symptoms, but these drugs rarely have a direct effect on the course of an upper-respiratory illness. Some of the ingredients in cold remedies are considered safe during a pregnancy, but you should check with your physician and pharmacist before using any of them. Rest, fluids, and time will take care of the vast majority of these infections. However, you should also contact your doctor if your runny nose, sore throat, or cough continues for more than a week; if you are producing thick, discolored drainage from nose or chest; or if you are running a fever over 100°F. If the doctor you speak with is not the one who is caring for your pregnancy, be sure that he or she knows you are pregnant.

Antacids. Many pregnant women develop heartburn and indigestion because of changes in the intestinal tract produced by the growing uterus. Antacids are generally considered safe during pregnancy when used in recommended doses, but they may provoke diarrhea and can interfere with the absorption of iron supplements as well as prescription drugs.

Laxatives. Constipation is common during pregnancy, but chemical laxatives are not the preferred method of treatment. Lots of fluids and juices, additional fiber in the diet (whether directly from food sources or psyllium-seed supplements such as Metamucil or Citrucel), and regular exercise are the best first-line remedies. If you are not able to have a bowel movement for a few days at a time, you should review additional options with your physician.

Are you exposed to any environmental hazards?

During the course of your pregnancy, and especially during the first three months, you should minimize your exposure to **X-rays** (also called **ionizing radiation**). Exposure to very large doses during the early weeks when the baby's tissues and organs are under construction could lead to birth defects. Fortunately, the X-ray exposure involved in common medical examinations is a tiny fraction of the amount generally considered risky. If you have had one or more diagnostic X-rays and then discover you were pregnant at the time, it is extremely unlikely that your baby will be affected. Nevertheless, if this occurs you should review with your physician what procedures were done.

Some reasonable precautions to minimize your (and your baby's) exposure to X-rays include these steps:

- If X-rays (including those in the dentist's office) have been recommended, be sure to tell both your physician and the X-ray technician if you are or might be pregnant.
- If at all possible, postpone X-rays until after the baby is born, or at least wait until the first three months of pregnancy have passed. Procedures that do not utilize ionizing radiation, such as **ultrasound** or **magnetic resonance imaging (MRI)**, may be alternative options that can supply the necessary diagnostic information. (It is currently assumed but not proven that an MRI study is safe in early pregnancy.) If X-rays are needed in an emergency situation, techniques that limit exposure (such as shielding the abdomen with a lead apron or limiting the number of films taken) may be utilized. (It is generally recommended that a woman of reproductive age have her abdomen shielded when she has *any* type of X-ray.)
- If you work around sources of ionizing radiation (for example, in an office or hospital area where X-rays are taken), be sure to follow carefully the occupational guidelines in your facility for minimizing and measuring any ongoing exposure.
- Depending upon location, dose, and timing during pregnancy, radiation therapy for cancer may—or may not—pose a significant hazard to a developing baby. The difficult problem of managing a cancer arises only in about one in one thousand pregnancies. Should this occur, however, the benefits and risks of any proposed treatment—as well as the consequences of postponing

treatment—must be reviewed in detail, and decisions made after careful deliberation and prayer.

Over the past several years concerns have been raised about the effects of exposure of pregnant women to **nonionizing radiation**—microwaves, radio waves, electromagnetic fields (such as those associated with power lines), and infrared light. Thus far, problems arising from these forms of radiation have not been clearly demonstrated. Specifically, research has not shown an increased risk of birth defects among pregnant women who work at video display terminals (VDTs) such as computer monitors for several hours per week. Similarly, adverse effects of living near power lines have not been established.

Some concerns have been raised about prolonged exposure to high temperatures in **hot tubs, whirlpools,** and **saunas**. Excessive heat can alter maternal (and therefore placental) blood flow. Additionally, body temperature elevation to 104°F or beyond during the first three months of pregnancy may increase the risk of a baby having a neural tube defect (see page 8). Because a maximum safe amount of exposure to high temperature cannot be established with complete certainty, it is best to avoid hot tubs or extremely hot baths altogether during the course of your pregnancy (and especially during the first three months).

Do you have any medical problems that need to be addressed?

Before 1900, a pregnant woman typically had only one prenatal visit with a physician prior to her delivery, during which her due date was determined—and little else. When next seen, she might be near term and in perfect health—or severely ill with an infection or a complication of her pregnancy. One of the major advances in public health in the early twentieth century was the recognition that a number of health problems that affect both mother and child could be detected, and in many cases corrected, through screening during pregnancy.

Many experts now not only advocate starting prenatal care as soon as possible after a pregnancy is diagnosed but even recommend a preconception visit for those who are thinking about starting a family. Whether before or during pregnancy, a thorough history and physical examination, including a review of important areas such as family background, habits, lifestyle, and general health, are wise. Some basic laboratory tests may also be done. Since all these areas can affect the health of a pregnancy and thus the quality of a baby's start in life, an ounce or two of prevention and protection can save several pounds of costly cure. Areas to consider include:

Family background. If there is a history of any diseases that are passed by inheritance (such as cystic fibrosis, sickle-cell disease, or Tay-Sachs disease) within the family of either parent-to-be, genetic counseling can help to determine the potential risk of having a baby with a similar problem. This information can in turn guide decisions about having certain tests done during pregnancy to detect possible problems in the child. Of course, testing for congenital defects and chromosomal anomalies does not mean the couple would (or should) choose to terminate a pregnancy should an abnormality be detected (see chapter 3, pages 90–95).

Previous pregnancies. If you have had a prior pregnancy loss, a complication during labor or delivery, or a child born with a congenital problem of any type, specific tests and preparations may be in order before or during another pregnancy.

General health. Pregnancy is not a disease, of course, but it does have a significant impact on the way a woman's body functions. Furthermore, a number of medical problems can have a profound effect on her pregnancy and the health of her baby. The most important of these are diabetes, high blood pressure (hypertension), epilepsy, heart disease, asthma, kidney disease, and the so-called autoimmune disorders such as rheumatoid arthritis or systemic lupus erythematosus. Any of these problems should be addressed and controlled, if at all possible, *before* becoming pregnant or as soon as possible after pregnancy is confirmed.

Infections and immunity. Most acute illnesses (such as colds) that might occur during a pregnancy are weathered without difficulty by both mother and baby. However, some types of infections in a pregnant woman can have adverse effects on her unborn child. When one of these occurs, the ultimate outcome will depend on (among other things) the type of organism, the severity of the infection, and the stage of pregnancy during which it occurs. While the more troublesome infections are uncommon, it is well worth taking some basic precautions in order to avoid them.

Rubella (German or three-day measles) is a viral infection that causes fever, aches, and a rash for a few days. If a woman becomes infected with rubella during the first month of pregnancy, her baby will have a 50 percent risk of developing one or more serious defects, which together are known as **congenital rubella syndrome.** These can include delayed growth, mental retardation, eye disorders, deafness, and heart disease. If the infection occurs in the third month or later, the risk drops to 10 percent.

Any woman who might become pregnant should have a blood test to see if she is immune to this disease. A vaccine against the rubella virus has been available since 1969, so most young women have had one or even two MMR (measles/mumps/rubella) injections during childhood—*but this does not guarantee that they are protected.* If the blood test does not detect antibodies to rubella, she should have an immunization *before* she becomes pregnant. Most experts recommend waiting for three months after the injection before becoming pregnant, although congenital rubella syndrome has not been reported even when the injection has been accidentally given during pregnancy. (If a woman is breast-feeding, the rubella vaccine can be administered without any apparent risk to the nursing child.)

Chicken pox (varicella) is another viral infection that usually occurs during childhood, although susceptible adults (including pregnant women) can also develop this illness—often with a more difficult course than their younger counterparts experience.

A developing baby can be infected with the mother's chicken pox, and the consequences will depend on the timing of the illness. During the first twenty-six weeks of pregnancy, there is about a 2 percent risk of developing a congenital varicella syndrome, which may include any of several defects of eyes, heart, and limbs. There is no way to determine whether the baby has been affected at the time of the mother's infection. Unfortunately, women who are infected with chicken pox during the first half of pregnancy may be told that they should have an abortion without being told that the risk of a congenital problem is quite low.

After twenty-six weeks of pregnancy, chicken pox in the mother does not result in harm to her baby unless the infection occurs from five days before to two days after delivery. (Before birth, the baby can be infected through the mother's blood via the umbilical cord. If the mother is infected shortly after giving birth, the baby can contract the illness by direct exposure.) When this occurs, a severe infection can result, because the baby may acquire the virus without also receiving any of the mother's protective antibodies. If this occurs, the baby should receive an injection called varicella-zoster immune globulin (or VZIG), which provides a temporary protective dose of "borrowed" antibody.

If you are pregnant and do not believe you have had this disease, you should be careful to avoid any child who has, or might have, chicken pox, as well as any adult who develops

LAB TESTS COMMONLY DONE DURING PREGNANCY

- A complete blood count (CBC) to check for anemia and other abnormalities of blood components.
- A urinalysis to check for infection, protein (which normally is minimally present in urine), blood, or other signs of disease.
- Blood type and Rh factor. This is important because differences between your blood type or Rh and the baby's could lead to complications in the newborn. For women who do not have the Rh factor (that is, they are Rh-negative), additional screening is done later in the pregnancy.
- A blood test for immunity to rubella (German measles).
- Tests for syphilis, hepatitis B, and HIV, and possibly cultures for chlamydia and gonorrhea (see chapter 4, page 97).
- Blood glucose to check for diabetes.
- A Pap smear to check the cells of the cervix (the opening of the uterus) for abnormalities, including cancerous or precancerous cells.
- Screening for bacterial and viral infections in the vagina and cervix is often performed during the second half of pregnancy. Specifically, testing to detect bacterial vaginosis, which could increase the risk for premature rupture of membranes and subsequent labor, and a culture for group B streptococcus, which can infect and harm the newborn after delivery, may be done during your pregnancy.
- Other tests may be appropriate, based on your history or exam findings. For example, if you have high blood pressure, an assessment of kidney function and other tests may be necessary.

shingles, which can spread the same virus. If you are uncertain whether or not you have had chicken pox in the past and wish to find out prior to or during pregnancy, your doctor can order a blood test that detects antibodies to the virus.

Group B streptococci are bacteria that are present in the vagina of approximately 20 to 25 percent of pregnant women and can infect the baby during birth, especially if labor is premature or if the woman's membranes (the "bag of waters") are ruptured for more than eighteen hours prior to delivery. Overall, about one of every one thousand infants is infected during birth, often with severe consequences including pneumonia and meningitis. Your doctor may recommend a culture to detect this bacteria at some point during your pregnancy. Of the 20 to 25 percent of women who carry this bacteria, only 1 to 2 percent of their babies will be infected. Therefore, antibiotics can be administered to the mother during labor to decrease the rate to 0.5 percent.

Toxoplasmosis is an infection caused by a parasite that may contaminate undercooked meat or dead animals and thus can appear in the feces of cats that eat rodents and decaying meat. If a woman develops toxoplasmosis during pregnancy, her baby has about a one in three chance of becoming infected, and of those, about one-third will show some signs of the disease. Significant problems in these infants can include premature delivery, a small head (microcephaly), encephalitis (inflammation of brain tissue), weak muscles, an enlarged liver and spleen, and inflammation of the retina. If recognized in mother and/or infant, toxoplasmosis can be treated with antibiotics. Unfortunately, this infection can be difficult to diagnose, and treatment doesn't usually change the outcome.

The most important take-home lesson about toxoplasmosis is that prevention is possible through two simple measures. First, any meat you consume during pregnancy, or *any* time, should be well cooked. Second, you should avoid any contact with cat droppings if you are pregnant or might be in the near future. This means staying away from the litter box and avoiding close contact with cats, especially if they spend much time outdoors.

Parvovirus causes an infection, seen commonly in school-children but also in other age-groups, called **erythema infectiosum**, or "fifth disease." Typically seen in winter and spring months, fifth disease is most well known for producing a so-called slapped-cheek rash on the face, although a lacy eruption may be seen on the arms, legs, and upper body as well. Adults who are infected may develop the rash but also typically develop aching joints. However, both children and adults can become infected without any symptoms at all. Unfortunately, this disease is contagious for up to three weeks *before* the rash breaks out, so it is virtually impossible to prevent exposure of other family members.

If a woman becomes infected with parvovirus during pregnancy, it's very likely (better than an 80 percent chance) that there will be no adverse effects on her baby. However, sometimes the mother's infection results in a severe anemia in the baby, which in turn can cause congestive heart failure. Therefore, a pregnant woman who is exposed to this infection should have a blood test to determine whether she is immune to it. If she is, there should be no cause for concern. If not, testing may be recommended later in the pregnancy to determine whether she has become infected.

If infection with parvovirus appears to have taken place during pregnancy—with or without symptoms—the baby should be monitored with ultrasound exams prior to birth for signs of heart failure resulting from anemia. Should either or both of these develop, the baby may require medication, early delivery, or even a transfusion prior to birth (one of the many forms of medical intervention now available for the preborn).

Cytomegalovirus (CMV) has the dubious distinction of being the most common congenital viral infection in the United States while being both untreatable and rarely (if ever) preventable. Fortunately, significant CMV disease in newborns is very uncommon. Approximately 1 to 2 percent of pregnant women experience a primary (first-time) infection with CMV, but the vast majority have no symptoms. About 30 to 40 percent of infected mothers transmit the virus to their babies, but only about 10 to 15 percent of infected infants will have some form of noticeable disease at birth. The overall risk of any infant having a serious disease related to CMV (that may involve the central nervous system, vision, hearing, pneumonia, or liver disease) is between one in ten thousand and one in twenty thousand.

At the present time, pregnant women are not screened for their susceptibility to CMV because there is no effective treatment for this infection. However, if a woman develops an illness during pregnancy that resembles mononucleosis—with fever, sore throat, enlarged lymph nodes in the neck, and marked fatigue—her physician may at some point request blood tests or even cultures to help determine if CMV might be involved. If this diagnosis is made, she will need careful and accurate counseling regarding the risk of the baby having congenital disease.

Approximately twenty different **sexually transmitted infections (STIs)** pose significant risks to both mother and baby. Many STIs are passed during intimate contact with people who look perfectly well and have no signs of illness. *Unfortunately, the first indication that an infection has taken place may be the birth of a very sick baby, a miscarriage or stillbirth, or even a woman's inability to become pregnant.* Chapter 4 on page 97 has details about STIs and pregnancy, including descriptions of their symptoms, risks to an unborn child, treatment, and prevention. Even if you consider yourself at low risk for having a sexually transmitted infection, you would be wise to review this information.

A common annoyance for both pregnant and non-pregnant women is vaginal infection with the common yeast *Candida albicans*, which can produce both itching and a clumpy ("cottage cheese") discharge. While this is not a risk to the baby, one common treatment—a single dose of the antibiotic Diflucan—is not recommended during pregnancy. Also, the cream Terazol (terconazole) should not be used during the first twelve weeks of pregnancy. It is very important that a woman being treated for this or any other infection inform her doctor that she is pregnant, or if there is a possibility (however remote) that she *might* be pregnant.

PERSONAL AND SPIRITUAL PREPARATIONS: WHAT SORT OF WORLD WILL YOUR CHILD LIVE IN?

As important as it is to have a safe and satisfactory childbirth, in the long run the most critical assignments of parenthood involve much more than preparing for the delivery date. Once the cord is cut and the first breaths of air are taken, your child's world has permanently and dramatically changed. If she is going to thrive, and not merely survive, that world needs to be safe, stable, and loving, especially during the first three years of life.

It is a tragedy that the world at large is anything *but* safe, stable, and loving. It is full of "many dangers, toils, and snares," to quote the writer of the hymn "Amazing Grace," so much so that some young adults are not sure they are willing to bring a child into a world so torn by upheaval and uncertainty.

But for children (especially the very young), the world they experience is primarily the creation of the people around them. The sights, sounds, and touches of parents and family and a general sense of order, comfort, and predictability can be an island of love and sanity, even when the culture outside the front door is volatile or even violent. The reverse is also true: The prettiest home in the nicest neighborhood may be hell on earth for a young child, who will carry the aftermath of damaging experiences into adulthood.

Whatever else you do as you bring up your child, you must convey a crucial message that she can hear, see, and *experience* in hundreds of different ways, especially when she is young:

> You are loved, you are important, and you always will be, no matter what happens. I care enough about you to provide for you, stand with you, coach you, correct you, and even die for you if necessary. My commitment to you is not based on what you do or don't do, how you look, whether your body is perfect or handicapped, or how you perform in school or sports. It is based on the fact that I am your parent and you are my child, a price-less gift that God has loaned to me for a season. Eventually I will release you to live your own life, but while you are growing up, I consider caring for you an assignment of utmost importance.

Obviously, a newborn baby will not understand these words, and even an older child will not fully grasp their meaning. But embracing these words as a mind-set and a fundamental attitude toward your child will shape thousands of interactions that ultimately convey its message. Indeed, most of the other details and techniques of child rearing—feeding, toilet training, education, and the rest—pale in comparison to the importance of communicating this attitude to your child, week in and week out for years.

The question to ponder, therefore, is this: Are you ready to deliver this message to your child and to strive to make your child's world safe, stable, and loving?

This is certainly a more complicated question to answer than "Are you smoking cigarettes?" or "Is your blood pressure too high?" The answer has a lot to do with how *you* were brought up and with the decisions you have made up until now. The answer is also tied up in how you see yourself in relation to the baby, to any other children you may have, to your mate, to your own parents, to the world in general, and, ultimately, to God. To get a better grasp on this issue, consider carefully the following questions, perhaps writing down your thoughts in a journal for future reference:

- What did your mother and father teach you about love, safety, and security? Did you see them express affection for one another? Did they build one another up or barrage one another, and everyone else, with criticism? (If you were reared by one parent, the same questions apply in connection with that parent or other caregivers.)
- Did you hear and feel that you were loved unconditionally? Were consistent limits set and enforced? Was discipline administered in a context of teaching and love, or did unpredictable punishments occur in outbursts of anger? Were you abused as a child—or as an adult?
- Are you expecting your baby to give you love? Are you hoping to derive significance from the role of being a mother or a father? Or do you already feel loved and believe that your life is significant and useful?
- How do you feel when
    you are interrupted frequently?
    someone needs you constantly?
    you have ongoing responsibilities?
    sudden changes rearrange your plans?
    you don't get enough sleep?

The messages you received from one or both parents can have a profound impact on the messages you in turn give to your own child. If your world was safe and secure, and if you felt loved and accepted by the most important people in your life—even when you were being corrected or disciplined—you are more likely to transmit that same sense of belonging and security to your own child. If the opposite was true, you may have a difficult time communicating that message to a child because you are probably still seeking it yourself.

You may be looking for love, acceptance, and significance from the role of being a mother or a father (and the recognition from others that ideally should come with the role) or even directly from your child. *But for babies or small children, nearly all of the loving and caring flows in a one-way direction: from you to them.* The newborn baby in particular is totally incapable of offering any affection before the first genuine smile appears at about the age of one month. His or her crying—especially if there is a lot of it—may sound downright hostile to the mother or father who is looking for a little appreciation for all the effort, pain, and sleepless nights.

If you are not sure—or are not happy—about your answers to these questions, you are not alone. No one has had perfect parents, and no one has lived a life free of mistakes and bad decisions. We are all on a learning curve, especially with parenting, and it's never too late to make course corrections. Here are some ways to get started:

Tap into a support team. By seeking guidance and input from your pastor, a professional counselor, a relative, or someone with parenting experience whom you respect, you can gain valuable encouragement and support. Many churches have ongoing small-group studies available for young parents, and these can be water in the desert during some of the challenging periods of child rearing. A counselor may be efficient at sorting through your particular personal issues, but a great deal can also be accomplished with a person (or a couple) who is willing to serve as a mentor. If you have been verbally, physically, or sexually abused as a child (or adult), it is particularly important that you work with someone who is qualified to help you in the process of healing the wounds that are an inevitable consequence of such experiences.

Take advantage of books, audio cassettes, and videotapes that can be utilized at your own pace. There is an abundance of materials that can educate and inspire you or supplement counseling about a particular problem.

Maintain a regular quiet time. Setting aside time to read Scripture, reflect, and pray elevates the entire project of caring for a newborn to a different plane. Some planning, creativity, and perseverance will definitely be necessary. For example, this activity may have to take place while the baby is napping (assuming that you can stay awake yourself). Or you may try to think and pray while taking a walk around the block, with or without a stroller. Whatever effort is spent carving out some time for personal renewal will definitely pay off—perhaps in ways you may not appreciate until months or years have passed.

God is clearly presented in both Old and New Testaments as the perfect parent: not only our Creator but a loving, patient, wise Father who cares enough to guide and correct His children on a daily basis. When we truly begin to grasp the lengths to which God has gone in expressing His love for each of us and His desire to be involved in the details of our lives, our ultimate sense of identity, security, and significance takes on a whole new meaning. If we were brought up in an atmosphere of inconsistency, neglect, or hostility and violence, God is willing and able to parent us, even as adults. And that in turn leads us into a new capacity for loving and cherishing our own children.

Prayer forges powerful links not only to God but also to

those we most care about. It's never too late to give thanks for
our children, to release the health and well-being of each child
to God's provision since they ultimately belong to Him anyway, and to pray for those who will influence that child in the
future—friends, teachers, pastors, and eventually, a mate.

**For the parent who is married: Cultivate your relationship
with your spouse.** Kids whose parents are openly affectionate,
do kind things for one another, and respect one another will
feel secure indeed. *Your relationship with your husband or wife
cannot be put on hold when children begin to arrive.* Eventually
they will leave the nest, and you will want to have a healthy
and thriving marriage, with a long-lasting supply of conversation and worthwhile projects, after they are gone.

Some thoughts for the expectant and new father

As your wife progresses through her pregnancy, your original
commitment to "love, honor, and cherish" will take on some
important new dimensions. She is going through some significant physical changes, including radical variations in hormone
levels, which can affect energy, appetite, and mood. At any
given time, she may feel tired (especially if there are other
small children at home), nauseated, ungainly, and unattrac-
tive. After your baby is born, she may feel terrific, but she
could also feel exhausted or depressed. Unfortunately, for all
of these reasons, pregnancy and the months that follow are
when there may be an increased risk of infidelity. Your job,
therefore, is to honor the commitments you made at the altar
on your wedding day and to say and do things that communicate a consistent message:

> You are loved, you are important, and you always will
> be, no matter what happens. I care enough about you to
> provide for you, stand with you, protect you, and even
> die for you if necessary. My commitment to you is not

based on how you look, whether your body is perfect, how much you accomplish, or whether we can have sex. It is based on the fact that I am your husband and you are my wife and that our union is a priceless gift that God has so graciously provided. I consider looking out for your well-being to be an assignment of utmost importance as long as we live.

Sound familiar? Cultivating this attitude toward your wife is the foundation for communicating the same message to your child. Some practical suggestions include:

Take the time to communicate. If you have been separated from your wife all day, debriefing with her is far more important than browsing through the evening paper or watching the six o'clock news.

Learn how to listen. If she's had a bad day, hear her out. It's more important to let her vent her feelings and find out what she needs rather than to try and "fix" everything.

Offer to take on some tasks that might not normally be your "turf" at home. Better yet, just do them without saying anything about it. Shoo her out of the kitchen, straighten things up, or offer to do the grocery run if you're not doing so already. Give her the opportunity to go out for a few hours to do something she enjoys or simply let her put her feet up or take a warm, uninterrupted bath.

Maintain (or start) a "date night" every week or at least twice a month. Spending a lot of money is not the object—but spending time together is. She needs to know that she is still desirable and that you appreciate her.

Unexpected flowers and cards always make an amazingly positive impact, as they have for generations.

Pray regularly for, and with, your wife.

On the warnings and cautions side, remember the following:

Learn to deal with conflict constructively. Most people do not automatically know how to discuss differences of opinion, especially strong ones, in a manner that is mutually respectful. If you find that discussions are generating more heat than light, take the time and effort to work with a pastor or counselor on your specific issues. Better yet, find a husband-wife team you both respect and who would be willing to serve as mentors, particularly in improving the basic way you approach disagreements.

Choose your timing carefully when you discuss conflicts and problems. If you are both tired, distracted, or irritated, the conversation will likely be unproductive.

Eliminate from your vocabulary words and phrases that insult or degrade your wife. If common courtesy would prevent you from saying them to a coworker or a complete stranger, you have no business saying them at home.

Never, under any circumstances, strike, shove, or in any way make physical contact with your wife as an expression of anger or an intention to injure her. There is never justification for taking this type of harmful action, but it is particularly destructive when she is pregnant. If you are angry and have run out of words, walk away from the situation and calm down. If you have hit your wife (or any woman in your life) in the past or feel the urge to do so, seek help from a pastor or counselor; such problems don't get better by being ignored or denied.

For the mother-to-be who is single
All of the recommendations mentioned earlier—finding a support team, taking advantage of helpful books and tapes, and establishing a quiet time—are especially important for

you and perhaps worth reading again. It is a courageous but often very difficult task to raise a child on your own, and you should not hesitate to seek whatever help is available within your family, church, or community at large. Most significantly, on many occasions you will also need to remember that God is keenly aware of all your needs and that He will be your "silent partner," standing beside you during those times when you feel you've reached the end of your resources.

At the same time, you will need to be careful with your attitude about your child. Watch out for the dangerous but all too common feeling that he is a burden, a hassle, or an obstacle to what you *really* would like to do with your life. (This viewpoint isn't unique to single mothers, by the way.) Because you might not have someone to share the workload, the time your child is dependent upon you may seem like an eternity. In fact it is but a season, and one that will never return. It may take effort to do so, but remember—especially when what you want most is a good night's sleep, one that isn't interrupted by crying—to cherish this new person in your life.

SO . . . ARE YOU READY TO BRING UP A CHILD?

This is a trick question.

As important as it is to plan ahead and prepare for parenthood, it is impossible to be *completely* ready. Even those who feel ready, willing, and able, who have had all their checkups, have gone to the childbirth classes, and have decked out the nursery to look like a designer showcase may be thrown a major curveball with the arrival of their new baby. An unexpected physical abnormality, a sudden medical problem during or after delivery, or perhaps a difficult temperament in an otherwise normal child can turn the lives of the most well-equipped parents inside out.

For most parents, there is never a perfect time to have a

baby. There will *always* be problems and circumstances to deal with: education, career paths, money, living space, health problems, and most of all, the basic maturity to nurture a child—especially the first one. Unfortunately, our culture has become so fixated on idealized notions of what constitutes a "wanted" pregnancy that in the United States there is one abortion for every three babies born.[2]

Many women have not actually been trying to become pregnant when they find out they are carrying a child, and a number are in difficult circumstances. This is a particularly acute issue when the mother is young, single, and limited in resources. Those who need help dealing with the circumstances surrounding their pregnancy should not have to fend for themselves. Over the past decade, hundreds of independent crisis pregnancy centers have been established across North America, all dedicated to helping pregnant women (both single and married) and those close to them tackle challenges of pregnancy and parenthood. Their services, all given without charge, range from locating a shelter and medical care to providing baby supplies and single-parent support groups.

The bottom line is that circumstances will *never* be perfect. No pregnancy, childbirth, or newborn baby will be flawless. But one major advantage of having nine months between conception and delivery is that it allows both Mom and Dad time to adjust and prepare for this major change in their lives. With time to reflect and draw on inner resources and assistance from family and community, the most turbulent beginnings of parenthood can ultimately have a successful outcome.

NOTES

1. H. Klonoff-Cohen et al., Journal of the American Medical Association 23 (March 8, 1995).
2. "Abortion Surveillance: Preliminary Data—United States, 1993," MMWR 45 (Washington, D.C., GPO, 1996): 235-238.

CHAPTER 2

Developing a Birth Plan
and Preparing the Nest

Just as every child is a unique and irreplaceable creation, each baby's entry into the world is a one-of-a-kind event. No two births are alike, even for parents who have had a number of children and feel like old pros. One critical aspect of child-birth never changes: Everyone involved in this momentous process wants the same outcome—a healthy baby and a healthy mother. Whether everything has moved like clock-work or nothing has gone as planned, this outcome is what matters most. This goal must be kept in mind during all phases of planning and experiencing birth and must override every other consideration.

There are many possible routes to the destination called healthy baby—healthy mother. A number of choices must be made along the way, although some parents may have more options than others. Who will provide the prenatal and deliv-ery care? What type of childbirth-preparation classes are avail-able? Who will be present at the delivery, and who will serve as coach? Will medications or anesthesia be used to relieve pain? Who will check on and follow the baby after delivery? Will the baby stay with Mom constantly or spend time in the nursery? What about breast-feeding versus bottle-feeding?

You may have strong convictions about all of these topics, or they may seem like a bewildering array of details to sort through when all you care about is getting everyone through the big event safe and sound. No doubt you will receive, if you haven't already, an earful of opinions from friends and relatives. There is no shortage of books, magazine articles, videotapes, and other materials available containing information and opinions about childbirth and all that follows it.

Like everything else in parenthood, wisdom about childbirth begins by avoiding extremes. Ignoring the inevitable due date and letting it happen without any preparation could result in a truly unpleasant experience, if not a full-blown disaster. But holding rigid expectations about every detail of the perfect birthing experience could lead to disappointment and frustration—or even skirmishes in the labor-and-delivery area. Either of these approaches will get the parent-child relationship off to a shaky start.

Instead, thoughtful consideration of the following questions will help you formulate a sense of direction as you approach the due date. Write down some of the things you would like—and not like—to be part of your birthing experience, as well as the areas about which you are uncertain. Seek advice from a few mature people who have been down the road before you and don't be dismayed if you hear differences of opinion. Be sure to review these topics with your health-care provider, preferably before the first contractions of labor begin!

WHO IS GOING TO PROVIDE YOUR CARE DURING PREGNANCY AND CHILDBIRTH?

Depending upon the community in which you live and the type of health-care coverage you have, you will be dealing with one or more of the following types of providers:

An **obstetrician/gynecologist (ob/gyn)** has completed four years of medical school, followed by at least four years of residency training specializing in the female reproductive system. An ob/gyn is prepared to handle both routine and problem deliveries and can perform cesarean sections. Some have additional training in treating infertility. A **maternal-**

fetal medicine specialist is an ob/gyn who has expertise in dealing with unusually difficult or high-risk pregnancies. **Perinatologists** may follow a pregnancy from beginning to end or may serve as consultants to other ob/gyns in their community.

Many **family physicians** (FPs, also called **family practitioners**) provide care for pregnant women. (In Canada, FPs take care of most uncomplicated deliveries.) Following medical school, an FP completes a three-year residency that encompasses the gamut of health care, including adult internal medicine, pediatrics, ob/gyn, and surgery. A family physician can provide routine obstetric care and baby and child care as well. Most do not take care of women with high-risk pregnancies or complicated deliveries, so FPs will routinely have an ob/gyn available for backup if trouble arises.

While most obstetricians and family physicians hold the familiar M.D. degree, a number of doctors who hold a **D.O. (Doctor of Osteopathy)** degree are equally qualified to serve as primary-care physicians during pregnancy and childbirth. However, this is not the case with chiropractors, naturopaths, and other alternative practitioners, whose training does not qualify them to provide prenatal care or deliver babies.

Nonphysician providers of prenatal care include the following:

A **certified nurse-midwife** (CNM) is a registered nurse who has additional hospital experience in labor and delivery and a year of training in midwifery. After passing a certification exam and obtaining a state license, a CNM can follow a normal pregnancy through delivery. The practice patterns of midwives in a given community will vary, depending upon the facilities and medical backup available to them. In a best-case scenario, they collaborate actively with ob/gyns and FPs, providing care for patients in hospitals and/or adjacent birth centers that handle uncomplicated deliveries.[1]

In some physicians' offices, a **nurse-practitioner** or **physician's assistant** may provide basic prenatal care under a doctor's supervision but will not actually deliver the baby.

WHO IS GOING TO PROVIDE CARE FOR THE BABY?

Your options for the baby's health-care provider may include the following:

Pediatricians have a medical degree and have taken at least three years of residency training in the care of infants, children, and adolescents. Like family physicians and ob/gyns, pediatricians are considered **primary-care physicians**—that is, they serve as the point of entry into the health-care system. They provide routine checkups and manage the vast majority of illnesses and other health problems of children. Some spend additional years developing expertise in subspecialty fields such as pediatric cardiology, neurology, and gastroenterology. (These physicians normally serve as consultants for specific problems, rather than providing primary care. In Canada pediatricians generally function as consultants.) A **neonatologist** specializes in the care of premature infants and sick newborns, usually in an intensive-care unit.

Family practitioners (whether holding M.D. or D.O. degrees) care for all age-groups, including infants and children. Depending upon their practice setting, FPs may request consultation from pediatricians or subspecialists when dealing with more difficult cases.

Pediatricians and family physicians may also employ **nurse-practitioners** and **physician's assistants**, who are trained to provide basic services in an office setting. They can carry out routine exams, treat common medical problems, and prescribe medication under the supervision of a physician. Some parents wonder whether they get their money's worth if they do not actually see a doctor during their visit. But often these

allied health professionals, as they are called, are actually able to spend more time answering questions and working through common problems.

CHOOSING HEALTH-CARE PROVIDERS FOR MOTHER AND BABY

This is a very important issue because the qualifications of your health-care providers and the quality of your relationship with them can have a major impact on your childbirth—and child rearing—experiences. Ideally you will be working with someone (or a team) who

- is competent. The greatest bedside manner in town can't compensate for lack of knowledge or poor judgment.
- treats you with respect. Courtesy, willingness to answer questions and explain clearly what is going on, and a feeling of collaboration rather than condescension are essential to good health care.
- is available. Whether you are dealing with a solo practitioner or a multispecialty group, you should be able to make contact with someone who can answer questions or respond to a problem within a reasonable period of time. That person may be the doctor, a colleague on call, an office nurse, a nurse-practitioner, or a physician's assistant.
- shares, or at least respects, your basic value system.

Finding all of these qualities in a practitioner may be easier said than done. Depending on their community and health insurance coverage, some families will have more choices than others. If you have options—for example, a list of preferred providers available through your insurance—don't hesitate to make inquiries. Most hospitals have referral lists of physicians who are permitted to admit patients to their facility. This will tell you that they have passed some level of scrutiny regarding their basic competence but not much else about their practice patterns or office routines.

If you already know someone in the medical community—a longtime family physician or a neighbor who is a nurse, for example—ask for recommendations. Take an informal poll of families with children in your church or neighborhood to see which names are mentioned most often. Families with pro-life convictions often prefer to see physicians who do not perform abortions. Local crisis pregnancy centers or other pro-life organizations usually maintain a list of these physicians.

If you have narrowed your list but aren't sure of your choice, you may want to set up a meet-the-doctor session. Such a visit should allow you to:

See how you are treated on the phone. Does the person at the other end of the line sound friendly, pleasant, and willing to talk, or harried and hostile?

Check out the office itself. Do you (or any of your children, if they are going to be seen there) feel comfortable and welcome? Is the waiting area tidy or a wreck? Does it feel like a bus station, a funeral parlor, or a nice place to relax? If children are going to be seen, are there things for them to do or look at?

Meet the doctor. If you make it clear up front that you want to talk briefly and not become a patient yet, you can also ask whether there will be a consultation fee. You may not be charged, in which case you shouldn't expect a half-hour conference. If you have a lot of questions about the practice, someone on the office staff may be able to answer them for you. A large, multidoctor practice may even have a designated patient-relations representative who will be more than happy to answer questions and show you around. Whatever you do, don't set up a get-acquainted visit and then suddenly ask, "By the way, can you look in Johnny's ear?" If you want medical attention, ask for it ahead of time and sign in as a patient.

Questions you may want to ask the physician who is going to take care of you during pregnancy and childbirth:

- What is the routine for prenatal visits?
- With whom does he or she share after-hours coverage? Ideally you should have a chance to get to know any and all of the people who might deliver your baby.
- What will happen when labor begins? Are there routines, such as electronic fetal monitoring, that are expected as a part of every childbirth? Any problems with moving around during labor? If you want to have an unmedicated childbirth, will the physician support that decision? If you desire pain relief, what options will be available? What is the physician's approach to an **episiotomy** (an incision to widen the opening of the birth canal just before delivery)?
- Don't be afraid to bring up the M word—*money*. How much will the prenatal and delivery care cost? How much more will it cost if a cesarean section is necessary? Is a checkup afterward included? How much will be covered by the insurance plan? (Before this discussion takes place, you would be wise to become familiar with the extent of your health insurance coverage.)
- How long should you expect to stay in the hospital after the delivery?

Questions you may want to ask of the physician who is going to care for the baby:

- How soon after birth will the baby be examined? If there is a need for cesarean delivery, will another doctor be called to care for the baby? (Some hospitals allow only pediatricians to tend to the newborn at the time of a cesarean birth. In these facilities, if a family practitioner had originally been designated as the baby's physician, he or she would usually assume care after the baby's condition has been judged stable.)

- What are the physician's views regarding breast or bottle feeding? Will you receive support for either decision? Any opinion regarding feeding on demand as opposed to attempting to establish a schedule?

HOW TO HAVE A GREAT RELATIONSHIP WITH YOUR DOCTOR

The best relationships between physicians and their patients, both young and old, are built on two basic qualities: mutual respect and flexibility. From the health-care provider's side, these are manifested by listening to you (and your child), providing understandable explanations, answering questions, and being willing to discuss options and alternatives to normal routines. From the patient's side, respect and flexibility involve acknowledging the value of the provider's training and experience, being willing to change course (especially during labor and delivery) if things are not going the way you had expected, and understanding that no one can guarantee a perfect outcome.

If you find yourself seeing a doctor who insists on "my way or the highway," who talks down to you like a schoolteacher addressing a misbehaving child, who races in and out of the exam room like the White Rabbit in *Alice in Wonderland,* or who won't give your questions the time of day, you might consider choosing another practitioner.

Assuming that you have a decent working relationship with your health-care provider, you can get even more out of your visits by following a few basic suggestions.

- What is the routine for checkups and immunizations after the baby is born?
- Does he or she have strong opinions about discipline? (This topic may be too far-reaching to cover during a visit of this type, although it should be brought up as the baby approaches the toddler months.) Are there any books or other materials regarding child rearing that he recommends? (This may provide you a glimpse of the practitioner's worldview and approach to basic values.)

- DO let the doctor know at the outset of your visit what you want to talk about. If you have a number of concerns and want to make the most of your time, give him a list of your questions, letting him know what's most important to you.
- DO make friends with the nurses and other office staff. They'll often be able to help you solve problems more quickly than the doctor will.
- DO respect your doctor's off-call boundaries. If you run into him at church or in a supermarket, don't ask for medical advice.
- DON'T utter the dreaded phrase "By the way . . ." at the end of the visit. That new problem may need more time than the other things you've already discussed.
- DON'T bring surprise patients. ("While I'm here, could you look at Billy's throat?")
- DON'T insist you will "talk with the doctor and no one else," except in very unusual or highly confidential situations. Many physicians rely heavily on a nurse to screen calls and questions, and refusing to talk with her may delay getting your problem solved.
- DON'T challenge every recommendation he makes. Good dialogue is healthy, but if you find yourself arguing more than agreeing, you should probably seek care from someone else.

WHERE WILL YOUR BABY BE BORN?

While interest in birth centers and home deliveries has waxed and waned over the past few decades (see page 54), in North America hospitals remain the most widely utilized birth setting for a number of reasons. The first and most obvious is that most pregnant women seek care from obstetricians and family practitioners—all of whom are trained, and for the most part continue to practice, in hospitals.

But a more compelling reason, and the overwhelming advantage of a hospital delivery, is the availability of definitive care for both mother and baby if something goes wrong. This is particularly important when a pregnancy is known to be complicated by medical problems such as diabetes, high blood pressure, prematurity, twins or multiples, or an unusual position of the baby in the uterus. Even a straightforward pregnancy can have a stormy conclusion, especially if it is your first, and the rapid availability of a full range of medical, surgical, and pediatric services is a reassuring safety net. If you have been told that you have a high risk pregnancy, it would be wise to ask your obstetrician whether the hospital in which you are planning to deliver the baby is equipped to handle problems that might develop before or after the birth. Hospitals that offer a wider range of resources (such as a neonatal intensive care unit) may be better suited to handle complex problems in both mother and newborn.

In addition, more options for pain relief, if needed, are available within the hospital than in other settings.

Some expectant parents have concerns about interventions and procedures they might experience during a hospital delivery, perhaps wondering if they leave their autonomy and options at the door when they check in. But over the years most hospitals have revised their maternity-care policies to become much more parent-friendly.

In response to patients' desires (and common sense), most

hospitals have drastically altered their maternity-care areas to create **labor/delivery/recovery (LDR) rooms.** Traditionally, women in hospital maternity-care areas have labored in one room, delivered the baby in another, recovered and stabilized in a third, and finally spent one or more days in a regular hospital room. In contrast, LDR rooms are usually large and nicely decorated (often with a couch, TV, and ample space for family members). The entire labor-and-birth process can proceed without the disruption of moving in and out of four different rooms.

In some facilities, mother and baby remain in the LDR for the duration of their stay, in which case the room is called an **LDRP,** the *P* standing for *postpartum,* meaning "after delivery." Because they combine the best of both worlds—a family-friendly environment with high-tech capabilities—LDRs (or LDRPs) in hospitals have enjoyed wide acceptance by both parents and health-care providers. In addition to the more pleasant surroundings, labor-and-delivery policies in most hospitals have also shifted to a more family-friendly, flexible, collaborative approach.

You can take a number of steps to become better prepared for a birth experience at a hospital:

Visit the facility and become acquainted with the labor-and-delivery area. Familiarity with the environment and the staff can greatly increase confidence and comfort during labor. Most hospitals host prenatal classes, tours, maternity teas, and other outreach activities. Hospital staff enjoy caring for women in labor, so get to know them, look things over, and feel free to ask lots of questions.

See if the hospital has specific policies regarding the number of people allowed in the delivery area. A husband's participation is almost always desired by the hospital, but you may wish to have other family members or close friends present as well. Are there any restrictions?

Find out what will happen to your baby after the birth. Will your baby stay with you? Is "rooming in" the rule or the exception? What routines are part of the baby's care? Is the hospital equipped to handle medical problems of the newborn? If your baby is premature, has an infection, or needs intensive care, will he be transferred to another facility?

Ask about the kind of teaching and assistance available after delivery. Does the staff provide "basic training"? If you have trouble nursing, is there a consultant available to help?

Take care of the paperwork ahead of time. Most hospitals allow you to preregister, check insurance coverage, and deal with other business details so this won't be a distraction during labor. Also, find out from your insurance carrier how many days in the hospital they will cover, assuming there are no unexpected problems. Some policies are more restrictive than others, and your doctor should be aware of any financial constraints you may have.

Ask the doctor about the possibility of obtaining some of the baby's blood from the umbilical cord at the time of delivery, for possible use in the future. When the cord is cut (See chapter 6, "The Moment Arrives," page 115), some of the baby's blood is routinely collected from the placenta (not from the baby herself) for certain tests. There are now facilities which will freeze a sample of this blood (a process called *cryopreservation*) for use in the future as a source of *stem cells*. These cells could potentially be very useful in the treatment of certain diseases—especially disorders involving blood cells, such as leukemia—should your baby develop one of these illnesses later in life. Cryopreservation companies charge both initial and annual fees for this service. While the odds are remote that your baby/child might ever need these cells, it is reasonable to discuss this option with your doctor, especially if there is a history of leukemia, lymphoma, or other blood disorders in your family.

WHAT TYPE OF CHILDBIRTH CLASSES WILL YOU TAKE?

Notice that the question was not *whether* you will take child-birth classes. The normal process of moving a baby from the womb to the outside world is called labor for a reason—it's work. One reason so many women were heavily sedated during childbirth a few decades ago is that few were adequately prepared for what would happen once labor started. As the contractions of the uterus became more uncomfortable, fear and anxiety would multiply the pain until virtually all control would be lost. In 1944 the groundbreaking book *Childbirth without Fear* by British physician Grantly Dick-Read introduced the concept that a woman who understood what was happening during labor and learned how to work with it could have a calm, controlled, and far more comfortable birth experience.

Over the next several years, a variety of prepared childbirth approaches and techniques were developed as the goal of having a natural childbirth gained popularity and acceptance. Some advocates of natural childbirth campaigned for labor and delivery completely devoid of any medical intervention, at times putting expectant parents who subscribed to these ideas at odds with their physicians. In response, many doctors complained about "natural childbirth fanatics" who challenged every detail of the hospital routine. But over time, physicians observed that well-informed couples working as a team had a much better experience—and usually had an easier time from a medical perspective—than terrified, unprepared patients who spent the entire labor and delivery in a state of panic and uncontrolled pain.

Childbirth classes are now considered a routine component of prenatal care. They come in all shapes and sizes and may be presented in hospitals, homes, or community centers.

WHAT ABOUT BIRTH CENTERS AND DELIVERIES AT HOME?

Some hospitals have established **birth centers** on or adjacent to their campus, staffed by midwives, family physicians, and/or obstetricians who are affiliated with the hospital. These facilities are geared toward women with low-risk, straightforward pregnancies, offering pregnancy-and-delivery care in one location. Usually prenatal visits are carried out in the same location and by the same health-care providers as the childbirth. The cost of birth-center care may be significantly less than the formal hospital setting. There is a relaxed familiarity to the surroundings and typically few surprises for the parents-to-be. Should a significant problem develop, however, mother and baby can be moved quickly into the main hospital for definitive care.

A number of **freestanding birth centers** operate independently and geographically separate from hospitals, offering similar services but with one distinct disadvantage: If a major problem should arise, mother and baby must be transferred to the nearest hospital. This process can be upsetting, time-consuming, costly (if an ambulance is needed), and potentially risky.

One study analyzing the outcomes of more than twelve thousand births at eighty-four freestanding birth centers in the United States showed a satisfactory safety record for low-risk pregnancies—although one out of four women delivering her first baby required transfer to a hospital. Since only 7 percent of women who already had one or more vaginal deliveries required transfer, *freestanding birth centers would be best*

Instructors may emphasize one or another school of thought or blend ideas from several sources. Needless to say, some classes will be more organized and detailed than others. The

utilized only for low-risk pregnancies in women who have already had at least one child.

Furthermore, it is imperative that the health-care practitioners not only be well trained in normal childbirth but also be capable of recognizing significant problems and be willing to transfer you promptly from the facility should the need arise.

Home birth is usually chosen by those with a fervent conviction that this is the most natural and least intrusive way to bring a child into the world. But home birthing compromises safety for the sake of a particular style of birth experience. If a serious problem develops suddenly—an unfortunate but very real possibility in maternity care—the home team is at a major disadvantage, and a catastrophe could occur in the time it takes to pack up and move to the nearest hospital. Even if a problem is less severe or develops more slowly, resources at home are extremely limited. Because home birth is not considered mainstream health care in our society, it may attract fringe practitioners whose credentials and skills are questionable.

If you are thinking about having your baby at home, you should carefully review your reasons and ask whether several hours of convenience and comfort at home are really worth the potential for a lifetime of damage—or a loss of life. All things considered, choosing to proceed with a home birth is not a wise decision.

In the final analysis, if you really have your heart set on a nonhospital type of delivery, a birth center directly affiliated with an adjacent hospital would be the better option— assuming, of course, that your pregnancy is uncomplicated.

leader should be a certified childbirth educator. Your doctor will probably have a referral or two, but you would be wise to ask some parents who have recently experienced childbirth for their recommendations as well.

Some hospitals or large medical groups also offer early-pregnancy classes dealing with nutrition, exercise, and general self-care. If available, these are well worth attending.

Normally you will begin childbirth-preparation classes during the sixth or seventh month of pregnancy, with a goal of being finished two weeks before the baby's due date. Most meet one evening per week for eight to twelve weeks, though in some communities late starters can take a crash course in one or two weekends. Childbirth preparation is intended to be a team effort of the mother and another person who will be available for the entire course, including the birth itself. Usually this team will be a husband-wife pair, but in some situations (especially with a single mother), a relative or close friend may be serving as the teammate.

The following areas should be covered as part of the curriculum:

- What happens during pregnancy and childbirth: basic anatomy and physiology, including the development of the baby, changes in the mother, and the stages of labor and birth.
- Basic self-care: nutrition, exercise, sexuality, and maintaining a healthy lifestyle.
- Managing the contractions: relaxation, breathing, and pain-control techniques; positions during labor; and the final pushing stage.
- Details of the birth setting: when and where to go, what will happen in the labor-and-delivery area (or birth center), how the labor will be monitored, possible interventions, and pain-medication options if and when needed.

- Possible problem areas and their treatment: failure to progress, fetal distress, premature labor, prolonged rupture of membranes, or cesarean section and its aftereffects.
- Preparing for the first days of baby care, including feeding techniques.

The approach most commonly taught in childbirth classes is the **Lamaze method** or some variation of it. This method was introduced by French obstetrician Fernand Lamaze in his 1958 book *Painless Childbirth*. In America, Lamaze's techniques have been called *psychoprophylaxis* (literally, "mind protection"), and the organization that accredits its teachers is the American Society for Psychoprophylaxis in Obstetrics,

ATTENTION FATHERS: BE AVAILABLE WHEN THE TIME ARRIVES

As has already been mentioned, fathers are no longer routinely shuttled off to a smoke-filled waiting area while their children are being born. They are now encouraged to play an active role in the delivery process through attending childbirth classes and acting as coaches (or at least loving supporters) during labor. But one additional, very practical detail involves being careful with the calendar.

The last month of your wife's pregnancy is probably not the best time to schedule several double work shifts or back-to-back business trips to the other side of the country. Obviously, no one can know for sure the exact due date, but it's a shame to work diligently through the preparation process and then miss the actual event. This may require giving your employer a fair amount of advance notice about the upcoming delivery and your desire to be present for it. The same type of advance planning is also important for the person who serves as coach for a single mother during her labor.

or ASPO. Along with other information, ASPO/Lamaze teaches a technique of distracting the mind from pain by using special breathing patterns and actively focusing attention on an external object.

Another widely utilized method was launched in 1965 when Denver obstetrician Robert Bradley published *Husband-Coached Childbirth*. Along with stressing the involvement of the mother's husband as a coach (a term men could relate to), the **Bradley method** teaches deep relaxation techniques rather than focusing attention away from the body. Of these two approaches, the Bradley method tends more to discourage pain medications and other interventions.

Some childbirth educators teach their own homegrown blend of both approaches. Regardless of the method you choose, the object of your preparation should not be to become a walking encyclopedia, reform the entire health-care system, or nurture unrealistic expectations of a problem-free childbirth experience. Training should combine a broad base of general knowledge, adequate time to practice pain-reducing techniques, reassurance that you can handle both normal and unexpected developments, and a healthy dose of reality.

If you truly desire an unmedicated childbirth but find that you can't manage the pain, accepting medication is not a moral failure.[2] If you forget some of the finer points of your breathing technique during the heat of the moment, you're not the first to do so. If an uneventful labor suddenly takes a surprise detour at the last minute, you need to be ready to ask intelligent questions, weigh the options, make an informed decision, and remain calm if things don't turn out the way you expected. *Remember: A healthy baby and a healthy mother are ultimately more important than a perfect childbirth experience.* You want to be as prepared as possible, and you should work diligently toward a controlled labor and joyous delivery, but you're not going to be graded on your performance.

As was already mentioned in chapter 1, this book does not contain step-by-step information about the childbirth process. You should be learning those details through your physician and childbirth classes.

What Does the New Arrival Need at Home?

As important as it is to prepare for the birth itself, there are some important and practical details to consider about life *after* your baby's arrival. New parents-to-be are often concerned about the amount of clothing and equipment they will need when their son or daughter finally arrives—and how much it will cost. If you have the financial resources to outfit a designer nursery and a four-season infant wardrobe, you will find no shortage of catalogues and showrooms to accommodate you. But most young couples with growing families are stretching their pocketbooks in several directions. You should be relieved to know that it is possible to meet a new baby's needs exceptionally well without creating a newborn penthouse. After all, infancy is the one stage in a child's life when he is not interested in material things. The newborn doesn't care where his clothes and equipment came from. Modest surroundings that are rich in parental love and tenderness will yield far better results than showcase environments that are emotionally impoverished. Remember—the greatest person who ever lived was born in a stable.

Actually, it is extremely unlikely that you will have to buy everything you need and want for the new baby. If you have older children, or friends and relatives with children, a number of items can usually be borrowed or handed down for the new arrival. Friends may throw a baby shower or two for you before the delivery and, after the big event, indulgent grandparents and other well-wishers will perhaps descend on you with all manner of gifts. If you are a single parent or you have had to deal with opposition and obstacles to your pregnancy, your local crisis pregnancy center (CPC) can assist you with a variety of baby supplies. Many new parents are able to obtain needed supplies at a fraction of the original cost by visiting local garage sales and thrift shops. Babies and children outgrow their clothes so quickly that many secondhand items that have been worn very little (and look brand-new) can be purchased for a few dollars. Used nursery furniture and equipment can also be picked up at bargain prices, but make sure that whatever you buy meets current safety standards, especially if it is more than a few years old (see pages 64–65).

It's a good idea to create your need/wish list *before* you start purchasing items for the nursery. You can use your list to keep track of what you've already acquired so that shopping trips for baby gear will be shorter and more focused. The goods you will need, commonly referred to as a **layette**, will fall into the following basic categories:

Clothing
While there is no magic formula for deciding how many of each type of garment to acquire, the following list covers the basics:

- Small, lightweight (receiving) blankets—3 or 4
- Sleeper sets with feet—3 or 4
- Light tops (gowns or sacques)—2 or 3
- T shirts or undershirts—3 or 4
- Socks or booties—3 or 4
- Sweaters—2 (heaviness depends on climate)
- Hats—2 (level of protection depends on climate)
- Infant sleeping bag (bunting)—1

As you acquire clothing for your baby, remember three important principles:

Think ahead. Most newborns outgrow newborn-size clothes

in a very few weeks, if not days, so favoring somewhat larger sizes for much of the wardrobe is a wise idea. This is especially true for those cute but costly dress-up outfits that may hang idly in the closet after a few outings. If you receive a number of

SHOULD YOUR CHILDREN WATCH THE BABY BEING BORN?

A few decades ago, only doctors and nurses welcomed the vast majority of American newborns into the world. Once the "husband barrier" was broken and fathers became active in the delivery process, some couples wanted childbirth to become a family affair. Why not let the other children watch the birth of their new brother or sister?

Some enthusiasts describe positive experiences with children as young as four years of age watching siblings being born. But the likelihood of an emotional jolt for the children, the potential distraction for the adults, and the issue of violating the boundaries of modesty within a family are all good reasons to keep your kids out of the delivery room. A better option would be to have the children prepared to see their new sibling soon after delivery—when both mother and baby appear to be okay and have had a few minutes to allow things to settle down.

If you choose to video the delivery for future viewing by your children or other family members, consider carefully who ought to see what. A living-color, full-frame shot of Mom's pelvic region isn't exactly appropriate viewing for the general public. There are lots of other interesting things to capture (especially facial expressions) during childbirth, and it would be prudent to talk over your wishes with whoever is shooting your video for you. If your video does indeed directly view the moment of birth, consider creating an edited G-rated version for the kids to see later on. This might include, for example, shots of the birth from a vantage point looking over the mother's shoulder.

these as gifts, don't remove the tags and boxes and consider doing some discreet trades for bigger sizes at the store where they were bought. If you are buying outfits for the next few months, consider what the future may hold weather-wise.

Think safety. Be sure that no garment is too snug around your baby's neck, hands, and feet and completely avoid any accessory such as a necklace or a long ribbon that could become tangled around the neck. Buttons, beads, and other small objects attached to shirts or pants may be a hazard if they can become detached and find their way into little hands, mouths, and airways; it's a good idea to reinforce buttons and bows, which requires only some time, a needle, and thread. Snaps are safer and handier. Infant and toddler clothing should be flame-retardant—a safety feature that will be stated on the label. Prewash the baby clothes you buy, whether secondhand or fresh from the department store. Use detergents without perfumes or other ingredients that might irritate the baby's skin. Many brand names offer such products; this information will appear on the label. This will assure not only that used garments are sanitary but also that new clothing is free from any detergents or other chemicals used during the finishing processes.

Don't worry about shoes at this point. Not only are they unnecessary before a baby can walk, but they may interfere with normal growth of the feet.

Think convenience and comfort. Since diaper changing is a frequent activity with babies, easy access is preferable to a complicated, multilayered outfit when cleanup is necessary.

Diapers
You will need to decide whether you want to use cloth or disposable diapers, or at least which you would like to start with.

Disposable diapers are abundant in every supermarket and most notable for their convenience. When it's time for a change, take them off, dump any solid waste into the toilet, fold them up, and throw them away. Manufacturers also compete with one another to see who can create the most leak-proof diaper by combining super absorbency with cleverly engineered plastic linings that prevent urine or stool from escaping onto bedding or furniture. For all of these advantages, however, disposable diapers have their drawbacks. Not only are they more costly than cloth diapers, but their plastic liners do not disintegrate, raising environmental concerns. (Over two thousand diapers enter dumps and landfills every year for each baby using disposables.)

Cloth diapers are less expensive, even when you use a diaper service. But they must be laundered by someone. If that someone is you, wash them separately from other clothing after rinsing them out in the toilet. Use hot water and a double rinse and avoid fabric softeners and scented additives, which can provoke rashes on some infants' skin. Since newborns will soil as many as ten or more diapers a day, you will need a stockpile of three or four dozen. You will also need pins or clips (unless you use the newer models with Velcro fasteners) and some type of waterproof protective covering, unless you buy the all-in-one versions.

Diaper services bring the convenience level of cloth diapering nearly up to that of disposables and still at less cost. Shop around for prices, delivery schedules (twice weekly is typical), and policy regarding whether you rinse first or simply toss the diaper, waste and all, into the pail the service provides. The price of the service should be weighed against the cost of laundry supplies and utility bills when you do the job yourself, as well as your time and energy, which may be in very short supply. While cloth diapers may appear kinder to the environment, it should be noted that diaper services (or parents at home) must consume considerable amounts of water and energy to clean them. Ultimately your choice between disposable and cloth diapers should be compatible with your family's time and budget constraints.

Furniture and other hardware

This is where your biggest onetime expenses may lie and where some judicious borrowing of equipment from friends and family will be helpful.

A **cradle** or **bassinet** is a portable sleep space, allowing you the convenience of changing your newborn's sleeping quarters relatively easily. In some families, a cradle whose gentle rocking has calmed restless infants for many decades is handed down from generation to generation. Bassinets don't sway, but they do have the advantage of being portable. Be certain that the legs of the bassinet are stable and sturdy so it cannot accidentally collapse.

If you want the new baby right next to your own bed or elsewhere in the house, a cradle/bassinet will allow you more flexibility. However, within three or four months your baby will outgrow it, and he will need to graduate to a crib.

A **crib** can be the newborn's sleeping place from day one and will be in use for two to three years. Since your baby will spend time in a crib without direct supervision, this must be a completely safe environment. In order to prevent falls and other types of accidents, cribs manufactured over the past several years have had to comply with a number of safety requirements. If your baby is going to be using an older model, you will need to check the following:

- The **slats** in the crib should be no wider than two and three-eighths inches apart.
- Unless they are supporting a high canopy, **corner posts** that extend above the rails are a potential hazard because they may entangle loose clothing. They should be unscrewed or cut off.
- **Paint** on an old crib may contain lead, and any flakes

of paint accidentally swallowed by a curious baby could cause lead poisoning. When in doubt, sand off the old coat (taking care not to inhale it yourself) and apply some high-quality enamel in its place.

- The **headboards** and **footboards** should be solid and without decorative cutouts that could trap a head, hand, or foot.

In addition, you should check the following before you place your baby in any crib, new or old:

- The **mattress pad** should fit snugly into the frame. If you can wedge more than two fingers between the pad and the crib side, the mattress pad is too small. Remove any extraneous tags and thin plastic wrappings. If you use a mattress cover, be sure it is made of thick plastic that, ideally, can be zipped around the pad. Don't place pillows or any soft bedding material other than a fitted sheet under the baby. His head or face might become accidentally buried in the soft folds, especially if he happens to be face down, which could lead to suffocation. (This may be one of the conditions leading to the tragedy of sudden infant death syndrome, or SIDS. See sidebar, pages 216–217.) Sheepskin, down mattresses, feather beds, and wavy water beds pose similar risks.
- **Bumper pads**, securely tied into place, should line the inside of the crib. When your baby can pull up to a standing position, the pads should be removed, since they can assist a baby's attempts to climb over the rail. The same is true of large stuffed animals that a toddler might use as a soft step or launching pad for a trip over the side.
- The **side rails** should latch securely in place, with the release mechanism out of reach of exploring fingers.

When fully raised, the rails should extend at least twenty inches above the top of the mattress. As your baby grows and eventually stands up, the mattress will need to be lowered.

- If you hang any **mobiles** above the crib, be sure they remain out of reach a few months from now when your baby begins to move toward (and grab for) interesting objects.
- For many reasons—sun exposure, shades, cords, and, worst of all, the possibility of a disastrous fall—*never put a crib next to a window, whether open or shut.*

A **changing table** can be a convenient one-stop location for diaper duties at home. But it is also notorious for being the place from which a baby takes his first fall. If you use a changing table:

- Never step away, turn around, or otherwise divert your attention from the job at hand unless you pick up the baby to do so. Babies seem to choose this moment to show off their new ability to roll over—and then take a fast trip to the floor. Never answer the phone or the door if it means walking away from your baby.
- To reduce the likelihood of such a fall, make sure you have all the changing gear—new diaper, wipes, etc.—within reach before you start.
- The table should have a two-inch guardrail around its edge and a safety strap to help you secure the baby. However, these should not be considered a substitute for your undivided attention when your infant is on the changing table.
- Don't distract an older baby by letting him handle a can of baby powder (which he might accidentally unload into his or your airspace), play with a disposable diaper (whose plastic liner he might rip off and choke on),

or suck on some other miscellaneous object on the changing table.

Car seats

Unlike a changing table, a **car seat** is an absolute necessity. Automobile accidents are a leading cause of death in children, and proper use of car seats could prevent hundreds of tragic losses every year. As a result, every state has passed laws requiring their use. Most hospitals will not allow you to take your new baby home without one, and many will loan or rent you a seat if you cannot buy one.

Each infant, toddler, and young child must be properly secured into an appropriate car seat *every* time he rides in a car—*no exceptions*. Holding a baby in your lap, even if you are wearing a seat belt, can cause him to be crushed between you and the dashboard in an accident—assuming that he hasn't been thrown through the windshield first. Even if the time needed to buckle everyone in place will be far longer than the drive itself, *do it anyway*, because most accidents occur within a few miles of home at speeds below thirty miles an hour. The death of a child for any reason is always a horrendous loss for a family, but the pain is greatly magnified when that loss could have been prevented.

The car seat for a newborn should be either an infant or convertible model manufactured since 1982, the year federal safety regulations were enacted. Because the newborn has no head control, he must face backward to prevent dangerous, rapid forward movement of the head during a sudden stop. The seat should position him so that his upper body is angled upward but not sitting upright, since he can't keep his head from flopping forward. You may need to use small rolled-up towels or diapers to pad the seat and keep him from slouching. The center of the backseat is the safest location for him, and thus you should avoid putting him in the forward passenger seat. This means that, should he start to fuss, you will have to resist the temptation to turn around and tend to him while your vehicle is in motion.

An infant car seat can have the distinct advantage of doubling as a carrier or even a comfortable napping spot for a small baby when you're not in the car. However, the reverse is not true: You should never use an infant carrier as a car seat. Once your baby outgrows the infant car seat (usually between nine and twelve months of age, or about twenty pounds), it will have little use until another baby enters your life. A convertible seat can be reconfigured to face forward when your baby reaches his first birthday and will accommodate him until he weighs forty pounds. It will be, however, too heavy and cumbersome to serve any other purpose.

It is very important to read directions carefully, to make certain the seat can be anchored securely in the car(s) that will carry your baby, and to see that any prospective chauffeurs (grandparents, for example) know how to use the seat properly.

Other safety measures to consider in regard to baby car seats include:

- *If your car has a passenger-side air bag, you should never place your baby—or for that matter, any child younger than twelve years of age—in the forward passenger seat.* As was just noted, even without the air bag, the backseat is a safer location for an infant seat. But if an air bag is present, it can cause serious or even fatal injuries to a baby if the bag inflates during an accident.
- When your car is sitting in the sun, cover the infant seat with a towel, since plastic and metal parts can become hot. Even if a towel has been used, check the temperature of the seat, belts, and buckles with your hand to be sure you're not depositing your baby into a veritable frying pan.

- At some time (or perhaps most of the time), your baby will wail indignantly when put into the car seat. Make sure there is nothing physically annoying him (such as a hot buckle or a stray toy poking his leg), talk or sing sweetly to him, and press on. But do not give in and take him out of the seat to restore calm to the car. If for some reason your baby's crying has reached an unusually distracting pitch, pull off the road and tend to his needs. But then buckle him in before you continue.

- *Do not, under any circumstances, ever leave your baby—or any children—unattended in your car.* Amazing and terrible things can happen while you "just dash into the cleaners for thirty seconds." Aside from physical risks to your baby, such as becoming overheated on a warm day or chilled when it's cold, there's always the exciting possibility that an older child will discover how to release the brake—or at least find the horn. And, while we would rather not think about such horrific possibilities, children left unattended in a car present a prime opportunity for a predator who is seeking his next victim to abduct and abuse.

Baby carriers—front and back

Many parents find front and back carriers extremely helpful during the first several months of a child's life. They allow a parent to tend to a variety of activities with hands free and baby close and secure. Front carriers are most useful for the first three to six months, after which a baby's increasing size, weight, and activity may begin to strain a parent's back and shoulders. Carriers may be configured so the baby is in an upright position with legs dangling through leg holes (like a backpack worn backwards) or in a "sling" arrangement in which the baby can lie horizontally as in a hammock. Of the two, the sling is somewhat more versatile; the baby can be placed in a variety of orientations (not merely staring at Mom's or Dad's chest), the weight can be adjusted or shifted to either shoulder, and some parents are able to continue carrying babies this way comfortably well past the first birthday. One variation on the sling is configured to allow an infant four months or older to be carried on one hip, an arrangement some parents find more comfortable.

When buying a front carrier, you may want to wait until you can take your baby with you and then "try him on for size." Pay attention to these details:

- How would you rate the padding, distribution of weight, and general comfort? Would you be able to walk around for extended periods of time with your baby in this particular carrier?
- How easy (or difficult) is it to put on and adjust, or remove, the carrier?
- How well supported are the baby's head and body?
- Does your baby seem contented in this arrangement? Some babies will be more calm and comfortable in a sling, while others may seem to prefer a vertical carrier.

If you choose a front carrier, you may find that carrying your baby for extended periods of time in a front pack is convenient for you, soothing for your new baby, and a bonding experience between the two of you. Some parents whose babies seem to cry a great deal if not held may find that a comfortable front carrier calms the infant—and maintains the parents' sanity. However, *you must not use a carrier when you are driving or riding in a car.*

A back carrier is most useful after a baby has gained steady head control, at which point you won't need to worry about the position and support of the head (which you cannot see). If both parent and passenger find the carrier agreeable, it may remain in service through the toddler months. As with front carriers, it is a wise idea to try on various models with the baby in place. One potential disadvantage of this arrangement is that you can't see or talk directly to the baby. This may become a bigger problem if he is irritable or begins to shift himself around by pushing against the frame. When using a back carrier you must also remember to bend your knees if you are tending to something close to the ground. If you bend at the waist, the baby may topple out of the carrier.

Carriages and strollers

These familiar items are useful when you have some distance to cover with your baby and you don't want to carry him. They come in a variety of shapes, sizes, and prices, some plain and simple and others loaded with bells and whistles. There are convertible models that can be changed from a carriage to a stroller when a baby becomes mobile and jogging (or even racing) strollers for those who want to do some serious exercise while the baby comes along for the ride (see color insert).

Unfortunately, according to the U.S. Consumer Product Safety Commission, there are more than ten thousand emergency-room visits every year involving children under five who have been injured in carriages or strollers. If you acquire one of these now or during the coming months, look beyond price and durability to these safety features as well:

- Look for a wide base that will not tip over easily.
- Check the seat belt. Is it securely attached to the frame? Is it strong? Is it easy for you to fasten and unfasten?
- Check the brakes. Do they securely lock the wheels? Are there brakes on two wheels rather than on just one? Are they easy to use? Will they be out of reach of inquisitive fingers when your baby becomes a curious toddler?
- If there is a basket that holds your supplies or parcels, for stability it should be placed low and in front of or directly over the rear wheels.

Your safety awareness will need to continue as you utilize a carriage or stroller for months into the future:

- Make sure the equipment is appropriate for the baby's size. Once a baby can sit up on his own, it won't be long before he can fall out of a carriage, so he must graduate to a stroller into which he can be more securely fastened.
- Always use the seat belt, even if your baby (or older child) protests.
- Don't hang a purse or shopping bag over the handle— the leverage may tip the carriage or stroller backwards.
- Keep older children away from the stroller as you fold or unfold it.

"READY OR NOT, HERE I COME!"

In a few short years you will probably hear your child call out this familiar phrase during some energetic neighborhood game. But now as you await your baby's arrival, you will also hear (and feel) the same message as your baby begins the inevitable passage from the womb to the outside world. Ready or not, your daughter or son will soon be arriving.

We hope that well before the delivery date you will have the time (and energy) to make some of the important physical, financial, emotional, and spiritual preparations that have been outlined in this and the previous chapter. If you haven't yet, and the due date is fast approaching, don't panic. You can jump on the learning curve at any time—even well after your baby has been born.

NOTES

1. *Lay midwives* do not have a nursing degree. They may or may not have formal training, a state license, or physician backup. Skill levels vary, and health-care professionals generally have serious qualms about their capabilities should any problem develop.

2. One approach that relieves pain while allowing you to remain awake and alert is the **epidural anesthetic**, which may be given either by the

obstetrician (if he or she is trained to do so) or an anesthesiologist. This involves the injection of pain-relieving medication through a small plastic catheter into the space just adjacent to the fibrous sack that surrounds the spinal cord. Pain is dramatically reduced without paralysis of the lower half of the body, and the ability to push during the final stage of labor is usually not affected. The catheter can be left in place if more medication is needed, and if a cesarean birth takes place, this medication can provide a great deal of nondrowsy pain relief.

CHAPTER 3

Birth Defects and Prenatal Testing

Every parent-to-be anticipates the arrival of a new son or daughter with a strong sense of anticipation and excitement but also with a certain level of concern in the back of his or her mind: *What if there is something wrong with my baby?* For some, a known family risk of a particular disease or a child already born with a birth defect usually brings this concern to the forefront of prenatal considerations: *How can we find out ahead of time whether or not this baby will be normal?*

WHAT ARE BIRTH DEFECTS?

Birth defects, also called **congenital disorders**, are abnormalities that are present at birth, whether or not they are diagnosed at that time. According to the March of Dimes Birth Defects Foundation, some type of birth defect is present in one out of every twenty-eight newborns. More than three thousand specific birth defects have been identified, ranging from conditions that are barely noticeable to some that are catastrophic. (Birth defects are the most common cause of infant death in the United States, claiming more than eight thousand lives every year.[1]) These disorders sometimes involve visible changes in one or several parts of the body, or they can affect the baby on a less visible metabolic or microscopic level.

WHAT CAUSES BIRTH DEFECTS?

While the underlying causes of many types of birth defects are understood, *in roughly two out of three cases the specific reason is unknown* and thus assumed to be the result of a complex interaction of genetic and nongenetic factors during the intricate process of the baby's development within the womb. Birth defects in which a specific cause can be identified fall into the following categories:

Genetic abnormalities

Genetic abnormalities, which arise directly from the transmission of genetic information from one generation to the next, account for 20 to 25 percent of all birth defects. In what is truly a marvel of engineering, all of the information necessary to form and maintain a human being is coded on long strands of the spiral molecule known as **deoxyribonucleic acid**, or **DNA**. An extended segment of DNA that serves a specific function (such as providing the blueprint for a certain protein) is called a **gene**, and an estimated fifty to one hundred thousand of these genes govern the physical attributes of each individual. Rather than being randomly dispersed throughout the cells whose functions it governs, DNA is packed into forty-six dense bodies known as **chromosomes**, all of which easily fit within the nucleus of a cell. Our forty-six chromosomes consist of twenty-three pairs, of which twenty-two are known as nonsex or **autosomal**, while one pair consists of the sex chromosomes designated X and Y.

Each of our 60 trillion cells contains *all* of our genetic code, with the exception of egg and sperm cells, which contain only a single set of twenty-three chromosomes. At the time of conception, twenty-three chromosomes from the mother's egg and twenty-three from the father's sperm combine to begin a new human being. These include an X chromosome contributed by the egg, and either an X or a Y chromosome from the sperm. If the final product contains two X chromosomes, the baby will be a girl, while an XY combination of chromosomes will result in a boy.

While this extraordinarily complex activity normally proceeds without mishap, at times it does not function as originally designed. This might result in profound abnormalities in the number or structure of the chromosomes, such that the fertilized egg may fail to divide properly, may not implant within the mother's uterus, or may not develop beyond a very early stage. In such cases a woman will have an early miscarriage or the new life will end without her ever being aware that it had started. However, a number of genetic abnormalities do not end this way, and the pregnancy may continue to term. There are two main types of genetic abnormalities:

Single-gene abnormalities involve a defect in a particular strand of DNA, which in turn causes a specific malfunction within the body. These abnormalities are further subdivided into three categories: dominant, recessive, and X-linked. These variations arise from the fact that genes are paired—that is, the genes on a chromosome inherited from the mother have a corresponding gene on the chromosome provided by the father. The effect of one gene may override the other, or they might make an equal contribution to a particular trait.

A **dominant genetic disorder** (for example, Huntington's-chorea) needs only one gene (which can come from either parent) to be manifested. If one parent is affected, there is a 50 percent chance that his or her child (of either gender) will have the same abnormality. Some dominant disorders run in families, while others result from a mutation that occurred in an individual egg or sperm.

A **recessive genetic disorder** (for example, cystic fibrosis) is one that will occur only when an abnormal gene that causes it is contributed by both parents. A child who receives an abnormal recessive gene from only one parent usually will not manifest that defect, although he or she will be a *carrier* of the disorder. If both parents of a child are carriers of a recessive disorder, the child has a 50 percent chance of being a carrier, a 25 percent chance of having two normal genes, and a 25 percent chance of being affected. Recessive genetic defects often cluster in particular racial, ethnic, or geographic groups.

X-linked genetic disorders (for example, hemophilia) are carried only on the X chromosome and may be dominant or recessive, although the latter are more common. Females with an abnormal X-linked gene usually are not affected by the problem because they typically have a normal gene on their other X chromosome, which will override the abnormal gene.

Chromosomal abnormalities involve significantly larger amounts of genetic material than do single-gene defects. Either part or all of a chromosome may be missing or duplicated. Often the results are not compatible with development of the fetus within the womb, and a miscarriage results. (It is estimated that half of all miscarriages that occur during the first three months of pregnancy are caused by chromosomal abnormalities.) The abnormality may be passed on from one or the other parent or may occur during the development of egg or sperm.

The risk of a child having a chromosomal abnormality increases steadily with the age of his mother. The risk of a twenty-five-year-old woman having a baby with Down syndrome—the most common disorder of this type—is 1 in 1,250, and the risk for all significant chromosomal disorders is 1 in 476. At age thirty-five, the numbers are 1 in 378 for Down syndrome and 1 in 192 for all chromosomal disorders. At age forty-five, those numbers drop to 1 in 30 and 1 in 21 respectively.[2]

Infections
Infections that are passed from mother to baby prior to birth account for about 3 to 5 percent of all birth defects and are discussed in detail in chapter 1.

Medical problems in the mother, such as diabetes, high

blood pressure, and heart disease, can affect the development of the baby growing within her. Detecting and managing any maternal conditions are key factors of prenatal care and a major reason regular visits with a qualified physician are so important during pregnancy.

Substances that pass from mother to baby
While the uterus, placenta, and amniotic fluid are usually very effective in providing a safe environment for the growing baby before birth, certain chemical compounds that enter the mother's bloodstream are capable of causing harm to her preborn child. The degree of damage can vary enormously depending upon the amount of the substance involved and the stage(s) of development at which the exposure to the unborn child takes place. These substances include:

- Drugs—prescription and nonprescription, legal and illegal
- Alcohol and tobacco
- Chemical and occupational pollutants

The use of drugs, alcohol, and tobacco is discussed in detail in chapter 1 (see pages 14–19). The gamut of potential environmental exposures, especially in the workplace, is well beyond the scope of this book. However, if you are pregnant (or might become so in the near future), you should become knowledgeable about any chemical compounds to which you are exposed on a regular basis.[3]

HOW ARE CONGENITAL DEFECTS IDENTIFIED PRIOR TO BIRTH?

A few decades ago, an expectant mother had little to inform her about her baby's condition other than the size of her abdomen, the movements that she felt inside it, her own sense of well-being or illness, and some very rudimentary input from her doctor. Advances in medical technology have changed

that situation dramatically so that even the most uneventful
pregnancy is now likely to be assessed with one or more prenatal screening tests.

   This section will briefly describe a number of screening and
diagnostic procedures utilized during pregnancy, along with
their potential benefits and risks. Their role and significance
in *your* pregnancy will depend upon your personal and family
history as well as how far your pregnancy has progressed. You
should be aware that tests will vary in their accuracy and pre-
dictive value. *Depending upon the procedure, abnormal results
may not predict defects with absolute certainty, nor do normal
results guarantee a problem-free baby.*

Ultrasound

Diagnostic ultrasonography (also called ultrasound or **sono-
gram**) is an extremely useful tool that utilizes high-frequency
sound waves to create images of a woman's uterus and the
baby growing within it. Sound waves are sent through a
handheld transmitter called a transducer that is gently applied
to a woman's abdomen or early in pregnancy may be placed
inside the vagina using a narrow probe. (Placing the ultrasound transducer inside the vagina does not pose any risk for
either mother or baby.) The sound waves reflect back to the
transducer from internal structures in patterns that vary depending upon their shape and density. The images are dis-
played on a monitor and may even be recorded on videotape.
(Some of the images may be printed for the expectant parents
to take home as their first "baby picture.")

When is it performed? Ultrasound may be carried out during
any stage of pregnancy. The timing for this procedure will depend to some degree upon its purpose, the state of your pregnancy, any problems that are developing, and your
physician's approach to following a normal pregnancy. Many
doctors recommend routine ultrasonography between the

sixteenth and twentieth weeks of pregnancy, at which point many details (including the chambers of the baby's heart) can be visualized.

How is it performed? A woman having an ultrasound will normally be instructed to drink a few glasses of water and hold off on voiding until the procedure is completed because a full bladder serves as a useful landmark. (A full bladder is not necessary for a vaginal ultrasound.) A conducting gel will be applied to the abdomen and the transducer then gently pressed against it in a number of locations. A basic evaluation, which can be carried out in the doctor's office, will usually not take more than twenty minutes, while a more detailed (sometimes called level two) study could take an hour or more. The latter might be done if there is concern about an abnormality for which more detailed information and sophisticated equipment are needed.

Normally you will be able to see the monitor during an ultrasound, and the technician or physician will usually point out a variety of highlights of your "tour" of the uterus and its occupant. Parents are often delighted and deeply moved by the first sight of their new child and may be surprised by the amount of movement if the baby is active at the time of the procedure.

Is it safe? Ultrasound has never been reported to cause harm to mother or baby, even during the earliest stages of pregnancy. No X-rays are involved, and the mother's skin is not punctured. Sometimes there is mild discomfort when the transducer is pressed against a full bladder.

What information does it provide? This test can provide a great deal of information:

- Verification that pregnancy is in fact under way within the uterus. A tiny sac can be visualized three weeks after

conception, and a week later the baby's body can be
seen within it. Ultrasound is also useful in diagnosing
an **ectopic pregnancy** (one that is growing in an
abnormal location).

- An accurate determination of the age of the baby and
  whether or not more than one baby is present.
- An assessment of the growth rate and movements
  of the baby.
- Detection of major structural abnormalities of the
  head, spinal cord, chest, abdomen, or limbs.
- The location and appearance of the placenta and the
  amount of amniotic fluid.
- Identifying structures (such as the placenta) that are
  important to visualize during diagnostic tests such
  as amniocentesis and chorionic villus sampling (see
  pages 85–90).

**Maternal blood tests: Alpha-fetoprotein,
beta-HCG, and estriol**

These tests are known as the "triple screen," and they are considered *screening* tests because:

- They are relatively easy and inexpensive to perform.
- While they detect pregnancies in which the baby may be
  at higher risk for certain problems, they do *not* make a
  specific diagnosis.
- They can be carried out on large numbers of pregnant
  women to determine who might benefit from more
  complex diagnostic testing.

Screening for **alpha-fetoprotein** (or **AFP**) is the most widely
used test. Alpha-fetoprotein is one of two major proteins that
circulate in the blood of the developing fetus. The other protein, **albumin**, is found also in the bloodstream of adults, while
AFP is unique to the fetus. Normally during pregnancy a small

amount of AFP finds its way into the **amniotic fluid** (fluid surrounding the fetus in its closed sac) and from there into the mother's bloodstream. A certain amount of AFP can thus be measured in the mother's bloodstream, and the level gradually rises during the first twenty weeks of pregnancy. A number of conditions can increase the amount of AFP that passes from fetus to mother at any given point in the pregnancy:

- A leak of fetal blood into the amniotic fluid or a defect in the placenta that allows more AFP to pass into the mother's bloodstream.
- Twins, because the two fetuses produce more AFP than one.
- An abnormality in which some of the fetus's internal tissue is exposed, allowing an increased amount of AFP to escape into the amniotic fluid. Examples of such conditions are open neural tube defects (anencephaly or spina bifida), which expose nerve tissue at the top or bottom of the spinal column (see page 8), or abdominal wall defects (omphalocele or gastroschisis) in which part of the intestinal tract may be present outside of the abdomen.

The screening test for a mother's blood level of AFP is quite sensitive: 80 to 85 percent of fetuses with neural tube defects can be detected through elevated levels of this protein in the mother's blood. However, the test is not very specific, since so many other conditions also cause the AFP to be elevated. As a result, out of one hundred cases in which maternal AFP is abnormally high, approximately sixty to seventy will prove to be false alarms in which no neural tube defect or other significant problem is identified.

How is the screening done? AFP is measured in a sample of blood drawn from the mother. The screening is most accurate if done between sixteen and eighteen weeks after the last menstrual period, but it can be carried out between fifteen and twenty weeks. Because of the steady rise of AFP during pregnancy, *accurate dating of the pregnancy is very important for a meaningful interpretation of this test.* In addition, the mother's age, weight, and race are taken into account when determining what level of AFP should be considered normal.

What if the AFP level is abnormally high? Your physician may want to repeat the test to confirm that the results are definitely abnormal. Even when the lab results are consistently high, however, a high AFP does not necessarily mean that the baby has a significant problem. Usually the next step will be an ultrasound examination, which can help specifically to

- confirm the accuracy of the date of the pregnancy. One of the most common reasons for an unexpectedly high level of AFP in a mother's bloodstream is that her pregnancy is actually farther along than was originally estimated.
- determine whether there is a multiple pregnancy (twins or more).
- detect abnormalities such as neural tube defects.

If the ultrasound study does not provide an explanation for the high AFP level, an amniocentesis (see below) may be carried out to determine the level of AFP in the amniotic fluid. This test is much more accurate than maternal AFP levels at predicting the presence or absence of neural tube and abdominal wall defects. But a serum-AFP and ultrasound may be adequate to make the diagnosis. A combination of normal amniotic fluid AFP and normal ultrasound would indicate that one of these problems is extremely unlikely. (However, an elevated AFP not caused by an open neural tube defect or twins has been associated with a greater chance of late-pregnancy complications.)

What if the AFP is abnormally low? A low AFP might indicate an increased risk of Down syndrome, although this is not a highly accurate test. (It will identify only about 20 to 30 percent of fetuses with Down syndrome in pregnant women under age thirty-five.) However, some confirmation of this risk may be obtained from two other maternal blood tests, which can be carried out at the same time. **Estriol** is an estrogen hormone whose level in the mother will be affected by the status of both the fetus and the placenta. **Beta-HCG (human chorionic gonadotrophin)** is a hormone produced by the placenta soon after conception, rising to levels that are detectable by the time the first menstrual period is missed.

If a low maternal AFP is present in combination with a low level of estriol and a high level of beta-HCG, the likelihood that the baby will have Down syndrome is definitely greater than if the AFP alone is abnormal. The results of these tests are combined with the mother's age to determine the probability that her baby will have Down syndrome. *Remember, however, that these tests cannot actually make this diagnosis.* This requires other studies, which will be discussed shortly.

Amniocentesis

Amniocentesis is the withdrawal of a small amount of amniotic fluid from the sac that surrounds the fetus. Both the contents of the fluid and the fetal cells that are present within it can be studied to diagnose a variety of problems before birth.

How is it done? When used to diagnose birth defects, amniocentesis is usually carried out between the fourteenth and twentieth weeks of pregnancy. Whether done in a physician's office or in a hospital, an ultrasound is routinely done first to assess (among other things) the size and position of the fetus, the location of the placenta, and the amount of amniotic fluid present. Then an appropriate site is selected on the mother's abdomen, antiseptic solution is applied, and often a local anesthetic is injected. (However, the anesthetic cannot numb the wall of the uterus, so a brief stinging or cramping pain might be felt when it is punctured.) Under ultrasound guidance, a long needle is inserted through the abdominal wall and into the amniotic fluid. Between 15 and 30 ml (or 1/2 to 1 ounce) of fluid is removed before the needle is withdrawn.

What kind of information is obtained from studying amniotic fluid?

- *Chromosome analysis.* Fetal cells within the fluid are cultured for one to two weeks and then specially treated so the chromosomes within them can be identified and studied. Extra or missing chromosomes are seen in disorders such as Down syndrome, in which the nucleus of each cell contains three chromosome 21s rather than the usual two. The analysis can also provide advance notice of the baby's gender, although amniocentesis will not be done strictly for this purpose. Results of chromosome analysis may not be ready until four weeks after the procedure.
- *Measurement of alpha-fetoprotein (AFP) in the amniotic fluid,* when screening tests done on the mother's blood reveal abnormal levels of this protein, as just described.
- *Identification of genetic markers for certain diseases* (for example, cystic fibrosis) where there is a family history or increased risk.
- *Assessment of the maturity of the baby's lungs.* This is evaluated toward the *end* of pregnancy in situations where a need to induce labor must be weighed against the possibility that the baby's lungs will not be mature enough to function normally once out of the womb. The compounds lecithin and sphingomyelin are

measured within the amniotic fluid, and when the **lecithin/sphingomyelin (or L/S) ratio** is more than 2, the baby can be expected to breathe adequately on his or her own after birth.

What kinds of birth defects will amniocentesis not detect?

- Specific, isolated structural abnormalities that do not have genetic or chromosomal causes. Examples would be cleft lip or palate, club foot, absent fingers or limbs, or heart defects.
- Disorders in the fetus arising from alcohol, tobacco, or drugs used by the mother.

What are the risks of amniocentesis? The mother might experience mild cramping for a few hours after the procedure. Occasionally local infection or leaking of amniotic fluid occurs at the puncture site. Unfortunately, the risks for the baby due to amniocentesis are more significant. Between one in 200 and one in 400 amniocentesis procedures in early pregnancy will result in a miscarriage. The risk of this complication occurring in a specific pregnancy will depend upon a variety of factors, including the size of the baby and the experience of the physician who performs the test. Miscarriage most commonly results from damage to the placenta, which may bleed and separate from the uterus, or from infection, which can begin if bacteria are accidentally carried by the needle into the amniotic fluid. Rarely, amniocentesis provokes early labor.

In what situations might amniocentesis be recommended for detecting a birth defect?

- When a woman has had another child with a chromosomal abnormality.
- When either parent has a chromosomal abnormality.
- When the mother's alpha-fetoprotein screening or

triple screen is abnormal and the reason cannot be
determined by ultrasound alone.

- When there is an increased risk of a genetically
  transmitted disorder for which additional information
  may be provided through analysis of amniotic fluid or
  the cells it contains.
- When a pregnant woman is over thirty-five years old.
  At this age, the chances of finding a chromosomal
  abnormality (one in 378 for Down syndrome, one in
  192 for all chromosomal defects) are roughly equal to
  the risk of a miscarriage from the amniocentesis. This
  is the most common reason that amniocentesis might
  be recommended during the first half of pregnancy.
  Unfortunately, in some instances a woman may be
  given the impression that she *must* have amniocentesis
  if she is over age thirty-five and that the pregnancy *must*
  be terminated if an abnormality is found. However,
  there is no requirement, legal or otherwise, that this
  test be carried out, regardless of a pregnant woman's
  age, and certainly no situation in which an abortion
  is mandated.

Chorionic villus sampling

Chorionic villus sampling (CVS) is a procedure in which
cells are taken from tiny, fingerlike projections of the placenta (called villi, which means literally "shaggy hairs").
These cells contain the same genetic material as the baby and
can be cultured for chromosomal analysis and other genetic
tests.

When and how is it done? CVS can be carried out between
the ninth and twelfth weeks of pregnancy. Using ultrasound
for guidance, a needle is introduced through the abdominal
wall into the uterus to the edge of the placenta, where a small
amount of tissue is aspirated. An alternative procedure

involves the insertion of a small catheter into the vagina and through the cervix (the opening of the uterus) to the placenta, from which the cells are withdrawn.

What information can be obtained from CVS? The cells obtained from chorionic villus sampling can be cultured and then analyzed for chromosomal and genetic abnormalities, yielding information similar to that gained from amniocentesis. However, this procedure can be carried out more than a month earlier than amniocentesis, and more cells are available at the outset, so results can be ready within a week to ten days. But CVS cannot diagnose neural tube defects because it does not obtain amniotic fluid. Also, while normal results can be considered highly reassuring, when abnormal results are obtained there is a 5 to 10 percent chance that the baby will in fact be normal. (This can occur because of chromosomal changes in the placenta that are not present in the fetus.) Thus when tests run on a CVS specimen are abnormal, a follow-up amniocentesis later in the pregnancy may be considered to verify these results.

What are the risks of CVS? As with amniocentesis, the mother may experience some cramping as well as pain at the puncture site if the specimen is obtained through the abdomen. (The vaginal approach is generally painless.) Vaginal bleeding and local infection are possible complications of the abdominal approach. Of greater concern is the risk of miscarriage, which occurs after about one in 100 procedures—at least twice the rate for amniocentesis. In addition CVS has been linked to limb abnormalities (missing or undeveloped fingers and toes) in the baby and cases of severe infections in the mother's uterus.

These risks, along with the slight but not insignificant possibility of a false positive result (that is, one that suggests an abnormality when the baby is in fact normal), raise particular concerns about CVS. The presumed advantage of this test over amniocentesis is that it allows for an earlier identification of the baby's genetic status—and thus an earlier abortion if the mother has decided that she will end her pregnancy if the baby is abnormal. If abortion is not an option that she intends to exercise, however, there would appear to be little purpose to expose her and her baby to this procedure's risks.

HOW DO I DECIDE WHETHER OR NOT TO HAVE CHORIONIC VILLUS SAMPLING OR AMNIOCENTESIS TO LOOK FOR A BIRTH DEFECT?

Make this decision carefully, prayerfully, and with all the facts you can possibly gather. You should be properly counseled and fully informed regarding the following:

- What potential birth defect(s) will the procedure help to identify?
- How high is the risk that the baby might be affected with a particular defect?
- How does the risk of the baby's having the abnormality compare with the risk of the procedure? It would be of questionable value to perform any procedure if the chance of provoking a miscarriage was significantly greater than the likelihood of identifying a problem, and it would be undeniably sad to lose a normal baby under such circumstances.
- What have the complication rates been for the specific physician or medical center that would be performing the procedure? CVS, in particular, requires special expertise and experience.
- What would be the specific benefits of having information about the defect prior to birth? Are there interventions available that might help the baby while

still within the uterus? Would preparations be needed for expert care at the time of delivery or shortly thereafter? Would it help the parents to learn about the condition ahead of time and make their own adjustments to cope with it?

- Is the primary purpose of the procedure to determine whether or not to continue the pregnancy? CVS is done to identify genetic abnormalities early in the pregnancy so that an abortion, if chosen, might be carried out with less difficulty. Amniocentesis, on the other hand, in a number of situations provides information that can improve the care of the baby either before or after delivery. There could thus be instances in which a woman who knows she would not have an abortion might nevertheless benefit from having an amniocentesis.

- What costs would be involved with this procedure? These would include not only physician fees but also laboratory costs and other expenses incurred at the facility where the procedure is to be performed.

With this information clearly in mind, you need to consider not only the medical aspects of the decision but also the personal and ethical dimensions. Your own values will significantly affect your response to the information you receive from prenatal testing—or whether you decide to have one or more procedures done in the first place.

In particular, you should consider ahead of time how you might respond to the unsettling news that your baby might have a birth defect. This is an extremely difficult question, even for those who value human life at all stages and in all conditions. How do you currently view people who have a significant physical, intellectual, or emotional handicap? How would you feel if such a person were your own child, living with you and depending on you for his daily needs, possibly for many years?

On a much broader scale, how do you view adverse events that occur in your life? Are they the meaningless cruelties of a mechanical universe? Are they divine punishment for something you have or haven't done? Or are they the fallout from a broken world, trials that God nevertheless can redeem and even use for a greater purpose in your life—and perhaps in the lives of many others?

These might seem rather weighty considerations to bring into a discussion of the pros and cons of a few medical tests, but these questions apply profoundly to the realm of prenatal evaluation of the baby. If you feel that a baby who will be born with one or more significant defects represents a biologic mistake—a life that shouldn't be lived—and that caring for him would be an exercise in futility, this viewpoint will seriously influence your response to any bad news you hear from your physician. Your reaction to such news could be quite different if you believe that life's trials are not pointless or punitive and that (to quote the apostle Paul) "we also rejoice in our sufferings, because we know that suffering produces perseverance; perseverance, character; and character, hope. And hope does not disappoint us, because God has poured out his love into our hearts by the Holy Spirit, whom he has given us" (Romans 5:3-5).

Undoubtedly, some people undergo prenatal testing in order to identify a significant disorder in time to abort the fetus. However, depending on the specific condition, there may be other measures that can help the less-than-perfect child (and the parents) before the birth. In certain situations knowledge that a baby will be born with a particular defect will allow physicians to prepare for his arrival and begin corrective measures in a timely manner. Advances in medical and physical therapy may also change the long-term outlook for a child with a particular defect.

WHAT IF THE RESULTS OF PRENATAL SCREENING OR DIAGNOSTIC TESTS ARE ABNORMAL?

Your response will, of course, depend on the test that was done and the specific defect that may be involved. It is important, first of all, to have a clear understanding of the reliability of the test(s) and the implications of the results. Was the test a screen, such as the alpha-fetoprotein blood test, that could prove to be a false alarm after further testing? Is there more than one possible explanation for the results? Does a repeat test or follow-up study need to be done to confirm the diagnosis? All of these questions should be reviewed carefully after receiving the news of abnormal results on any test.

Assuming that a birth defect has been identified with some certainty, what else might you do upon receiving this information? Again, this will depend significantly on the type of problem and its long-term implications. The diagnosis of Down syndrome, for example, which has a relatively normal life expectancy, is vastly different from anencephaly, in which most or all of the brain is missing and death follows very soon after birth. You will, in fact, need to deal with news of a birth defect on a number of levels.

Your emotional response will probably be intense and will need to be acknowledged and expressed among those whom you love and trust. Don't be surprised if you experience a wide range of feelings, including:

- Shock
- Denial—*This can't be happening.* Accepting the diagnosis might be extremely difficult, even when the same diagnosis is given by further testing or another consultant.

- Sorrow and grief—over many losses: the loss of hopes and dreams for a normal child or for the baby's life itself if the defect is one that will seriously shorten her life.
- Anger—at oneself (*What did I do wrong?*), at someone else, or even at God (*Why have You allowed this to happen?*).
- Impatience—wanting more information, answers to difficult questions, and perhaps more testing immediately.

This is the time for solidarity and teamwork between husband and wife. Blaming or finger-pointing is a luxury no one can afford.

Your practical and problem-solving response should be to find out more about the defect. What does it involve? Can anything be done to correct or improve it before or after birth? Reading about it, doing research in the library or on the Internet, or talking with other parents who have dealt with the same problem can help you understand more clearly what you may be dealing with later on.

Your support-gathering response is extremely important. An impending birth defect is not the type of problem that is discussed easily. Those with whom you are closest among family, friends, and church members need to be brought up to speed on your problem. You will need shoulders to lean (and cry) on, open ears and hearts, and knees ready to bend in prayer for you and your child.

Finally, *your spiritual response* is crucial. During this time you may wonder if God is making any sense or if He hears your cries and prayers. Don't be surprised (and try not to get upset) if you hear simplistic or unkind "answers" from well-meaning individuals; don't let such responses prevent you from drawing near to God, who really does care about this situation more than you can imagine. Indeed, its ultimate significance—what it will mean, how it will affect you and your family, what you will learn from it, and how this difficulty and sorrow will be redeemed—may not be clear for many years or even during this lifetime.

A SPECIAL ENCOURAGEMENT

You might feel a great deal of pressure to end a pregnancy by means of abortion, especially if the defect is severe. You wonder if it wouldn't be more merciful to all concerned if this imperfect life and all the trials that will accompany it would not be brought into the world in the first place.

We certainly don't want to trivialize the sorrow, difficulty, and expense involved when a child has a serious defect. But it is important to remember that no child you bear will be free of defects and imperfections. Even if all the body parts and systems are completely normal when a baby is born, other profound problems could develop later in life. A "normal" child might suffer injuries and illness after birth or break your heart eventually by making poor lifestyle choices. On the other hand, a baby who is malformed or destined for subnormal intelligence or a very short life could become the greatest blessing of your life.

NOTES

1. While not minimizing the untold sadness that such a loss brings to a family, it is of some comfort to know that the number of deaths caused by congenital disorders represents a very small fraction of the approximately 3.5 million births that take place every year in the U.S.

2. The American College of Obstetricians and Gynecologists, *Planning for Pregnancy, Birth, and Beyond* (New York: Signet, 1994), 94.

3. The Occupational Safety and Health Administration in Washington, D.C., which has established standards designed to reduce the likelihood of work-related injury or harm, requires that information be made available to any employee regarding potentially harmful compounds present in the workplace. In order to arrive at a "bottom line" that reduces risks to your (and your unborn child's) health, you may need some help from your physician in interpreting the Medical Safety Data Sheets (MSDS) or any other input you receive regarding harmful materials to which you may be exposed.

CHAPTER 4

Sexually Transmitted Infections (STIs)

Their Impact on You and Your Unborn Child

Syphilis is caused by a spiral-shaped organism known as a **spirochete**, which easily passes from mother to baby during pregnancy and can cause serious problems in many of the baby's organs or even stillbirth. Fortunately, the infection can be detected by a blood test, which is normally obtained as part of the first prenatal visit. If the test is positive, additional tests are necessary to confirm the diagnosis. If a woman becomes infected later in her pregnancy, however, the diagnosis might be missed, with disastrous consequences for the baby. Many of the problems caused by syphilis can be avoided if this infection is promptly diagnosed and treated (usually with penicillin).

Gonorrhea is a bacterial infection that continues to infect more than one million Americans every year. A pregnant woman with an active infection can transmit it to her baby during childbirth. The eyes of the newborn are extremely sensitive to this bacterium, and severe damage or even blindness can result if they become infected. For this reason antibiotic eye ointment or drops (required by state law) are given to every newborn, regardless of the mother's history. Gonorrhea prior to or during pregnancy can be treated with antibiotics; the type of antibiotic, dose, and length of treatment will depend on the extent and severity of the infection. Note: Antibiotics from two families, the quinolones and the tetracyclines, should not be used during pregnancy because of the potential harm that they might cause to a developing/growing baby. It is very important that a woman being treated for this or any other infection inform her doctor that she is pregnant, or that there is a possibility (however remote) that she might be.

Chlamydia is an organism that has risen from relative obscurity in the 1970s to become the most common bacterial STI in the United States. As with gonorrhea, a chlamydia-infected woman may pass the organism to her baby during delivery. Not only may the baby's eyes become infected, but a stubborn pneumonia can also develop. When an infection with chlamydia is diagnosed, treatment with antibiotics can and should be carried out. As was noted regarding gonorrhea, a woman who is (or *might* be) pregnant should not take antibiotics from the tetracycline or quinolone families.

Herpes simplex virus (HSV) is notorious for a property it shares with a number of other organisms: Once a person is infected, HSV remains for life. HSV type 1 typically causes eruptions known as cold sores or fever blisters around the mouth or nose, although it can also cause genital infections through oral-genital contact.

A baby born to a mother with HSV could be infected during vaginal delivery if there is a herpes outbreak on the mother's genital area. The risk of transfer is much higher (50 percent) if this is the mother's first outbreak rather than a recurrence (3-5 percent). For the newborn, an HSV infection can be disastrous. About 20 to 30 percent of infected infants will have surface (skin and mucous membrane) involvement only. In the other 70 to 80 percent, the virus spreads throughout the body and central nervous system, with a strong likelihood of major consequences including blindness, seizures, mental retardation, and death.

If you have a history of genital herpes, it is important to inform your physician, and both of you should be watchful for any recurrences. If there is an outbreak within a week before birth, your physician will probably recommend a cesarean delivery to minimize the risk of contact between virus and newborn. While cold sores around the mouth are less likely to cause trouble, you should be cautious if one is present when you give birth. You should avoid touching your mouth, wash your hands frequently, and wear a surgical mask over your mouth when handling your baby until the sore heals. (Be sure to check with your doctor to confirm that you are dealing with an HSV outbreak.)

Genital warts are caused by the **human papilloma virus (HPV)**. This infection is extremely common among sexually active individuals. HPV causes soft, wartlike growths in the genital area. Occasionally, large warts may obstruct the birth canal and necessitate a cesarean section. During pregnancy these may grow dramatically, and surgery, cautery, or laser treatment may be needed to remove them. Fortunately HPV transmission from mother to newborn during delivery appears to be extremely uncommon; however, if it does occur, it causes recurrent growths on the vocal cords. Of greater concern is the association of HPV with cancer of the mother's cervix (the opening of the uterus). Any woman who has ever had one or more genital warts or has ever had sexual intercourse should have regular Pap smears to detect early changes that might be caused by HPV infection in the cervix, which can be treated before developing into a cancer.

Bacterial vaginosis is an overgrowth of bacteria in the vagina that can be (but is not always) sexually transmitted. Because this condition can increase the risk of premature rupture of membranes and/or preterm labor, screening for it may be performed during the second half of pregnancy.

Acquired immune deficiency syndrome (AIDS) is caused by the **human immunodeficiency virus (HIV)**. The vast majority of HIV infections are transmitted during sexual contact, through contaminated needles and syringes used during the injection of illegal drugs, or by transfer from infected mother to baby during pregnancy. (Transmission of HIV during blood transfusions is now extremely rare.) A small number of cases in infants have been attributed to nursing from an infected mother.

After gaining access to the body, HIV multiplies quietly within the immune system over a period of many months or years, gradually destroying its ability to deal with invading microorganisms. The eventual result is full-blown AIDS, in which a person becomes vulnerable to a variety of devastating infections and some forms of cancer. Although this condition has been almost universally fatal, the development of new drug regimens may extend the life span and improve the quality of life for those with this disease, while researchers continue to seek a cure. Pregnancy does not increase the progression of HIV infection to AIDS but can worsen the disease in a woman who is already severely ill.

A pregnant woman infected with HIV has a 25 to 35 percent risk of transmitting the virus to her baby. If she has progressed to active AIDS, the risk can be as high as 60 to 70 percent. About one in five infected newborns will develop AIDS-related illness by one year of age and die from overwhelming infection before another year passes. The rest develop AIDS later in childhood, with the risk increasing by 8 percent each year.

Screening tests for HIV detect a person's antibody response to the virus and not the virus itself. If such screening indicates that one has the HIV virus (is HIV positive), further investigation will be necessary to determine the status of the infection and guide treatment decisions. It is strongly recommended that testing for HIV be carried out as part of routine prenatal screening for the following reasons:

- A woman can become infected with HIV even if she has not been involved in a high-risk lifestyle. A single sexual encounter with an infected individual or a onetime experiment with intravenous drugs can transmit the virus.
- The signs and symptoms of HIV/AIDS may not appear for years after the initial transmission, so a woman may have no idea that she is infected.
- Medical treatment of an HIV-infected pregnant woman may decrease her odds of transmitting the virus to her baby to less than 5 percent.

Hepatitis B is a viral infection of the liver that is transmitted through the same mechanisms as HIV. The majority of cases resolve completely following a flulike illness with fever, nausea, and **jaundice** (a yellow discoloration of skin). However, about 5 percent develop a chronic infection that can lead to **cirrhosis** (scarring) or even cancer of the liver. Furthermore, chronic carriers—of which there are about one million in the United States—can transmit the virus to sexual partners or from mother to baby during pregnancy or delivery. Most babies who are infected at birth become chronic carriers as well and risk developing long-term complications.

A blood test for hepatitis B surface antigen should be a part of routine prenatal screening. If it is positive, further testing can determine if a woman has a new infection, an old infection that has resolved, or a chronic infection. Depending on the results, appropriate plans can be made to help protect the newborn with an antibody injection if needed, along with the routine hepatitis B vaccine normally given shortly after birth.

A final word on STIs

Sexually transmitted infections can have lifelong and life-threatening consequences both for parents and their children. Yet they are definitely preventable for those who are willing to commit to a "no-risk" sexual lifestyle. In a best-case scenario, this means that a man and a woman abstain from sexual relations until marriage and then remain strictly monogamous in a mutually exclusive relationship. Medically, this eliminates a significant number of risks, and greatly enhances the stability of the environment for raising children.

The threat of HIV/AIDS has sparked an ongoing national campaign for what has been called "safe sex," placing a heavy emphasis on condom use to prevent the spread of STIs. But while condoms offer some degree of protection some of the time, they are far from foolproof. Condom failure rates for preventing pregnancy are widely reported to be 10 percent or higher per year, meaning that at least one out of ten sexually active women using condoms as their only form of birth control will be pregnant within a year. But a woman can become pregnant only two or three days per month, while STIs can be transmitted *every day*. Furthermore, some STIs, such as syphilis, herpes simplex, and human papilloma virus (HPV) infection, can occur on areas of the genitals that are not covered by condoms. Most authorities, even those who strongly advocate condom use, consider condoms to offer little, if any, protection against infection with HPV, herpes simplex virus, and syphilis. If you are unmarried, it would be wise to remain abstinent until you enter a permanent, monogamous relationship.

If you have had one or more sexual partners prior to marriage, you should discuss STI screening with your physician. This is especially important if you are pregnant, because so many STIs have more serious consequences for the baby if they are acquired during pregnancy. In addition, it is important for a pregnant woman to be both candid and thorough in reviewing her sexual history—including any prior symptoms of vaginal discharge, pelvic discomfort, or surface changes in the genital area—with her physician, because important screening tests may be recommended based on this information.

CHAPTER 5

The Adopted Child

Approximately fifty thousand native-born and many more foreign-born children are adopted every year in the United States. Each of these adoptions represents a unique set of circumstances in which the paths of adults and children who (with rare exception) do not share biological ties converge. Adopting a child can fulfill a couple's most cherished dreams and desires while meeting a child's deepest needs for love and stability. But as honorable, compassionate, and joyous as this process might be, it is also rarely accomplished without considerable effort, significant (but surmountable) challenges, and occasional heartaches.

Because this book is primarily concerned with rearing children, most of the issues and details of events prior to bringing an adopted child home will not be discussed here. Concerns related to adoption agencies, attorneys, regulations, foreign governments, finances, paperwork, the home study,[1] and, above all, the endless patience often required of adoptive parents-to-be are all very important but ably covered in a variety of other books and materials. One topic that will be addressed is the nature of the relationship between the adoptive parents and the birth parents[2] (especially the mother), assuming that one or both of the birth parents are involved in the adoption process, since their interactions can have a significant impact on the child's upbringing.

CLOSED AND OPEN ADOPTIONS

When a pregnant woman decides that she is going to release her baby for adoption, two basic scenarios may occur, each having many variations. In what is called a **closed adoption**, the birth mother has very little (if any) contact with her infant immediately after delivery, and no contact with the adoptive parents. Confidentiality regarding the parties involved in the adoption prevents future interactions between them. Closed adoptions were the norm in previous generations (and remain so in Canada) and are still carried out in significant numbers in the United States. Those who favor this approach feel that it brings about more timely and effective closure for all concerned, allowing the birth mother to move on with her life and the adoptive parents to focus their attention exclusively on the baby. Others raise concerns that closed adoption may leave the birth mother with a significant emotional crater to fill, as she can only imagine what her child's life will be like during the ensuing months and years. Also, unless specific arrangements have been made (as is done in Canada and in some adoption agencies in the United States through a registry system), the child of a closed adoption would be unable to fill an important gap in his own personal history if he should desire to meet his birth mother when he is an older adolescent or adult.

In recent decades the partially or completely **open adoption** has become more common. This means that there is some degree of interaction between the birth mother or both birth parents and the adoptive family. In many cases, the birth mother actually selects who will rear her child from a number of potential candidates presented by an adoption agency. The couple may then become involved with the birth mother through an extended period of her pregnancy, and one or both adoptive parents might even attend the birth of the baby. The birth mother or both birth parents may relinquish the baby directly to the adoptive parents at the hospital or shortly after the birth in a physical gesture of release. Such a relationship can be fulfilling for all concerned, and it will also offer the adoptive parents more knowledge of the baby's prenatal care and family health history. But it is not without potential pitfalls. Childbirth and adoption are emotionally charged events, and open adoption raises the possibility for complications in both the immediate and distant future. If you are going to be involved in an open adoption, consider the following:

The relationship between the adoptive parents and the birth mother, and everyone's expectations for the future, should be carefully considered and discussed before the baby is born.

For example, if the prospective parents offer a generous amount of attention and affection (and even material goods within the legal limits set by the state) to the birth mother prior to the delivery, they might satisfy some deep needs in the birth mother's life. But once the baby arrives, the parents' attention quite understandably shifts dramatically to the infant. The birth mother may then feel like a nonentity, someone who was valued only because she was carrying the prized baby inside her. Depression, bitterness, even second thoughts about the adoption decision could result from this turn of events. If the adoptive parents do not want or intend to have an ongoing relationship with the birth mother after the birth, they should be careful about the signals they send beforehand.

It is very important that expectations be clarified regarding the amount of contact between mother and adoptive family once the baby is born. The birth mother may want to visit her baby, which can help her develop a clear mental picture of the setting in which her child will be brought up. But ongoing visits might also become uncomfortable for the adoptive parents if they begin to feel that they are "on trial" when the birth mother is present. These visits can also be emotionally difficult for the birth mother, who sees her baby relating to another woman as "Mommy."

What about long-term contact between the birth mother and the adoptive family? In some cases regular visitation continues for years, but it is more common for interaction to be limited to pictures and an update from the adoptive parents once or twice a year. For many birth mothers, the need for closure leads them to a decision to walk away both physically and emotionally, bringing ongoing contact with their child to an end. Many experts in this field argue that long-term contact can be unhealthy for the birth mother because it could prevent her from moving forward with her life. Furthermore, the birth mother's continued involvement in her child's life might become disruptive if she interferes with decisions the adoptive parents must make on a day-to-day basis. Everyone must have a clear understanding that the adoptive parents are the parents and that they have the final say in the way the child is brought up. Honest conversation and counseling will help clarify expectations and minimize the risk of conflict.

Everyone involved in an adoption must understand that the birth mother will undergo a significant grieving process that normally lasts many months, even under the best of circumstances.

It is very important for the birth mother to receive competent and compassionate counseling before—but especially after—the birth, to work through the grieving and releasing process. It is not enough for an agency or an attorney to say that counseling is available "if she needs it" and then leave it up to the birth mother to initiate the process. Adoptive parents would be wise to see to it that counseling takes place and to cover its cost if necessary. Not only does this ensure that the birth mother's emotional needs are taken seriously, but it also reduces the likelihood of a reversal—a heart-wrenching event in which the birth mother decides after a few weeks or months that she wants to keep her baby after all. All too often the seeds of a reversal are sown when the grieving process leads the birth mother to think that the adoption choice was a mistake.

All of these concerns, especially the need for counseling before and after the baby's birth, most certainly apply to the biological father also, assuming that he remains involved and is engaged in the ongoing decision making.

Sometimes the adoption process takes place much more rapidly, and adoptive parents may find themselves meeting a birth mother or both birth parents for the first time at the time of birth. While there might not be much opportunity for building a relationship on such short notice, the exploration of everyone's expectations should still take place, even if in a somewhat condensed time frame.

WHAT IF AN ADOPTION FALLS THROUGH OR IS REVERSED?

Two of the most emotionally charged events related to the adoption process are the "failed placement" (the placement that has been arranged with considerable effort, but then falls through for whatever reason) and the reversal (the baby has actually arrived in the adoptive parents' home for several days, or even a few months, only to be taken away when one or both biological parents have a change of heart before their legal rights to the baby have been terminated). Both of these situations (especially the reversal) can be extraordinarily difficult and will generate virtually the same full force of grief that would occur with the loss of any child. *The severity of the loss must be acknowledged, and the need for grieving not ignored.* (Although some may try to lessen your pain by saying or implying, "This wasn't really your child, after all," your loss is real, and lack of biological ties has nothing to do with it.) Counseling, whether individually or through a support group, can be very helpful, especially when the question of trying to arrange another adoption is to be broached.

COMMON CONCERNS OF ADOPTIVE PARENTS

Parents who are considering adopting a baby or a child often have a number of qualms and concerns, most of which are quite normal (and similar to those of parents anticipating caring for their own new baby).

Will I be able to love this child as if he were my own flesh and blood (especially if I already have one or more biological children)? The process of adding children to any family raises similar questions ("Is there enough love in me for this new baby on the way?"). But God is able to open a parent's heart to "make room" for the newcomer. After a very short while it becomes virtually impossible to imagine life in the family without him.

Will I be able to treat each child in my family the same way, especially if I have both biological and adopted children? Actually, no two children in any family can be treated in exactly the same way because each child is a unique creation. Remember that no child is perfect, that all children will give you grief at some point, and that one child will probably cause more overall difficulty than another. The issue isn't treating everyone exactly the same way, but rather being firmly committed to each child's well-being and surrounding each one with both unconditional love and appropriate limits.

Can I discipline a child who has been abused or abandoned? Absolutely—in fact, not doing so is a worse form of abandonment. Discipline does not merely consist of negative consequences or punishment imposed for misbehavior; it encompasses the entire process of building a child's character and imposing appropriate limits.

Am I up to this? Doubts and feelings of inadequacy about parenting are normal. (Even if you believe that you have child rearing completely figured out, the next bundle of joy God sends will most likely change that opinion.) However, if you feel major persistent qualms about your ability to parent, by all means spend time with a qualified counselor to sort through your specific concerns.

SPECIAL ISSUES IN CARING FOR ADOPTED CHILDREN

The most basic needs of an adopted child are the same as those of any other child: physical, emotional, and spiritual nurturing in an environment where love, stability, and appropriate limits are clearly evident. Nearly all of what you will read in this book or other resources about parenting will apply to your adopted child. However, several specific concerns that may arise during or after the adoption process are worth a brief review.

Unity of purpose on the home front

While in nearly every case the prospective parents share equally the desire to adopt a child, occasionally one may be less enthusiastic about this undertaking than the other. It is unwise for one person to merely "go along" with an adoption primarily to please one's spouse. The commitment of both parents to the adopted child should be as strong as if he were biologically their own.

Nursing an adopted baby

Believe it or not, it is not necessary for a woman to bear an infant in order to nurse one. A woman who would like to breast-feed an adopted baby may be able to produce her own milk through a combination of medication that stimulates lactation and repeated stimulation of her breasts, either by using a pump prior to the adoption or allowing the baby to nurse after he arrives.

This process is usually more successful with infants younger than eight weeks of age, although it can also be attempted with an older baby. While nursing an adopted child can yield many of the benefits that breast-feeding affords to infants and mothers (see chapter 8, page 149), it will also require considerable commitment and effort. Furthermore, it is very likely that the adoptive mother's production of milk will be less than adequate to meet all of the growing baby's nutritional needs. Supplementation with formula will thus be necessary in such cases. Needless to say, plans to nurse an adopted baby should be discussed in advance with a knowledgeable physician or lactation consultant.

Adopting an older baby or child

Parents of newborns are normally concerned about the process of bonding with their new baby, often wondering if even brief periods of separation will interfere with it. But what if you are going to begin parenting a baby who has lived with someone else for several weeks or months—perhaps one who cannot even understand your language?

In such circumstances you cannot necessarily expect an instantaneous bonding experience or a picture-perfect first meeting where a child throws his arms around your neck in a display of unrestrained gratitude. In fact, in some cases the initial contact will be strained. A baby might be frightened, fussy, fidgety—or oddly quiet, especially if he has been raised in an environment where crying yielded little response from his adult caretakers. In addition, a baby arriving from a foreign country may be tired, poorly nourished, and literally overloaded by the entire experience. Whether coming from across town or halfway around the world, he may actually show signs of grieving for whatever familiar faces and environment he has left behind.

Adopting a child with a physical, mental, or emotional handicap

A special-needs baby can be a great blessing to a family, but it is important to have a clear understanding of problems that are likely to arise during his life. (In some cases a handicap may require special education and care well into the child's adulthood.) Support services, including other parents who have raised a baby with similar problems, should be consulted both before and after the adoption.

Medical concerns
You should obtain as much information as possible about the medical history of the baby you are planning to adopt. Details of the family history, the mother's pregnancy and delivery, congenital problems, illnesses, and immunizations are helpful, if available. However, in some cases you may not even be certain of your baby's birth date, and some evaluation based on physical and behavioral characteristics will be necessary. (This may not be easy if the infant has been malnourished or raised in a deprived setting that has delayed his growth and developmental milestones.)

If your adopted baby appears to be well, you might want to wait for several days (or even a few weeks) before taking him for a medical evaluation, so that he can become comfortable with you before entering the unfamiliar realm of the doctor's office. An infant from a foreign country may require a more extensive examination soon after arrival—even if he has been examined before leaving his country of origin—because of the possibility that he might have acquired one or more infections (such as tuberculosis, hepatitis B, or intestinal parasites) that are more common in other areas of the world, or conditions (such as particular forms of anemia) seen in certain racial and ethnic groups. If the baby appears ill upon arrival, he should be evaluated as soon as possible.

Cross-cultural and cross-racial adoptions
From an infant's standpoint, his ethnic background is not initially a major source of concern, although the adoptive

parents might need to deal with occasional inappropriate reactions such as "Why would you adopt a child of a different
race?" As the child becomes older, however, you will need to
deal with questions raised by differences in appearance within
the family. Most can be handled during the ongoing process
of talking to him about his adoption (see next section). Exploring your child's racial or ethnic heritage as a means of
enhancing his overall understanding of his "story" would be
beneficial to both you and your child. Your child should be
encouraged to develop and maintain friendships within his
minority community. This will make him more comfortable
moving in and out of his own subculture. Keep in mind,
though, that your child's basic sense of identity should focus
primarily on qualities of character and bonds of love that have
been established in your family over a period of years.

TALKING TO A CHILD ABOUT
HIS ADOPTION

In bygone generations it was common not to reveal to a child
his status as an adopted child, apparently out of fear that this
would cause him undue pain or alienation. Unfortunately,
this approach usually had the opposite effect. Very often it
was during adolescence—a time already full of great upheaval, self-doubt, and issues of an emerging identity—that
he would learn of his adoption, often by accident (such as a
relative's careless slip of the tongue). And so, with all the other
concerns of this age-group already in full swing, he would
now have to contend with harrowing questions such as "Why
did my mother abandon me?" and "What else don't I know
about my family?"

Just as children should be given information about sexuality on a need-to-know basis that is age appropriate, so should
the adopted child's unique question "Where did I come
from?" be met with answers that are straightforward, tactful,

and truthful. Ideally, a child should not grow up remembering a time when he did not know that Mom and Dad were not his biological parents. *The events leading to his adoption should be described as a unique and positive story.* The decision of his birth mother very often can be understood as one born out of love and concern rather than an act of abandonment. But even if the child was abandoned by his birth mother, he can be told, quite truthfully, that *God did not abandon him and never will.* Whatever the circumstances might have been, a child can be led to understand that God not only "knit him together in his mother's womb" but also entrusted him to his adoptive parents, who are continually joyful that he has become an important member of their family.

Some adoptive families put together a scrapbook that tells the child's story. This might include pictures of the birth mother, if available, and if possible a note from her to the child explaining what she did, her feelings about him, how happy she was about the family that was adopting him, and so forth. Baby pictures, documents, a map of his country of origin if he came from a foreign land, and any other such memorabilia are of great interest to children, who will look through them over and over as they grow up.

NOTES

1. A home study is a detailed assessment of the prospective parents and their home, required by all adoption agencies in an effort to ensure that an adopted child will be brought up in a safe and nurturing environment.

2. Throughout this section the term *birth mother* will be used to designate the woman who is giving birth to the child. *Birth parents* refers to both the birth mother and the biological father.

The Moment Arrives

After months of anticipation, some emotional highs and lows, and (usually) a number of hours of labor, the waiting will finally be over. All your hopes and preparations are about to culminate in the arrival of the tiny new person (or perhaps more than one!) whom you will soon be holding in your arms. Without question, your first look, touch, and embrace of this newest member of your family will be an intense experience, one that we hope will be joyous and fulfilling as well. What can you expect to see?

WHAT HAPPENS DURING THE FIRST FEW MINUTES AFTER BIRTH?

The moment your baby exits the birth canal (or the uterus in a cesarean delivery), she will begin a rapid and radical transition from the warm liquid "inner space" of amniotic fluid—in which the placenta efficiently provided for all her needs by way of the umbilical cord—to the outside world. Within seconds she must begin breathing for herself, within minutes begin regulating her own temperature, and within hours begin actively taking nutrients.

As soon as her body is out (or sometimes when the head alone has just been delivered), her nose and mouth will be gently cleared of fluid. The umbilical cord will be clamped and then cut. (By prior arrangement, Dad may be offered this privilege.) In order to prevent heat loss and a drop in body temperature, the baby will be dried quickly, often while being checked to be sure she is breathing adequately. The mild rubbing that occurs during drying will actually stimulate breathing. (No one swats a newborn on the fanny after birth, by the way.) You may hear a little whimper, a continuous noisy howl of protest, or something in between during these exciting first few moments.

How quickly you are able to hold your newborn will depend on your condition and the baby's. In many uncomplicated births, the baby practically makes a nonstop flight from birth canal to mother's chest. In others, the need for some immediate attention to deal with a problem will delay this initial moment of contact. If the delivery was particularly difficult or was a cesarean birth, the mother may not have as much freedom or may be too preoccupied to attend to her baby. If the baby's breathing is slow to start or sluggish and inadequate, she will be quickly placed on a warmer. Further gentle stimulation will continue, and if needed, oxygen or assistance with a bag and mask will be given until the problem stabilizes.

Some babies need more attention to the vocal cords and airway because of the presence of **meconium** in the amniotic fluid. Meconium is a thick, tarlike material that accumulates in the baby's intestines starting at about the fourth month after conception. Normally it is not seen until after birth, but 10 or 15 percent of babies will pass some beforehand. Meconium is usually harmless to a baby, even if swallowed. But if a large amount is present before delivery, and if she makes any breathing or gasping attempts before birth or during delivery, meconium may have been inhaled into her airway. This can cause a number of respiratory problems, and thus if your baby exits the birth canal amidst some meconium-stained fluid, her airway should be cleared of this material as soon as possible. This may require the brief placement of a tube (called an *endotracheal tube*) into the airway of the baby in order to suction out this material. (While the need for these sorts of interventions is the exception rather than the rule, the possibility of an unexpected respiratory problem in the new-born is one of the reasons most health-care providers prefer not to deliver babies away from the hospital.)

Assuming things go smoothly, you should have an opportunity to spend time with your new baby immediately after birth. While keeping her warm and covered, both mother and father can gently touch and caress her, check out the tiny details of her hands and feet, allow her to grasp their fingers, and look into her eyes if they are open. This is a close, emotional time, and you should feel free to laugh, cry, say a prayer of thanksgiving, or just be silent and savor the moment.

The baby may or may not be interested in trying to nurse right away, but you need not be in any hurry. She has plenty of extra fluid in her body at the time of birth, and you may want to try the first feeding later when you are a little more comfortable. The doctor will usually be attending to some after-birth details—collecting a sample of blood from the umbilical cord, delivering the placenta, checking for and repairing any damage, and generally cleaning up, so this may not be the ideal setting in which to get positioned for the first nursing.

The baby's first report card and other details

At one minute and five minutes after birth, a nurse or doctor will do a quick survey of your baby and then assign an **Apgar score.** This simple point system was devised by anesthesiologist Dr. Virginia Apgar during the early 1950s as a tool to predict which infants might need closer observation or more intense care after birth. A baby is given zero, one, or two points on each of five variables: appearance (specifically color), pulse rate, response to stimulation, activity (including muscle tone), and respirations.

Few babies receive a perfect ten at five minutes because most have some dusky or bluish coloration of the hands and feet. (Note that references to pink or blue coloration in the table have nothing to do with the racial or ethnic origin of the baby.) If the score is six or less at five minutes, the baby will be given closer attention. Remember that the Apgar score is not a "grade" or a prediction of success in life. Rather, it serves as a cue or a red flag for the level of care a baby may need immediately after birth.

APGAR SCORECARD

Sign	0	1	2
Appearance	pale or blue	body pink, extremities blue	completely pink
Respirations	absent	slow or irregular	good, crying
Pulse	not detectable	below 100	above 100
Reflex irritability	no response to stimulation	grimace	cough, sneeze, or cry
Muscle tone	limp, or weak movement	some movement	active motion

Scores determined for each sign are totaled. The highest possible score is 10.
By five minutes of age, most healthy babies have scores of at least 7. A score less than that indicates that the baby warrants careful watching.

Eventually the health-care staff will weigh and measure your baby, take footprints, apply an armband, and carry out a few other standard procedures. There is no reason your baby should be unceremoniously carted off to the nursery for these details two minutes after birth. On the other hand, you don't need to be upset if you are separated from the baby for a few minutes once you've had a comfortable time to get acquainted.

Soon after the baby is born, the nurse will bathe her to remove the thick, whitish material called **vernix**, which served as a protective covering for her skin while she was in the womb. The baby will also receive three routine medical treatments:

- One dose of **antibiotic eye ointment or drops.** Eye infections caused by gonorrhea or chlamydia acquired during birth can be serious enough to cause blindness. These are effectively prevented by this treatment. Even if you feel certain that you could not possibly carry these organisms, all states by law require this treatment.

- A shot of **vitamin K.** Newborn infants have a relatively low level of this vitamin, which is necessary for blood clotting. Rarely, the level is so low that the baby may be at risk for internal bleeding that can cause significant damage (a syndrome known as **hemorrhagic disease of the newborn**). A single injection of vitamin K prevents this problem.

- A **plastic clip** on the remnant of the umbilical cord. The clip will be removed before discharge or will be left in place and removed at the doctor's office during a follow-up visit.

A closer look: physical appearance and behavior of your newborn baby

Your newborn will not look like the smiling image you have seen beaming from a jar of baby food. (The "newborns" you see in movies and TV-show delivery rooms are nearly always a few weeks old.) She, in fact, will have a unique appearance immediately after birth. Be sure to take plenty of pictures—this phase will be very short.

Depending on the course of labor, her head may develop an oval shape known as **molding**, resulting from compression of the soft bones of the skull during the trip through the birth canal. This may be accentuated if her head is large and if labor was long. Pressure against her mother's pelvis may also produce some puffiness of the scalp. If blood vessels break under the skin, a collection of blood called a **cephalhematoma** will form, although it may not be obvious for a day or two after birth. Normally all these conditions resolve without difficulty or any specific treatment. However, a cephalhematoma may take months to disappear and may harden in the process.

When you gently run a finger over the top of a newborn's head, you will feel the fontanelles—the two indentations where the bones of the skull have not yet joined. These so-called soft spots, the largest of which will be felt toward the front of the skull, are actually covered with a thick protective membrane. They are usually flat, but they may bulge slightly when the baby cries or pushes out a bowel movement. If you watch the hair on the scalp covering her anterior (or forward) fontanelle, you may even see some gentle pulsations.

A newborn may be nearly bald, be endowed with thick hair, or have an amount in between. Don't be too impressed (or upset) with the hair you see; color, texture, and amount will usually change to some degree during the first year. You may also notice some soft, thin, fuzzy hair called lanugo along the back and shoulders. Lanugo is more obvious in some babies than others, but if at first it looks conspicuous, you need not worry about your newborn growing a fur coat. This will disappear within several weeks.

Her face, and especially her eyelids, will be puffy. A closer look at the eyes usually reveals some shade of blue gray or blue brown in Caucasian babies, or brown in dark-skinned infants. Unless she is born with dark brown eyes, the final color of her eyes may not be known for at least six months. The newborn can focus on and follow a slowly moving object at close range and may be particularly attentive to a nearby face. Some of the most emotional moments in parenting occur when a new baby and a loving parent gaze into one another's eyes. Because her brain will need some time to assemble these visual images into meaningful patterns, your smile will not be returned for a while. (She will begin this direct socializing at four to six weeks of age.) You may notice some bright red spots on the white portion (the **sclera**) of one or both eyes. These are areas where tiny blood vessels ruptured during labor. They are not a sign of damage and will disappear on their own in several days.

A newborn has well-developed hearing and will appear startled (with sudden jerking movements) in response to a sudden loud noise. While her environment doesn't need to be hushed like a library, it is a good idea to keep the sounds around a new baby at a comfortable level. If a noise is loud enough to annoy you, it will certainly not be pleasant for her. Soothing voices, humming, singing, and soft music are definitely welcome in her world of new sounds.

The newborn's nose is relatively flat, and her nasal passages are quite narrow. Since she breathes primarily through her nose rather than her mouth, you may often hear a noisy, snorting type of breathing, especially if she is excited. Furthermore, she may sneeze from time to time, in order to clear mucus out of her nose. This by itself does not mean that she has a cold. However, if you notice mucus draining from the nose, or if you are not sure whether the breathing sounds are normal, ask the doctor to check it. You may also hear your baby hiccuping, as she may have done inside the womb. This does not require any specific treatment.

The skin of the newborn is usually smooth, but in postmature (late arriving) babies it tends to appear more wrinkled. Some (or much) of her skin may be covered by **vernix**, especially in the creases of the arms and legs. This material, which helped protect the skin while she floated in amniotic fluid, will be much more noticeable if she is premature. Many babies have areas of dry, flaky skin, especially on the hands and feet. These do not need to be treated with lotion, but dryness will persist if a baby is bathed too frequently. She may have a dusky color for the first few minutes until her newly functioning lungs send blood with higher levels of oxygen through her circulation. As this process continues, she will "pink up," although hands and feet may maintain a bluish tinge for a longer period of time. Some babies develop a ruddy coloration or may appear flushed when they cry. In nonwhite infants, the dusky color will be more pronounced, but lips, tongue, and fingernails will appear pink once the blood is carrying more oxygen.

When you have had time to inspect her from "stem to stern" in more detail, you may notice some unique markings on her skin. A small red **salmon patch** (some may call it a "stork bite") occurs on the nape of the neck in 50 percent of all infants. One or more of these may also appear on the eyelids or on the forehead between the eyebrows. Eyelid patches will disappear by three to six months of age, while those on the neck will fade but may last for years. Areas of increased pigmentation known as **mongolian spots** are common on the back and buttocks of dark-skinned newborns, although they may be found in all racial and ethnic groups. These spots may even have a greenish or bluish tinge like a bruise and will disappear gradually over a few years' time. Tiny cysts known as **milia** appear on the nose, cheeks, and forehead of many newborns. (The same type of cysts are nearly always seen on the roof of the mouth and have been dubbed **Epstein's pearls**.) Between one and two days of life, many newborns develop a number of red spots with a slightly raised pale center. This eruption, unique to newborns, is known as **erythema toxicum**, but it is not a sign of any illness or toxicity. Both milia and erythema toxicum disappear without treatment.

In baby boys the testicles will normally be present in the scrotum, having made a short but important journey from within the abdomen to the scrotal sac during the final weeks of pregnancy. When one (or both) has not moved into position at birth, the baby is said to have an undescended testicle, a condition that will be evident at the time of the first exam.

This occurs in approximately 3 percent of full-term male infants and is more common in premature newborns. Fortunately about 80 percent of undescended testes will enter the scrotum by the end of the first year of life.

The scrotum of a baby boy may appear puffy or even swollen, a change that normally resolves within a few days. In about 10 percent of male infants, a collection of fluid called a **hydrocele** may persist for six to twelve months. A hydrocele normally resolves on its own, but sometimes it is accompanied by a swelling in either groin that often appears during crying or straining. This is a **hernia**, a sac that may contain a small portion of bowel. If you feel that your infant may have a hernia, have his doctor check this area during an office visit. If one is indeed present, it will need to be corrected surgically. Rarely, the contents of a hernia sac become stuck (or **incarcerated**) in the abdominal wall, restricting blood flow and causing increased swelling and pain. Emergency surgery may be needed to prevent damage to the bowel. If your infant's groin becomes markedly swollen or tender (provoking crying when touched), you should call the doctor immediately.

The baby girl's genital area—specifically the **labia** or "lips" at the opening of the vagina—may also appear swollen. In addition, a little mucus, or even a small amount of blood, may drain from the vagina during the first few days of life. Both are caused by sudden changes in hormone levels after birth and will disappear on their own.

While a newborn is awake, his legs will tend to be flexed frog-style, with fists closed and drawn toward the face. In fact, he may accidentally scratch himself. Some newborn shirts enclose the hands to prevent scratching, but if necessary long nails can be carefully trimmed. A newborn's feet will tend to be turned inward and the legs bowed. During sleep, arms and legs will relax and unfold.

As you watch his arms and legs move around, don't expect

any purposeful movements. A newborn cannot deliberately reach for anything, kick in a specific direction, or turn the head toward a sound. However, he does have a number of reflex behaviors that are already programmed into the nervous system at the time of birth. When you gently stroke one of his cheeks, he will turn his head in that direction. This is called the **rooting reflex**, and it helps the baby locate his food source. Place a nipple (or fingertip) in his mouth, and he will begin to suck on it. This **sucking reflex** will in turn set off the **swallowing reflex**. These nourishment-seeking behaviors are necessary for survival.

The **Moro** or **startle reflex**, on the other hand, is not. If a newborn is startled or if his head or body moves suddenly downward, his arms will quickly arch over his chest, as if trying to embrace the nearest solid object. The Moro reflex will disappear after the first few months of life. The **grasp reflex** is easy to demonstrate: Place your finger in a newborn's hand, and he will grasp it tightly for a short period of time. This reflex will disappear around the age of two months, but shortly thereafter he will be deliberately grabbing everything within reach.

GETTING FURTHER ACQUAINTED WITH YOUR BABY: THE BONDING PROCESS

Over the past several years, much has been written about the importance of bonding with a newborn, especially in an era when family structures and commitments have seemed so shaky. What exactly establishes the deep emotional ties with a child that will cause a parent to spend untold hours feeding, bathing, rocking, changing, and attending to the seemingly unending needs of a new baby? Is the bond locked into the genetic code of mothers and set loose by the flow of hormones during pregnancy? Is it biologically preexistent in fathers, or does it develop through watching role models in his family, as an extension of his love for his wife, or by an act of the will?

Does it spring to life when the baby is first seen at the moment of birth? And what secures the attachment of a newborn to his mother and father?

Some have suggested that there is a critical time in the baby's first hours of life when a special connection will be made, especially between mother and child, that will affect the quality of their relationship for years to come. But this assumption raises a troubling question: What happens when mother or baby (or both) have special medical problems and cannot be together during those early hours or days? What if the new mother has a cesarean delivery and thus only momentary contact with her baby after birth, not to mention the potential distraction of pain during her recovery? What if the baby is born prematurely and must spend weeks in a high-tech hospital setting?

The answers hinge on the fact that human behavior is highly complex and not rigidly stereotyped or predictable like a computer program. As a result, bonding is a process that begins well before the baby is born and continues for years thereafter. It is certainly influenced by biology, hormones, and genetics. But it is also shaped by the upbringing of the new mother and father, their personal and spiritual values, their commitment to one another, and some everyday decisions they must make. Furthermore, human babies are not like newly hatched ducklings that attach themselves to the first object they see.

Throughout this book we will be looking at the process of building and nurturing the bonds between parents and children and suggesting practical ways to carry out this important assignment. Here are several specific ideas for during childbirth and the time immediately following it:

If at all possible, keep sedating medications to a minimum during the hour or two before delivery. It is indeed nice if both mother and baby are awake and alert when they meet for the first time. However, it is not a sign of moral failure to request pain relief during labor (especially in the later stages when discomfort can become much more intense). If you in fact receive medication that produces drowsiness immediately after birth, you will have plenty of opportunity to begin enjoying and interacting with your baby in very short order.

Stop, look, listen, and touch. Whether immediately after birth, a few hours later, or (better yet) many times over the next several months, take the time to sit quietly and enjoy your new family member. Study his features. Let him grip your finger. Smile and talk and sing to him. Count his toes. Marvel at the handiwork of God's creation and thank Him for loaning this child to you for a season.

Look into rooming in. Continuous contact with the baby in her room can give a new mother more practical and realistic preparation for the first few days at home. A pattern for nursing can be established, problems can be talked over with the nurses and other staff members, and (more important) there is more time for everyone to get acquainted with the new baby. Most hospitals today are flexible about these post-delivery arrangements, and some will assign a single nurse to attend both mother and child in a more coordinated fashion.

Some mothers prefer a variation on this theme, in which the baby spends most of the day rooming in and goes to the nursery during the late-night and early-morning hours. This can be particularly helpful for a mother who has had a long, exhausting labor. Occasionally when one or more small children are waiting at home and Mom already knows the basics of feeding and newborn care, she will actually prefer *not* to have full-time responsibility for the new baby, in order to get a time-out and rest for a day or two. However, this relatively quiet interlude should include a generous amount of one-on-one time with the newborn, since the other children will want some attention once everyone arrives home.

In one sense, it might seem easier to spend time forming attachments with the new baby by getting out of the hospital and returning home as soon as possible. But home is also where your responsibilities are. Someone needs to prepare meals, do laundry, feed the dog, maintain order, and tend to any other children in the family, all of which could compete with your attention to your newborn. Ideally, prior arrangements can be made with husband, relatives, friends, or live-in help to take on some of these daily assignments. Preparing for this phase of childbirth can be every bit as important as all the classes and exercises during the last months of pregnancy.

Feeding and bonding. There are numerous advantages to breast feeding, which will be elaborated on in detail in the next chapter. One that many mothers have described is a feeling of special closeness and nurturing that comes from a combination of skin-to-skin contact with the baby, the satisfaction of providing him nutrients and watching him grow as a result, and possibly the release of hormones triggered by nursing. For these and many other reasons, breast feeding is the form of nourishment preferred by medical authorities (at least for the first few months).

Because of the unique relationship between mother and baby during breast feeding, fathers may feel that they have less to offer, at least for the first several weeks. On the contrary, there are plenty of hours left in the day when the baby can be held, rocked, talked to, and generally enjoyed by his father. In addition, while Dad may be tired from hours of coaching, he will not have suffered the same physical exhaustion from the childbirth process that Mom did, and he should be given the opportunity to tend to their newborn child as often as possible.

If you cannot or choose not to breast-feed, you need not lose sleep wondering whether your bonding with your child is going to be impaired. For one thing, both parents can interact with the baby during bottle feeding. And remember that feeding is only one of many components of the attachment process.

What about bonding after a cesarean delivery?

The need to deliver the baby by cesarean section may arise suddenly, or it may be known for some time in advance. The reasons this surgery may be recommended and the techniques used to carry it out will not be detailed here. (They should be covered in detail in your childbirth classes.) However, in most cases there should be time to carry out an **epidural anesthetic,** which allows the mother to be awake and alert during the delivery. Furthermore, the father or coach is typically allowed to sit at the head of the operating table, near the anesthesiologist. Only a small minority are so-called "crash" surgeries, in which an emergency requires that a general anesthetic be given.

When your baby is delivered by cesarean section, as soon as her cord is clamped and cut, she will be taken to a warmer for a brief examination. (While this is going on, the obstetrician and an assistant will check your uterus and abdomen, then begin the process of closing the multiple layers of tissue between the uterus and skin.) If all appears satisfactory, the baby will be brought to the head of the table where you can look at and touch her briefly. Unfortunately, the logistics of a cesarean delivery make a prolonged time with her difficult, and any attempt to nurse immediately after birth is impossible. After the surgery, you will go to a recovery area, where you may have further contact with your baby.

The first minutes (or even hours) after a cesarean delivery are usually not what most couples hoped for as a postchildbirth bonding experience. But catching up can be done over the next few days. Here are a few suggestions to help the process go more smoothly.

Explore your pain-relief options. A cesarean is major surgery, and pain control will be necessary for the first few days. The traditional injections of meperidine (Demerol) or other narcotics every few hours can cause wide swings between drowsy relief and wide-awake discomfort, either of which can interfere with your interaction with your baby. If at all possible (and if available at your hospital), consider having the analgesic (pain-relieving) medication given through a **patient controlled analgesia (PCA)** pump. This is an intravenous system that delivers the medication at a rate you control, within specified limits. The effect is smoother, without extremes of pain or sleepiness. Some anesthesiologists will leave the small tube for the epidural block in place, allowing for very effective pain relief without any drowsiness at all.

Don't give up on nursing. Breast-feeding after a cesarean delivery is challenging because the usual positions for holding the baby can be quite uncomfortable. But it can be done and is worth the effort (see chapter 8, page 155).

Try to recruit some extra help at home. The discomfort and fatigue that are so common in the wake of major surgery can turn the most basic tasks at home into major projects, leaving little energy (or enthusiasm) for the pleasantries of bonding. If your husband can't take extra time away from work to be home, consider having someone lend a hand for a few hours a day or even serve as a live-in to take care of some of the daily necessities. This person could be a relative (perhaps one of the baby's grandmothers), a volunteer from church, or someone specifically hired for this job. (Some insurance plans will help fund this assistance through a home-health agency.)

ADDITIONAL EVENTS BEFORE GOING HOME

The newborn examination. Sometime during the first twenty-four hours after birth, your baby's pediatrician or family physician will carry out a formal examination. (Of course if problems are apparent at birth, an evaluation will be carried out immediately.) Unless you go home within a few hours, a second checkout exam may be done before discharge. You should receive feedback from these checkups, especially if there are any problems. In addition, you may have questions about basic care and follow-up visits. You will get more out of these conversations if you write your questions down ahead of time.

Routine blood tests. Most states require that your baby be screened for certain congenital metabolic disorders that can cause major problems if not detected very early. These include **phenylketonuria (PKU)**, which can cause mental retardation; **galactosemia**, which can lead to brain, liver, and kidney damage, as well as cataracts; **congenital hypothyroidism**, which, if untreated, can affect growth and intelligence; and **sickle-cell disease**, an abnormality of red blood cells that can cause a variety of problems in black children or children of Mediterranean ancestry.

Screening is usually done on a small sample of blood obtained from the baby's heel. Occasionally borderline abnormal results will require that the test be repeated, especially in a premature infant. If one of these uncommon metabolic problems is detected, your baby's physician will provide further information regarding the next steps to be taken.

Screening for hearing loss. Significant hearing loss affecting both ears is present at birth in one to three out of one thousand newborns (and in as many as two to four in one hundred who require intensive care). Because this can impair speech and language development, detection by the age of three months is recommended so that intervention can begin by six months. Unfortunately, it is usually difficult for parents or physicians to detect hearing loss before the first birthday. Therefore, most hospitals offer screening in the newborn nursery, using one (or both) of two methods which are painless, quick, and relatively easy to perform. If this is not available in the facility at which the birth took place, ask your baby's doctor about obtaining it during the first few weeks. If screening raises the possibility of hearing loss, follow up with more formal testing and referral to a specialist will be recommended.

Circumcision. Circumcision is the removal of the foreskin, the half inch of skin that covers the head of the infant's penis. It has been a religious and cultural tradition in many parts of the world for thousands of years and was the norm for newborn boys a generation ago. More recently, some consumer groups and professional organizations have questioned the wisdom of routine circumcision.

The advantages of circumcision are primarily hygienic. The circumcised penis is easier to keep clean, whereas uncircumcised boys and men must learn to retract (gently pull back) the foreskin to clean the head of the penis. Otherwise, the accumulation of debris and bacteria may lead to an inflammation known as **balanitis**. Some evidence suggests that uncircumcised children are at higher risk for infections of the urinary tract. In older men, cancer of the penis (a relatively rare disease) occurs almost exclusively in the uncircumcised.

On the other hand, circumcision is a minor surgery and thus carries with it a very slight risk of complications, specifically moderate bleeding, infection, or even injury to the penis.

If there is a family history of bleeding problems, the procedure should not be done until the baby's clotting status has been checked. Babies who have not had a vitamin K injection (sometimes the case when the baby was born at home) tend to bleed more freely after the procedure. (Interestingly, the biblical mandate for circumcision of male babies in the nation of Israel called for the procedure to be done on the eighth day—which, prior to the use of vitamin K, was precisely the time clotting-factor levels would peak, thus reducing the risk of bleeding.)

Typically, circumcision is done by the baby's pediatrician or family doctor, or by Mom's obstetrician, before the baby leaves the hospital, although it can be arranged anytime during the first few weeks. It should not be done if there is any question about the newborn's stability, especially during the first twenty-four hours. Some physicians use a local anesthetic to relieve pain, although the baby will normally stop crying immediately after the procedure is finished. Circumcision is generally carried out when the infant's stomach is empty, but he can be nursed immediately afterwards. A small dressing will be applied to prevent bleeding, and it will fall off on its own within a day or two. The head of the penis will appear somewhat raw, and a small amount of petroleum jelly will keep it from sticking to the inner surface of his diaper. If the circumcision has been done with a device called a Plastibell, the small plastic bell will fall off on its own in about three or four days, leaving a healed surface.

If a baby boy is not circumcised, the foreskin should be left alone until it can be retracted easily, which may occur anytime before puberty. Occasionally problems with the foreskin develop later in life, and in some cases a circumcision becomes a medical necessity for an older child or adult.

Whether or not to have a baby boy circumcised is a straightforward decision for some families and a quandary for others. Despite some potential health advantages, there is no medical consensus specifically supporting or condemning routine infant circumcision. For many families, religious or other traditions are the main considerations. In others, the father or an older brother has been circumcised, and the parents want everyone to look alike. Foreskin uniformity in the family, however, is not really necessary for a child's emotional well-being.

If you are uncertain about your decision, take some time to discuss the pros and cons with the baby's physician and (assuming you are married) with your spouse. The bottom line is that you can and should be comfortable with your decision.

WHEN DOES THE BABY GO HOME?

After a hospital birth, it is not uncommon for mother and baby to return home in one or two days following a vaginal delivery and three or four days after a cesarean. Obviously this will change if mother or baby needs further care. If the newborn is premature or develops an unexpected problem that requires a longer stay, most hospitals are prepared to offer parents as much ongoing contact with the baby as possible.

Whether after a few hours, a day or two, or an extended stay, the gathering together of mother, father, baby, other family members, and your assorted new baby gear (including flowers, balloons, gifts, and other items that may have suddenly appeared after the delivery) for the trip home is a true graduation, a family commencement. Savor the moment and make sure someone captures it in pictures or on video. You are about to begin the next great adventure in parenting.

CHAPTER 7

Baby Blues, Postpartum Depression, and Postpartum Psychosis

Many mothers who have just had a mountaintop experience in the delivery room are often dismayed to find themselves in a dark, turbulent emotional valley during the first weeks after the baby is born. Between 70 and 80 percent of women are affected by a temporary emotional slump commonly known as "baby blues," while 6 to 8 percent suffer from a more severe disturbance known as postpartum (literally, "after the delivery") depression. A much less common—but far more severe—disturbance known as postpartum psychosis occurs after about one in 1,000 deliveries.

When one considers all of the intense physical and psychological changes that accompany the birth of a new baby, it's actually surprising that storm clouds aren't a part of *every* mother's emotional weather after childbirth.

There are a number of physical factors that can affect the emotions of a new mother:

- Dramatic shifts in the levels of a number of hormones (estrogen, progesterone, prolactin, cortisone, and others) after delivery. No one has identified which one (or perhaps a combination) might play a dominant role. There are probably differences in the sensitivity of women to changing hormone levels, as occurs in premenstrual syndrome.
- Physical exhaustion following the demands of labor.
- Blood loss during and after delivery.

- Pain after childbirth, especially following a cesarean section. Drugs that may be needed to kill pain can also affect mood and energy level.
- Loss of sleep, perhaps starting with an all-night labor and continuing with the round-the-clock needs of a newborn.
- Genetic factors. Depression, anxiety syndromes, panic attacks, and even more severe disturbances have a definite biochemical component. Because vulnerability to these syndromes can be inherited, they may run in families, much like diabetes, heart disease, or other medical problems.

Personal and family issues that could also affect the emotions include:

- A difficult labor and delivery during which very little went according to plan.
- Problems with the baby. These might include a complex medical concern such as prematurity or a normal baby with feeding problems or unusual irritability.
- A mismatch of expectations. The amount of time and effort involved in caring for a newborn may come as a shock to some (especially first-time) mothers, who may have never experienced being on call twenty-four hours a day.
- Lack of family support. If Dad is gone most of the day (or there is no dad in the picture) and relatives are not available to lend a hand, taking care of a newborn can be overwhelming. This will be worsened if a marriage is shaky or if a new mother is getting negative input: "Why are you so tired? I've been working hard all day— all you've had to do is sit around with the baby!"
- Perfectionism. With a new baby (or even with one or more older children) it is not possible to be the Mother

of the Year, keeper of the showcase home, rising young executive, and amorous wife. Childbirth and baby care bring one's limitations into striking and sometimes distressing focus.

- Financial pressure. Budgets are often tight in new families, and the expenses surrounding childbirth will add new stress to the family finances.
- Feelings of being stuck or trapped in the new role. A woman who has been pursuing a rewarding career or who is accustomed to a relatively carefree lifestyle might begin to feel that nonstop responsibility for a helpless newborn is a ball and chain—especially if family support or financial resources are limited.

POSTPARTUM BLUES

Baby blues, the most common mood problem related to childbirth, usually develops during the first week after delivery. Symptoms can include irritability, tearfulness, anxiety, insomnia, lack of energy, loss of appetite, and difficulty concentrating. This emotional and physical slump typically resolves by itself within two weeks. However, it should not be met with an attitude of "ignore it and it will go away." Support and reassurance from husband, family, and friends are very important. In addition, help with the baby, housekeeping, and other practical details can make a major difference.

POSTPARTUM DEPRESSION

While many of its symptoms are very similar to those of baby blues, **postpartum depression (PPD)** is a more serious condition. Not only does it last longer, but its impact on both mother and baby is more profound. A mother with PPD may be so intensely depressed that she has difficulty caring for her baby, or she may develop extreme and unrealistic anxiety over the infant's health. Furthermore, ongoing disruption of mother-child interactions can have adverse effects on the infant's long-term development.

PPD can begin at any time during the first six months after childbirth. It is more common among women who have had a prior clinical depression, or a previous postpartum depression. While two out of three mothers recover within one year, this problem should not be left to run its course. Like a major depression occurring at any other time in life, PPD is not a situation in which a little "attitude adjustment" is all that is needed. If symptoms such as those listed above for baby blues continue for more than two weeks, professional help should be sought. Treatment might involve extended counseling, the use of antidepressant medication, or both. Medication is sometimes very helpful in normalizing biochemical mechanisms in the central nervous system that affect mood, sleep patterns, and fatigue. However, if a mother is breast-feeding, input from the baby's doctor will be needed if medications are being considered.

POSTPARTUM PSYCHOSIS

In the relatively rare but very serious disorder called **postpartum psychosis**, a woman experiences not only a disturbance in mood but also a break with reality. At some time during the first month after delivery, she may become confused and experience hallucinations and delusions. She may even consider harming herself or her baby. A woman who develops postpartum psychosis must be evaluated immediately by a qualified psychiatrist, although it might be difficult to convince her that this is necessary. This condition can and should be treated with appropriate medication. There is, however, a one-in-seven chance that it will recur with a subsequent pregnancy.[1]

It is important to note, however, that postpartum depression and psychosis can occur without warning. A woman's mood during her pregnancy does not necessarily predict how she will feel after the baby comes home. However, if a woman has a history of depression or other significant emotional problems or if they have occurred in her immediate family, those close to her should be alert for signs of turbulence during the days and weeks following childbirth. *A mother who has suffered postpartum psychosis in the past must be observed carefully for any signs of recurrence after future deliveries.*

PREVENTING EMOTIONAL PROBLEMS AFTER CHILDBIRTH

The first chapter of this book includes a section (see pages 34–36) that contains recommendations for parents anticipating the birth of their child. These include tapping into a support team, maintaining a personal quiet time, and (for married couples) building the relationship with one another. All of these are important *after* the baby is born as well. Fathers should pay particular attention to the items under "Some thoughts for the expectant and new father." Expressions of love and respect, help with the daily tasks of living, and ongoing prayer for (and with) a new mother can certainly help prevent an emotional upheaval during the weeks after a baby arrives.

NOTES

1. D. A. Bright, "Post-partum Mental Disorders," American Family Physician (1994): 50.

CHAPTER 8

The First Three Months, Part One

Family Adjustments, Feeding the New Arrival, and Dealing with Basic Health Concerns

Now that the efforts of labor and delivery are over, within a few hours or a few days after your baby's birth (with rare exception), you will be bringing your son or daughter home. You will most likely have some apprehensions about the coming weeks—or, for that matter, about the first night. Will he get enough nourishment? How often should he be fed? Where should he sleep? Will *we* get any sleep? What if he starts crying—and won't stop? If there are other children at home, how will they respond to the new arrival?

Many of these questions have already been addressed in a childbirth- or parenting-preparation class. But just in case you didn't get all the bases covered, the following two chapters will cover the ABCs of new baby care.

Before we begin, remember:

- The information in this book assumes that your baby is full-term, has been examined, and is basically healthy. If he was born prematurely or has medical problems that require special care, you should follow the specific directions of your physician.
- In the coming months you will be getting all sorts of advice from friends, relatives, and other resources. Much of it will be helpful and appropriate, at least for most babies. But if something you read or hear doesn't make sense or doesn't work, don't be afraid to get a second opinion. And if you get conflicting advice, don't

panic. Newborns are much more sturdy and resilient than you might think, and there are very few mistakes that loving, attentive parents might make that cannot be straightened out later on.

- While it is normal to feel some anxiety over the responsibility of full-time care for a new baby, the process of parenting a newborn should not be dominated by fear and uncertainty. Be confident that you and your baby can and will survive and thrive, even while all of you are learning. Since every parent-child combination is unique, some adjusting and improvising will be a necessary part of the process. But it is neither necessary nor wise to wade through the first months or years purely on blind instinct.

FIRST THINGS FIRST FOR COUPLES: MOM AND DAD'S PARTNERSHIP

With all the excitement and changes that come with the role of parenting, whether for the first time or with a new addition, *it is extremely important that mother and father continuously reaffirm the importance of their own relationship.* For many reasons, it is common for a new baby to take center stage and for parents, especially new ones, to put the maintenance of their marriage at the bottom of the daily priority list. Remember that the two of you became a family with the exchange of vows, before children were in the picture. You will remain a family after the children have grown and left your home. While they are under your roof, a rock-solid partnership, continually renewed and refreshed, will be the foundation for the security of any and all children you add to your original family of two. Your new baby is to be loved and cherished, but he must not, for his own sake, become the permanent center of gravity around which everything else in your home revolves.

Preventing turmoil in the nest

You might assume that the awe and wonder of having a new-born at home would automatically forge a powerful bond be-tween the proud parents. But it is also quite possible for the new demands of baby care to generate some unexpected fric-tion, resentment, or jealousy in the marriage.

If the new baby is breast-fed rather than bottle-fed, much of a young mother's time and energy will be occupied with feeding, not to mention the many other details of infant care. (This can also occur, of course, when a baby is bottle-fed, al-though in this case others can take turns with feeding ses-sions.) As a result, a father might begin to feel left out and could even resent a nursing child who seems to have displaced him from his wife's affections.

This may be aggravated by unspoken assumptions about mothers' and fathers' roles, especially with newborns. If one parent believes that tending to a baby is "women's work" and that Dad need not report for duty until his son can throw a ball or his daughter is ready to ride a bike, a wedge can de-velop between mother and father. He may become weary of seeing her attention directed toward meeting the newborn's seemingly endless needs. She may become irritated if he isn't pulling his weight at home, especially if he seems to expect her to meet a lot of his needs when she is thoroughly exhausted.

How can you prevent a newborn nest from becoming a "house divided"?

Hot tips for Mom: Make sure your husband knows that he hasn't been relegated to the back burner of your affection and interest. Beware of total and absolute preoccupation with your new baby, as normal as that desire might seem to you. If you nurse, carry, rock, caress, and sleep with your baby twenty-four hours a day without offering some attention to your mate, before long your marriage may be a shadow of its former self.

Whenever possible, try to freshen up if you haven't seen your spouse for several hours—even if you're pooped. It's important that you take care of yourself even in these early days of motherhood, because from now on it will be tempting to neglect yourself when there are so many needs and tasks surrounding you. Certainly your husband will appreciate seeing you take steps to maintain your health and appearance. But for your own sake it is important to cultivate good feelings about who *you* are by giving some priority to your personal needs and interests. Taking care of yourself, even in small ways, can help you avoid baby-care burnout—not only now but also in the days and seasons to come.

Hot tips for Dad: Pay lots of attention to your newborn, for whom you can do all sorts of things (such as cuddling, rocking, and changing). Wives tend to become very enamored with husbands who clearly cherish their babies. Don't expect to be treated like another child at home, waiting for a weary housekeeper to fix your meals, do your laundry, and clean up your messes. Roll up your sleeves and pitch in. Finally, take another look at the material in chapter 1 entitled "Some thoughts for the expectant and new father" (page 36). Your commitment to "love, honor, and cherish" has no expiration date.

Patterns you establish now in your marriage may well continue as your new baby and other children that may follow grow to maturity. Ultimately their sense of security will rise or fall with the visible evidence of stability, mutual respect, and ongoing love of their mother and father for one another. Overt demonstrations of affection not only fulfill deep and abiding needs between husband and wife, but they also provide a strong, daily reassurance for children that their world will remain intact. The same can be said of time set aside by parents for quiet conversation with one another *before* the children have gone to bed.

Equally significant is a regular date night for Mom and Dad, which should be instituted as soon as possible and maintained even after the kids are grown and gone. These time-outs need not be expensive, but they may require some ongoing creativity, planning, and dedication. Dedication is necessary because child-care needs, pangs of guilt, and complicated calendars will conspire to prevent those dates from happening. But the romance, renewal, and vitality they generate are well worth the effort.

Special note to single parents

Taking care of a new baby is a major project for a couple in a stable marriage. For a single parent—who usually, but not always, is the mother—the twenty-four-hour care of a newborn may seem overwhelming from the first day. But even without a committed partner, you can take care of your baby and do it well. The job will be less difficult if you have some help.

Hopefully, before the baby was born you found a few people who would be willing members of your support team. These might be your parents, other relatives, friends, members of your church, or volunteers from a local crisis pregnancy center (CPC). By all means, don't hesitate to seek their help, especially during the early weeks when you are getting acquainted with your new baby. If your parents offer room, board, and child-care assistance, and you are on good terms with them, you would be wise to accept. Or if a helpful and mature family member or friend offers to stay with you for a while after the birth, give the idea careful consideration. (Obviously, you should avoid situations in which there is likely to be more conflict than help.)

Even after you have a few weeks or months of parenting

under your belt, at some point you may need a brief time-out to walk around the block, or advice on calming a crying episode. But no one will know unless you ask. Many churches and CPCs have ongoing single-parent groups in which you can relax for a few hours on a regular basis, swap ideas, and talk with others who know firsthand the challenges you face.

LIFE WITH A NEWBORN: WHAT CAN YOU EXPECT?

Since you are bringing home a new baby for the very first time, you have probably been wondering what your life will be like on a day-to-day basis. Perhaps you have envisioned your new parenthood as a tranquil scene from a greeting card or a TV commercial: a contented mother and father sitting by the fireside, smiling softly at the tiny cherub who sweetly coos her love in return. Or you may have heard tales of misery from family or friends, describing endless sleepless nights, relentless fatigue, and no life at all away from the seven-pound tyrant who demands attention every moment. Some young mothers arrive at parenthood believing that caring for their new baby will be like bringing a puppy home from the pet store.

In one sense, a newborn has a relatively simple agenda: eating, sleeping, crying, being quietly alert, and eliminating urine and stool, repeated over and over each day. Therefore, it wouldn't seem all that difficult or complicated to care for her. After all, she won't be feverishly exploring every cupboard in the house, struggling with overdue homework assignments, or arguing with you over rights to the car.

But there are countless variations on these basic activities and some unpredictability in the way each baby behaves from day to day. Furthermore, the first few days of life at home may seem unsettled for both you and your baby. You may be coping for the first time with the profound reality of being responsible for a tiny, helpless human twenty-four hours a day and wondering if you will ever "have a life" again. It may take several character-building days for both baby and parents to establish a predictable pattern of eating and sleeping—or to become used to the absence of a predictable pattern. In response to her new surroundings, your baby may also be more fussy or sleepy after she first arrives home.

For all these reasons, cookbook approaches to baby care, with step-by-step directions for every situation, are unrealistic. Instead, as we look at the elements of your new baby's daily routine, we will outline some basic facts and principles that you can then adapt and fine-tune to your family's unique circumstances. Above all, try your best to relax and trust that you and your baby will in fact eventually settle in (and settle down) together.

FEEDING YOUR NEWBORN

For a new baby and her parents, feeding time represents far more than "open mouth, insert milk." In the course of receiving life-sustaining calories, nutrients, and fluids from multiple feedings every day, your baby is also having a series of important multisensory experiences. The receptors of sight, hearing, touch, taste, and smell are all actively gathering information during feedings. More important, emotional bonds are forming as the discomfort of hunger is repeatedly ended by a loving parent. As you become more familiar with your baby and more relaxed, you can look forward to each feeding as a special, satisfying, and relaxing event rather than a time-consuming chore or a source of anxiety. Like so many other aspects of parenting, how you approach and prepare for this activity will have a major impact on its success.

The vast majority of newborn babies are ready, willing, and able to take in the milk offered to them. As mentioned in the last chapter, they come equipped with rooting, sucking, and swallowing reflexes that are quite efficient at transporting milk from nipple to stomach. While babies may show differences in feeding styles and some may seem more adept than others at the outset, you should assume from the beginning that you and your baby are very capable of working together to accomplish this important goal.

Breast or formula?

Over the past few decades a mountain of scientific evidence has validated what is, in fact, a very straightforward observation: Human mothers are beautifully designed to feed their own babies. Breast milk, with extremely rare exception, is the best—and should normally be the complete—source of nutrition during the first months of a child's life, without additional water, juice, cereal, or other foods.

While there is clear medical consensus that breast feeding is the preferred source of fuel for the newborn, it should not be viewed as a sacred rite. If you need or choose to bottle-feed, you can do so with assurance that your baby will do well physically and emotionally. There are a variety of formulas available that will meet a baby's nutritional needs quite adequately, and both Mom and Dad or a single parent can provide a warm, nurturing experience while feeding an infant from a bottle.

Whether you feed your baby breast milk or formula (or a combination of the two), it is important to understand that *she does not need other types of food or fluids during the first three to four months.* Juice, cow's milk from the dairy case, cereal, fruit, and other solids are all unnecessary and/or inappropriate for your baby at this stage of her life.

Details about formula feeding begin on page 171. However, if you are planning to use formula but have the option to breast-feed or if you are not sure which approach to use, take time to consider carefully the following information before you make your final decision.

What are the advantages of breast feeding?
Human milk is uniquely suited to human babies. It is not only nutritionally complete and properly balanced, but it is also constantly changing to meet the needs of a growing infant. The fat content of breast milk increases as a feeding progresses, creating a sense of satisfied fullness that tends to prevent overeating. Furthermore, the fat and cholesterol content of breast milk is higher in the early months, when these compounds are most needed in a baby's rapidly growing brain and nervous system. The primary proteins in all forms of milk are whey and casein, but in human milk, whey, which is easier to absorb, predominates. Compared to cow's milk, the carbohydrate component of breast milk contains a higher percentage of lactose, which appears to play an important role in both brain development and calcium absorption.

Vitamins and minerals are adequately supplied in mother's milk. No supplements are needed for the breast-fed infant, although additional vitamin D may be recommended by your baby's physician if you live in a climate or geographical area where sunshine is rare. Trace elements, such as copper and zinc, are present in the right amounts, and iron is present in breast milk in a form that is easier to absorb than in any other type of milk.

Breast milk is absorbed extremely efficiently, with little undigested material passing into stool. Experienced diaper changers are well aware that formula-fed infants tend to have smellier stools, a by-product of the nutritional odds and ends (especially certain fats and proteins) that are not thoroughly absorbed on their trip through the bowel.

From day one, breast milk contains antibodies that help protect babies from infections. The first product of the breast after birth, known as **colostrum**, is particularly rich in antibodies known as **immunoglobulin A**, which help protect the lining of the intestine from microscopic invaders. As the mother comes in contact with new viruses and bacteria, her immune system generates the appropriate microbe-fighting antibodies and passes them on to her baby, thus reducing— but by no means eliminating—the newborn's risk of becoming infected. This is particularly important in the first several months of life, when the newborn's immune system is less effective at mounting a defense against microscopic invaders. While formula manufacturers have labored mightily to duplicate the nutritional mixture of breast milk, they cannot hope to supply any of these complex immune factors. Breast-fed infants, for as long as they are given breast milk, thus tend to have fewer infections (including ear and intestinal infections) than their formula-fed counterparts.

Breast milk is free. It is clean, fresh, warm, and ready to feed, anytime and virtually anyplace. It does not need to be purchased, stored (although it can be expressed into bottles and frozen for later use), mixed, or heated.

Stimulation of a mother's nipples by a nursing infant releases a hormone called oxytocin, which helps her uterus contract toward what will become its nonpregnant size. The hormonal response to nursing also postpones the onset of ovulation and the menstrual cycle, providing a natural—though not foolproof—spacing of children. Nursing mothers also tend to reach their prepregnancy weight more quickly.

Breast feeding lends itself to a sense of closeness, intimacy, and mutual satisfaction. The skin-to-skin contact, the increased sensory input for the baby, and the mother's satisfaction in being able to provide her child's most basic needs can help establish strong bonds between them.

Are there any reasons not to breast-feed?
There are a few medical situations in which breast feeding

poses a risk for the baby. HIV, the virus responsible for AIDS, has been reported to be transmitted from infected mother to noninfected infant through breast feeding. A mother with active hepatitis B or tuberculosis should not nurse her baby. Obviously, a serious illness in the mother may make breast feeding extremely difficult or even unsafe for both mother and child. Furthermore, virtually all medications show up to some degree in breast milk, and some are potentially harmful for infants. If one or more drugs that may be unsafe for a baby are needed to preserve the mother's life and health, formula feeding should be used. Careful consultation with both mother's and baby's physicians is in order when making this decision.

Previous breast surgery may affect a mother's ability to nurse. A biopsy or local lump removal in the past normally will not cause difficulty. Even after a mastectomy it is possible to feed a baby adequately using the remaining breast. Breast-reduction surgery, however, may result in an inadequate milk supply if the majority of milk-producing tissue has been removed. Previous breast-enhancement/implant surgery should not cause a problem for nursing unless the ducts that carry milk to the nipple were cut during the procedure.

Infants born with phenylketonuria (PKU) or galactosemia, rare metabolic disorders that are detected by routine screening tests after birth, must be fed special formulas to prevent a variety of serious consequences. Congenital problems such as a cleft lip or palate, heart disease, and Down syndrome can create special challenges for nursing. However, the benefits of mother's milk for these infants are usually well worth the extra effort needed to provide it for them, even if they cannot obtain milk directly from the breast. A team effort involving parents, physicians, and a lactation consultant will be necessary.

A number of nonmedical concerns might cause a woman to be reluctant to breast-feed or to consider abandoning it too quickly. These are worth some review and reflection.

A friend or relative's bad experience. "My sister had a baby who wouldn't nurse/couldn't nurse/didn't want to nurse. He wouldn't stop crying until we gave him a bottle. After days of frustration, tears, and sore nipples, she felt like a total failure."

If someone you know has had difficulty nursing a baby in the past, remember that each newborn is different. There is no rule that says history must repeat itself, and there are, in fact, very few women who simply are unable to supply enough milk to sustain their offspring.

Physical problems. "My breasts are too small/too big. My nipples are flat/dimpled/inverted."

Your milk is supplied by **mammary** (milk-producing) **glands** whose function is not related to breast size. In response to large amounts of hormones circulating during pregnancy—especially prolactin (literally, "for milk"), estrogen, progesterone, and human placental lactogen (which, as its name indicates, is secreted by the placenta)—the mammary glands enlarge, mature, and become capable of producing milk. However, the actual process of creating milk is held in check during pregnancy by these same elevated hormone levels. When your baby is born and the placenta delivered, the abrupt loss of placental hormones allows milk production to begin in earnest—whether you plan to nurse or not. This interplay between multiple hormones and structures within the body is intricately designed, and you can assume that it will function as intended.

Nipples may vary in shape, and some may be easier for infants to grasp and suck than others. Those that clearly protrude may look like better nursing candidates than those that are flat, dimpled, or inverted. What matters most, however, is what happens when the infant attempts to latch on and suck. To get a preview, gently squeeze *behind* the nipple using thumb and index finger.

When properly attached, a baby will grasp the entire **areola** (the dark area surrounding the nipple) and not just the nipple itself. If your nipple clearly extends outward in response to this squeeze, your baby should have little difficulty. If your nipple flattens or inverts further, however, you may have tiny adhesions under the skin that are preventing it from extending outward. Normally, changes in the breast related to pregnancy will help correct this problem. However, if the squeeze test is still yielding a flat or inverted nipple by the last trimester of pregnancy, a **breast shell** may help. This is a simple plastic device, worn inside the bra, that exerts constant gentle pressure on the areola and gradually helps the nipple protrude. If help is needed after birth, shells can be worn between feedings.

Don't try to toughen up your nipples by pulling or rubbing them before or during pregnancy. Not only will this fail to prevent any soreness during nursing, but it might stimulate the release of hormones that can cause the uterus to contract or even begin labor prematurely.

Lifestyle issues. "I don't want to be the only one who can feed the baby. I've seen women whose babies are like appendages stuck permanently on their chests. They have no life—they can't go anywhere or do anything without their baby."

Breast feeding does take more of Mom's time, but it need not be a ball-and-chain experience. After nursing has become a well-established routine, milk can be expressed into a bottle and stored for Dad, grandparents, or baby-sitters to use at a later date. And if you need to get away for a long evening or even overnight, it won't harm your baby to have a formula feeding or two if you don't have enough of your own milk in the freezer. Don't forget that nursing means being free from the hassle of buying formula; preparing it; and dealing with nipples, bottles, bottle liners, and other items.

Keep in mind that it is hardly a major setback if nursing slows your life down for a while. Your body needs time for rest and restoration after accomplishing the formidable tasks of completing pregnancy and childbirth. Do you really need to accelerate immediately back into the fast lane of your prepregnant lifestyle? This very dependent season of your child's life—whether she is breast- or bottle-fed—is relatively short, and it would be beneficial for both of you if you could settle back and enjoy it as much as you can. (This applies whether or not you need to return to a full- or part-time job outside the home.)

Returning to work. "I need to return to my job in two months, and I don't see how I can spend eight or ten hours in the office at the same time I'm trying to nurse."

Even one or two months of nursing are worth doing, and believe it or not, with some planning, creativity, and assistance on the home front, it is possible for a breast feeding mother to return to work. The adjustments will vary considerably with the age of the baby, the location of the job, and the hours involved.

BREAST-FEEDING BASICS

As mentioned in chapter 3, your new baby may be nursed for the first time immediately after delivery or some time later if you or the baby has medical needs that require immediate attention. A newborn is alert and most ready to nurse during the first two hours after birth; therefore many physicians recommend that a mother offer the breast during that time if at all possible. However, even if your first feeding must be delayed several hours or even days, you can still get off to a good start.

Whenever you begin, you and your baby should be able to find a position that not only is comfortable but also allows him to latch on to the breast properly. This occurs when his mouth closes over the areola and forms a seal with his gums. His tongue should be positioned against the underside of the nipple and then with wavelike motions, compress it, emptying the milk-containing ducts just below the areola.

If he repeatedly clamps down on the nipple only and not the areola, you will probably develop some major pain and cracking in the nipple before long—and have a frustrated baby as well because he won't get much milk this way. Some babies at first seem more interested in licking or nibbling than in grasping the breast properly. While it is a good idea in general to avoid bottle feedings during the first several days unless absolutely necessary, it is particularly important that these "lick and chew" newborns stay away from formula and pacifiers until they catch on to latching on.

If you nurse immediately after delivery, it will usually be easiest to lie on your side with the baby's entire body facing you, stomach to stomach. This position will also be very useful in the days following a cesarean delivery, in order to prevent the weight of the baby from pressing on your sore abdomen. In this position you will need to lift your breast with the opposite hand to move the areola next to his mouth. More common is the sitting cuddle position, in which the infant's head is cradled in the bend of your elbow with your forearm supporting his back and your hand holding his bottom or upper leg. An alternative sitting position, called the football hold, places your baby's body at your side supported by your arm with your hand holding his head. This is another helpful position if you have had a cesarean birth, since it minimizes pressure on your incision site. It is also useful for mothers of twins who wish to nurse both babies simultaneously.

Once you are positioned comfortably, gently lift your breast and stroke your baby's cheek or lower lip with your nipple. This will provoke his rooting reflex. When his mouth opens wide, gently pull him to you so that your areola enters his mouth. You will need to make this move relatively quickly before his mouth closes. Be sure not to "meet him halfway" by leaning forward, or else you will have a very sore back before long. It helps to compress your breast slightly between thumb and palm or between two fingers in a scissorlike position, using your free hand, but stay a couple inches behind the areola when you do so.

When your baby begins sucking, nerve endings in the nipple send a message to the pituitary gland at the base of your brain. The pituitary in turn secretes the hormone prolactin, which stimulates more milk production, and **oxytocin**, which causes tiny muscles that surround the milk ducts to squeeze milk toward the areola. This event is called the **let-down reflex**, which you will probably feel as a change of pressure or, less commonly, as a tingling within the breasts. Some women, however, can't feel the let-down reflex at all. Once your milk has come in, you may notice anything from a slow drip of milk to a full-blown spray during let-down. Many women will experience let-down not only in response to their baby's sucking but also when their baby—or someone else's—begins to cry. During the first days after delivery, you will also feel contractions of the uterus in response to the oxytocin released by the pituitary gland. While these might be uncomfortable, they are carrying out the important function of reducing the size of your uterus.

The let-down reflex may be inhibited by certain drugs, as well as by smoking. Let-down also may not function as well if you are upset or tense. It is therefore important that your nursing times be as relaxed and calm as possible. You might consider setting up a comfortable "nursing corner" at home, where your favorite chair (very often a rocker) and a table with soft light, a few key supplies, soft music, and even something to read are within easy reach. A small stash of healthy snack food and some water or juice may be a welcome addition as well. If you live in a multistory setting, you may want to set up one of these "nursing stations" on each floor. Take the phone off the hook and savor these moments, not worrying about whatever else you think you should be doing. Watch your baby, caress him, talk or sing softly to him, or take some time to pray quietly. These can be sweet times of reflection and meditation during otherwise busy days.

Remember that for the first three or four days you will be producing **colostrum**, the yellowish, high-protein liquid full of antibodies and white cells. With rare exception, this is all your baby will need, since he was born with extra fluid in his system that compensates for the relatively low fluid volume of colostrum. When your milk supply begins to arrive, you will notice some increased fullness, warmth, and probably tenderness. During this process your breasts are said to be **engorged**, and they may actually swell so much that your baby will have trouble latching on to them. Should this occur, you can gently express some milk from each breast, softening it so your baby can grasp more easily. To express milk, grasp the edge of the areola between thumb and fingers and then repeatedly squeeze while pushing gently toward your chest. (A warm compress or hot shower may be needed to get the milk flowing.) Engorgement typically lasts only a day or two (see page 162).

Nursing patterns

Each baby has a unique style of nursing, and yours may mesh easily with your milk supply and lifestyle or may require that you make some adjustments. Some infants get right down to business, sucking vigorously and efficiently without much hesitation. These "barracudas" contrast sharply with the "gourmet" nursers, who take their sweet time, playing with the nipple at first, sampling their meal, and then eventually getting started. Some babies vary the gourmet approach by resting every few minutes, as if savoring their feeding, or even falling asleep one or more times during the nursing session. The "suck and snooze" types may exasperate a mother who feels that she doesn't have all day to nurse. While it's all right to provide a little mild stimulation (such as undressing him) to get Sleepy back on task and complete his feeding, some downsizing of your expectations for the day's activities may be necessary to prevent ongoing frustration.

Newborns also vary in the frequency with which they need to nurse. A typical span between feedings will be two to three hours or eight to twelve times per day, but during the first days after birth, the interval may be longer, with only six to eight feedings in a twenty-four-hour period. The baby will feed more often than usual during growth spurts. The time involved in a feeding will also vary, but a typical feeding will take ten to fifteen minutes per breast.

As with nearly every aspect of life, what is said to be "typical" may not match with what happens in reality—especially with newborns. For example, your first nursing experiences in a hospital setting may be somewhat confusing, especially if you are not rooming in. Many hospital nurseries still adhere to the tradition of bringing out all the babies to their mothers for feeding on a fixed schedule. But most babies don't automatically synchronize to Nursery Standard Time and may be sound asleep for these nursing "appointments." The result is repeated frustration for mothers whose zonked-out newborns seem to have little interest in latching on, let alone sucking, during the first few days after birth. In a worst-case scenario, a baby who hasn't been ready to nurse with Mom might wake up and sound off when he's parked in the nursery, only to have his crying ignored or answered with a bottle. Many hospital nurseries now bring newborns to their mothers when they're hungry rather than in fixed shifts. Overall, however, rooming in gives everyone a better chance to get acquainted and, more important, nurse when the baby is awake and hungry.

Don't worry if your baby doesn't seem terribly interested in frequent nursing during the first few days. That will change, often just after you bring him home. The early phase of sleepiness that occurs as he adjusts to the outside world will usually give way to more active crying and nursing—sometimes every few hours—after the first week. Some parents are aghast when this happens. The mellow baby they enjoyed in the hospital suddenly seems wired and insatiable just a few days later. Don't panic. Instead, look at this as a time to hone your nursing skills with a very willing partner.

The newborn baby normally will announce his desire for milk very clearly, with some insistent crying every two to four hours. When this occurs, it is appropriate to tend to him promptly, change him if necessary, and then settle in for a feeding. Some infants make sucking movements or fuss for a while before overtly sounding off. There's no point in waiting for full-blown crying before offering the breast. For five to ten minutes you will notice him swallowing after every few sucks, and then he will shift gears to a more relaxed mode or even seem to lose interest.

At that point he can be burped, either by lifting him and placing his head over your shoulder, or by sitting him up with your hand under his jaw and gently patting him on the back. You can also place him face down across your lap, with head supported and chest a little higher than abdomen, and gently pat his back.

Once he burps, he may show interest in the other breast. (If he doesn't burp and yet he appears comfortable, you can still proceed with the feeding.) Since the first side may be more completely emptied during the feeding, it is wise to alternate the breast from which he starts. (A small pin or clip that you move from one side of your nursing bra to the other can help remind you where to begin next time.)

Relatively frequent nursing is typical after the first days of life, and it will help stimulate your milk production and let-down reflex. A newborn who seems to be very content with infrequent feedings (more than four hours apart) should probably be checked by your physician to confirm that his activity level is satisfactory. He may in fact need to be awakened to feed every three hours to ensure adequate weight gain during the first two or three weeks.

Problems and concerns with nursing

"How do I know if she's getting enough?" During the first few days after birth, this concern often prods new mothers toward bottle feeding, where they have the security of seeing exactly how much the baby is consuming. Remember that the quantity of milk you produce during a feeding will start with as little as half an ounce (15 ml) of colostrum during the first day or two and increase to an ounce (30 ml) as the milk supply arrives by the fourth or fifth day. After the first week, your milk output will range from two to six ounces per feeding. Obviously, there is no direct way for you to measure how much your baby is sucking from your breast, but other signs will indicate how the two of you are doing:

- When the room is quiet, you will hear your baby swallowing.
- Once your milk has arrived, you may notice that your breasts soften during a feeding as they are emptied of milk.
- After the first four or five days, you should be changing six to eight wet diapers each day. In addition, you will notice one or several small, dark green stools— sometimes one after every feeding—that become lighter after the first (meconium) stools are passed. As your milk

supply becomes well established, your baby's stools will take on a yellowish color and a soft or runny consistency. Later on, stools typically become less frequent.

- Tracking your baby's weight will give you specific and important information. *It is normal for a baby to drop nearly 10 percent of her birth weight (about eleven or twelve ounces, for example, for a seven-pound baby) during the first week.* Usually she will have returned to her birth weight by two weeks of age, and thereafter she should gain about two-thirds to one ounce per day. Obviously you can't track these small changes at home on the bathroom scale. Instead, it is common to have a checkup during the first week or two after birth, during which your baby will be weighed on a scale that can detect smaller changes. If there is any question about appropriate weight gain, your doctor will ask you to return every week (or more often, if needed) to follow her progress.

One of the most important—and hardest—things to remember if you are concerned about the adequacy of your nursing is to *relax*. If you approach every feeding with fear and trembling, you may have difficulty with your let-down reflex. Furthermore, newborns seem to have an uncanny sense of Mom's anxiety, and their jittery response may interfere with smooth latching on and sucking. Remember that for many women, breast feeding requires time, effort, and learning. Even if your first few feedings seem awkward or your baby doesn't seem to be getting the hang of it immediately, you should be able to make this process work. Take a deep breath, take your time, and don't be afraid to ask for help if you are truly having trouble getting started.

"It hurts when I nurse!" No one wants to spend a good portion of the day in misery, and a strong dose of pain with every feeding can demoralize even the most dedicated breast feeding mother. Some tenderness during the baby's first few sucks of each feeding is not unusual for a few days after birth while a callus is being formed.

Many mothers also feel aching during the let-down reflex, and some may even notice a brief shooting pain deeper in the breast after nursing as the milk supply is refilling. For some women the engorgement of the breasts prior to each nursing session can be very painful. It is possible, in fact, to have intense pain with engorgement even when your nursing technique is correct and nothing specific is wrong with your breasts. Some mothers who are unprepared for such severe discomfort may give up on nursing too soon. But becoming comfortable with nursing may, in fact, take a few days or even a few weeks as your baby learns and your body adjusts to this new function.

In most cases, pain serves as a warning that should not be ignored. If you have significant, ongoing pain with nursing, you should review this with your doctor and attempt to identify one of the causes that can and should be treated.

Intense discomfort can arise from traumatized, cracked, or inflamed nipples, which, of course, are sensitive areas to begin with. If the nipple is irritated at the tip, it is probably entering your baby's mouth at an upward angle and rubbing on her palate. During the latching-on process, try holding your breast so the nipple points downward. This is often easier if you are sitting, using the cuddle or football hold.

If the nipple is more tender at the base, it is more likely being chewed during feedings. Remember that your baby needs to take the entire areola into her mouth when she latches on, so your nipple lies against her tongue. If she won't open her mouth fully or slides off the areola after latching on, your nipple will be gummed continually while you nurse. To add insult to injury, your baby may not get enough milk when this occurs. The combination of miserable mom and crying newborn is often enough to send Dad out into the night in search of formula.

To help your baby latch on to the whole areola (and not just your nipple), wait for her to open her mouth wide enough and then gently pull her to the breast. If you are engorged and she is having difficulty forming a seal around the areola, you can express or pump some milk so that area will be softer. You may have to utilize the football hold (see page 155) to give your hand better control of her head and thus keep her from sliding off the areola. If she seems to lose her position during the feeding, don't be afraid to pull her gently from the breast and then reattach. If she has a strong hold, you should first loosen it by pulling downward gently on her chin or inserting a finger into the corner of her mouth to release the vacuum seal formed by her gums.

Other causes of painful irritation of one or both nipples, or even full-blown inflammation known as **dermatitis**, include:

- Overzealous use of soap and water that can remove the skin's own moisturizers. Rinse your breasts during your shower or bath but keep soap away from your nipples.
- Continuous moisture on the skin surface. This can occur when the breast is not allowed to dry off after a feeding or when the pads of a nursing bra are moist. Air drying for a few minutes after nursing is the simplest solution, while making certain that your nursing bra is dry as well.
- An allergic reaction to breast creams or oils. Paradoxically, traditional remedies for breast soreness such as vitamin E preparations or impure lanolin may make the problem worse if they provoke an allergic dermatitis. If your nipple develops redness, swelling, and a burning sensation, stop using any nipple cream. If the problem

persists or worsens, see your doctor. You may have to
use a mild anti-inflammatory prescription cream for a
few days to calm this problem down more quickly.

- An infection with the yeast organism known as **Candida
albicans**, which will also be present in the baby's mouth.
In this case the irritation may not only burn but also
itch. Candida may appear sometime after you have been
nursing without any problems. A tip-off is the presence
of small, white patches inside your baby's cheeks.
Candida infection in the baby's mouth (also known
as **thrush**) is not a dangerous condition, but it can be
a persistent annoyance. Candida infections usually
respond to treatment with an antifungal cream (check
with your doctor). At the same time, your baby should
be given antifungal drops by mouth. If both of you are
not treated concurrently for several days, the infection
may bounce back and forth between you. Furthermore,
in order to prevent reinfection, you will need to change
nursing pads after every feeding. If your baby is
receiving any feedings from a bottle or is using a
pacifier, you will need to boil the rubber nipples and
pacifiers every day until the infection clears.

- Rarely an ongoing **eczema** problem that has appeared
on other parts of your body will erupt on the breast
during nursing. You will want to consult with your
doctor about appropriate treatment, which may involve
the short-term use of a mild anti-inflammatory cream.

- A potentially more serious cause of pain is **mastitis**, an
infection caused by bacteria that gain entry into breast
tissue, usually through a cracked nipple. Symptoms
include pain, swelling, heat, redness, and tenderness
in a localized area of one breast, accompanied by
generalized aching and fever. If there is no fever,
it probably is a plugged duct and does not require

antibiotics. Should this problem develop, it is important
to contact your physician. Antibiotics that are safe for
both mother and baby will normally be prescribed, and
acetaminophen may be used to reduce both pain and
temperature. The use of warm, moist compresses can
assist in the treatment. *In addition, it is important to
continue nursing,* although you may be more
comfortable with more frequent, shorter sessions. Your
baby will not become ill by nursing from an infected
breast, and emptying the breast of milk helps clear the
infection. Ice cubes can be applied directly to the breast
(at first in quick, short strokes) above and below the
infected area. This can help reduce pain and swelling.

Aside from some of these specific treatments for breast and
nipple pain, how else do you spell *relief* until the cracking or
irritation heals?

- Don't attempt to toughen your nipples, either before
  or after the birth, by rubbing, stretching, or pinching
  them.
- Acetaminophen (or ibuprofen) may be taken thirty to
  sixty minutes before you nurse. Of course, it is wise to
  take medications only when necessary while nursing,
  but a short-term pain reliever that helps you continue
  nursing will be a worthwhile exception.
- Take some measures to "move things along" during
  your feedings. Express a little milk before your baby
  latches on and then gently massage your breasts while
  nursing to help them empty more quickly. Think in
  terms of shorter but more frequent feeding times.
- Air dry your nipples for several minutes after you nurse.
  Some mothers find that ice applied to the nipple just
  before nursing may reduce pain when the baby latches
  on. Many traditional remedies such as breast creams,

oils, vitamin E capsules, or even tea bags have fallen out of favor, especially since some may actually increase the irritation. However, a *pure* lanolin preparation applied after nursing may help restore skin moisture and decrease pain.

- If your baby forms a strong suction with her gums, be sure to release her grip before you pull her from your breast.
- If all else fails, consider pumping your breasts and allowing your baby to accept your milk from a bottle while your nipples are healing, especially if they have been bleeding. This is less desirable during the first several days while she is still learning the ropes, but it's better than giving up on nursing altogether.

Remember that a temporary time-out from breast feeding to allow for healing or for any other reason (for example, an illness affecting either mother or baby) does not mean that you cannot resume nursing when things calm down. Pumping your breasts at feeding time will help you maintain your supply. Furthermore, even if your baby has spent a fair amount of time with a bottle, she can learn (or relearn) to obtain nourishment successfully from your breast.

"My baby wants to nurse all the time. I'm getting sick of being a human pacifier." All babies derive comfort and satisfaction from sucking, but some are true enthusiasts who would be more than happy to turn every nursing session into a ninety-minute marathon. You may be happy with this arrangement, but more likely it can lead to sore nipples and a gnawing concern that your entire existence has been reduced to being a mobile restaurant. Fortunately, you are not without options.

A healthy newborn, properly attached to the breast and sucking continuously, will empty about 90 percent of the milk available on each side within ten minutes. You can usually

PUMPING AND STORING BREAST MILK

There will likely be at least a few, if not many, times during your breast feeding when you will not be able to nurse your baby for several hours (or days) at a time. These occasions might involve anything from an evening out for dinner, an unexpected trip, a time-out to allow irritated nipples to heal, or even the desire to supply breast milk to a premature infant who must be fed by tube. Nursing mothers who begin or resume work outside the home may have to contend with daily absences of several hours from their babies. While formula can be a satisfactory substitute in these situations, it is also possible to maintain your baby's nourishment with your own milk.

GUIDELINES FOR EXPRESSING MILK—
FOR IMMEDIATE OR FUTURE USE
- First, hands should be thoroughly washed with soap and water each time you collect milk. (The breasts do not need to be washed, however, but should be free of any lotions or creams.)
- Next, before any milk is expressed, each breast should be gently massaged. Using the palm of the hand, stroke several times from below, above, and sides of the breast toward the nipple, applying gentle pressure.
- After massaging, milk can be expressed from each breast, either by hand or with the assistance of a breast pump. Either method is acceptable, and the choice of one or the other approach can be based on effectiveness, convenience, and cost.
- As with the first days of nursing, you may find it easier to begin expressing milk for three to five minutes at a time and then gradually progress to ten- or fifteen-minute sessions if you are collecting milk on a regular basis.

To express by hand. Sit in a comfortable position and lean over the container into which you will be collecting the milk. Place the thumb and index finger of one hand about an inch to either side of the nipple and then press toward your chest while gently squeezing the fingers toward one another. At first, you may see a few drops, a literal spurt, or nothing at all.

When the milk stops flowing, release your fingers, rotate to another position around the nipple, and squeeze again. If you don't see much milk, keep trying and don't give up—becoming adept at expressing milk may take practice. You may find that massaging again improves your flow. It may also be helpful to alternate between breasts, rather than expressing all the milk from one before moving to the other.

To express using a breast pump. Breast pumps utilize a funnel or bicycle-horn-shaped apparatus that is placed against the breast. A vacuum is created, either by manually moving a piston or by an electrically powered device, and milk is sucked into an appropriate container. Electrical pumps are more expensive but may be more efficient, especially for a mother who needs to express milk on a regular basis. (Some models can pump from both breasts simultaneously.) It is usually possible to rent one from a medical-supply company, hospital, or other local resource in order to confirm its usefulness before actually buying one.

To make an airtight seal between the pump and your breast, a little water or milk can be applied to the skin where contact is made. The apparatus should be applied snugly enough to make a good seal but not pressed so tightly to restrict the flow of milk. Pumping can continue until after the milk has stopped flowing for a minute or so. After you are finished, use soap and water to wash whatever components of the pump came in contact with the milk and then allow them to air dry. (Check the manufacturer's directions for specific details about cleaning and proper handling of the equipment you are using.)

COLLECTING AND STORING MILK

Your milk can be collected in a clean baby bottle or a nurser bag that attaches directly to a nipple assembly. Your baby can immediately drink what you have just expressed (which would be the case, for example, if you are expressing milk while sore nipples are healing), but you can also store milk for future use.

Remember that breast milk is a perishable food. Here are some guidelines for handling it so it will maintain its nutritional value and not become contaminated:

- If you plan to refrigerate or freeze milk, do so as soon as you have finished collecting it. Label and date it.
- You may feed a baby fresh breast milk that has been left at room temperature for up to six hours, after which the milk should be discarded.
- Breast milk that has just been expressed may be kept in the refrigerator for seventy-two hours, but any that is thawed from the freezer must be used within twenty-four hours.
- Various time limits for safe storage of breast milk in the freezer have been recommended; they range from two weeks to six months. A reasonable guideline would be to store milk no longer than one month. Mark each bottle or plastic bottle liner with the date you collected it and use the oldest milk first.
- You can combine the milk from both breasts into a single bottle or plastic bottle liner. If a particular pumping session has not yielded enough milk, you

can freeze it and then add more cooled milk to the
same container later—but don't change the date
on your label.

- When you want to feed your baby expressed milk,
  thaw it by placing the bottle or bottle liner in warm
  water. Heating milk in a microwave is not recommended
  because of the potential formation of hot spots in the
  milk that could burn the baby's mouth.

hear and feel the transition from intense sucking and swallowing to a more relaxed, pacifying sucking after five to ten
minutes on each side, at which point you can decide how long
you want to continue. If you're both feeling snug and comfortable, relax and enjoy it. But if it's the middle of the night
and you need sleep or you're getting sore, you won't destroy
your baby's personality by gently detaching her.

A problem can arise, however, if your baby sounds terribly
unhappy and indignant when you decide enough's enough.
How do you respond? The answer depends on how far along
and how well established you are in your nursing relationship.
In the earliest days when milk is just arriving or you're not sure
whether she is truly swallowing an adequate volume, it is probably better to give her the benefit of the doubt and continue for
a while longer. This is especially true if you are blessed with
a casual "gourmet" or "suck and snooze" baby who may not
empty your breast very quickly.

But watch the various indicators of your progress: good
swallowing sounds, frequent wet diapers, weight gain, and
softening of your breast after feeding. If these are going well
and you feel you have developed a smooth nursing routine
after two or three weeks, you can consider other calming maneuvers, including the use of a pacifier (see sidebar on pages

172–173). *If your soothing maneuvers aren't working, however, or your baby doesn't seem to be gaining weight, contact your baby's doctor for further evaluation and recommendations.*

Some mothers make the mistake of assuming that every sound from a baby should be answered with nursing, when something else (or nothing in particular) may be bothering her. If, for example, she has just finished a good feeding thirty minutes ago and begins to fuss after being put down for a nap, it is reasonable to wait and listen for a while, since she may settle down on her own, rather than trying to nurse her again. Otherwise you may find yourself spending nearly every minute of the day and night with your baby attached to your breast. As the days pass, you will become more discerning about the meaning of your baby's various crying messages.

A final note: If you are having a significant problem with breast feeding—whether it be latching on, anatomy problems, sore nipples, sluggish nursers, slow weight gain, or anything else—seek out a **lactation consultant** for some additional help. This is a health-care professional whose wealth of knowledge and practical suggestions can help both mother and baby succeed at breast feeding, even when the going gets very tough. Your baby's doctor or a local hospital should be able to give you a referral.

BOTTLE-FEEDING BASICS

Choosing a formula

First things first: *For the first year, do not feed your baby cow's milk from the dairy section at the store.* Cow's milk that has not been specifically modified for use in infant formulas is not digested well by human infants; it contains significant loads of protein that your baby's kidneys will have difficulty processing, and it contains inadequate amounts of vitamin C and iron. It also contains inadequate amounts of fat, which provides 50 percent of the calories in human milk and formula.

Furthermore, the new baby's intestine may be irritated by cow's milk, resulting in a gradual but potentially significant loss of red blood cells. Finally, some of the protein in cow's milk may be absorbed through the baby's intestine in a way that can lead to allergy problems later in life.

The vast majority of bottle-fed infants are given commercial formulas, whose manufacturers have gone to great lengths to match mother's milk as closely as possible. The most commonly used formulas are based on cow's milk that has been *significantly* altered for human consumption. Among other things, the protein is made more digestible and less allergenic, lactose is added to match that of human milk, and butterfat is

---

PACIFIER POINTERS

Some parents say they could not have survived their baby's infancy without these gadgets, while others (and some breast-feeding advisers) see them as an abomination. While they are not exactly a threat to world peace, pacifiers can be overused. They are definitely not good for very young infants who have not established stable and efficient nursing patterns. The feel, texture, taste, and smell of a pacifier are clearly different from that of Mom's nipples, and sucking a pacifier too soon may interfere with a baby's learning the real thing. But after two weeks or more, assuming nursing is going well, a pacifier can help calm a baby who

- is already fed and full, but still wants to suck;
- doesn't have anything else, such as a wet diaper, bothering him; and
- will suck on it with apparent satisfaction.

Inserting a pacifier in an infant's mouth must not be a substitute for feeding, parental nurturing, or checking to see if something is wrong.

removed and replaced with a combination of other fats more readily absorbed by infants.

Soy formulas, which are based on soy protein, do not contain lactose, which is the main carbohydrate in cow's milk. These are used for the small percentage of infants who cannot digest lactose and who develop excessive gas, cramps, and diarrhea when they consume regular formula. In addition, bottle-fed infants who have diarrhea resulting from a viral or bacterial infection may develop a temporary difficulty processing lactose. During their recovery, these babies often tolerate soy formulas better than cow's milk formulas. Infants from families with a strong history of cow's milk allergy have

If you decide to use a pacifier, make sure you get a one-piece model with a soft nipple—either the straight bottle shape or the angled "orthodontic" type. Never use the nipple assembly from a feeding bottle as a pacifier because the nipple can come loose and choke your baby. Make sure you have the right size for babies younger than six months and that it is designed to survive boiling or trips through the dishwasher. For the first six months, you will need to clean pacifiers frequently in this way to reduce the risk of infection.

Babies are unable to replace pacifiers that fall out of their mouth, so you will have to do this for them. *Do not, under any circumstances, tie a pacifier to a string or ribbon around a baby's neck to keep it in place. Your solution to the wandering pacifier could strangle your baby.*

If you find a pacifier that your baby likes, buy several. They have a knack for disappearing into the sofa, under the car seat, or into the bottom of the diaper bag, so lots of backups are a good idea.

traditionally been started on soy formulas as a precautionary measure, but many of these may be allergic to soy formula as well.

There are a variety of formulas that have been designed for special needs. Infants who are allergic to both cow's milk and soy formulas may use what are called **protein hydrolysate** formulas, in which the proteins are essentially predigested. Special formulas are also available for babies with phenylketonuria (PKU) and for premature infants.

Check with your baby's physician regarding the type(s) of formula he or she recommends. Once you have made your choice, you can stock up with one or more of the three forms in which they are normally sold:

- **Ready-to-feed** is just that. Put it into a bottle if it isn't already packaged in one, make sure the temperature is right, and you're all set. While extremely convenient, this format is also the most expensive.

- **Concentrate** must be mixed with water in the exact amount recommended by the manufacturer. If it is too diluted (mixed with too much water), your baby will be shortchanged on nutrients. But if it is too concentrated (mixed with too little water), diarrhea and dehydration may result. The unused portion of an opened can of concentrate may be sealed and stored in the refrigerator for twenty-four hours, after which it should be discarded.

- **Powdered formula** is the least expensive form and must be mixed exactly as recommended, using the measuring scoop provided.

If you cannot afford formula and do not have access to community resources, it is possible to mix your own using evaporated (*not* condensed) milk, corn syrup, and sterile water. However, you must talk to your doctor about the specific combination of ingredients as well as additional vitamin supplementation.

You can prepare a day's worth of bottles at one time, storing the ones you don't immediately need in the refrigerator for up to twenty-four hours. The good news for today's bottle-feeding parents is that the laborious process of boiling water and sterilizing bottles, which consumed a great deal of time and energy in previous generations, is (with a few exceptions) usually not necessary to prepare formula safely today. However, these basic precautions will prevent your baby's formula from being contaminated by potentially harmful bacteria:

- Wash your hands before you begin handling formula, water, bottles, and nipples.
- If the formula you are using comes from a can, wipe the top before you open it. Use a separate can opener specifically designated for this purpose, and clean it on a regular basis.
- Unless there has been a recent flood, earthquake, outbreak of bacterial infection, or other local calamity, tap water is usually safe to use in mixing formula. (Check with your baby's doctor for a recommendation regarding whether your water should be boiled first.) Running the cold-water tap for a minute or two will decrease the amount of lead or other impurities that might have collected within the pipes. *Well water should be checked for bacterial contamination or excessive mineral content and should always be boiled before you use it.* If you have any doubts or concerns, use bottled water.
- After each use, bottles and nipple assemblies can be washed in the dishwasher or by hand with hot, soapy water, using a bottle brush to clean the inside thoroughly. Follow with a good rinse.

It's not necessary to warm a bottle, although younger babies prefer tepid or room-temperature formula. To warm a bottle you've stored in the refrigerator, let it sit for a few minutes in hot water. Warming the bottle in a microwave is *not* recommended because uneven heating may cause pockets of milk hot enough to scald a baby's mouth. Before feeding, shake the bottle well and let a drop or two fall on your hand. It should be barely warm and definitely not hot. Also check the flow rate from the nipple. An ideal flow is about one drop per second when the bottle is held upside down. If the nipple allows milk to flow too quickly, your baby may choke on it. If it flows too slowly, he may swallow air while he tries to suck out his meal.

You can use four- or eight-ounce bottles made from plastic or glass. (Later on, however, when he can hold his own bottle, glass bottles should be replaced with plastic.) Many parents prefer the nurser style in which formula is poured into a plastic bag that attaches to a plastic shell and nipple assembly. Babies tend to swallow less air from the bags, but they cost more in the long run. It is important not to use the bags to mix concentrate or powder because you cannot measure accurately with them.

As with breast feeding, bottle feeding should be relaxed and unhurried, preferably in a comfortable and quiet area of your home. Hold your baby across your lap with his upper body slightly raised and his head supported. A flat position during feedings not only increases the risk of choking but also allows milk to flow into the passageways, called **eustachian tubes**, that lead into the middle ears. Frequent ear infections may result. Stroke the nipple across his cheek or lower lip to start the rooting reflex, and be sure to keep the bottle elevated enough so the milk completely covers the inside of the nipple. Otherwise, he may start sucking air.

The fact that milk is flowing from a bottle does not mean that the feeding should switch to autopilot. Take time to lock eyes with your infant, talk or sing softly to him, gently caress him, and pray about this new life with which you've been entrusted. Your baby should not be left unattended with a bottle propped in his mouth. This practice puts your baby at an unnecessary risk for ear infections or choking.

Formula-fed newborns typically will consume two or three ounces every three or four hours, gradually increasing to a routine of taking about four ounces every four hours by the end of the first month. A general rule of thumb is that a baby will need between two and two and one-half ounces of formula per pound of body weight each day (up to fifteen pounds). Normally he will give crying or fussing cues when he is hungry and turn his head away or push the nipple out of his mouth with his tongue when he is full. If the bottle isn't empty, don't force the issue. However, during the first few weeks it is wise to awaken him to feed if he is sleeping for stretches of more than four hours during the day.

When (if ever) should the baby's formula be changed?

Most doctors will recommend that bottle-fed infants begin with an iron-fortified cow's milk formula, and if doing well with it, use it through the first year of life. (Iron is not absorbed as efficiently from formula as from breast milk, and the amount added to iron-fortified formula ensures that your baby will get what he needs.) Like their breast-fed counterparts, babies in this age-group do not need other vitamin supplementation.

One of the headaches that most bottle-feeding parents eventually face is figuring out whether irritability, especially if accompanied by gas or loose stools, means that baby and formula are not getting along. There are no clear-cut answers to this dilemma.

If you think your baby might be having a problem with the current formula, discuss it with his physician. It may be appropriate to try another brand, or even a different form of the same brand, and observe the results. Sometimes persistent crying, irritability, and poor sleep at night—definitely one of the most disturbing situations for new parents—will provoke a switch to soy-based formula. If it seems to help, stay with it. Beware of making changes too quickly or attributing every one of your baby's problems to his current formula, because you won't be able to sort out cause and effect, and you may over-look some other cause of his discomfort. Occasionally there may be such frustration and expense associated with finding a tolerated formula, that relactation may be considered. A lacta-tion consultant can assist even if several weeks without nurs-ing have passed.

HEALTH AND SAFETY CONCERNS: CHECKUPS AND IMMUNIZATIONS

Your pediatrician or family physician will ask that you follow a specific routine of well-baby visits; there is a definite purpose to this plan that involves monitoring the baby's progress and administering immunizations that are very important to her health. If you have been sent home from the hospital within twenty-four hours of your baby's birth, your baby should be checked within the next twenty-four to forty-eight hours. If all is going smoothly, you can expect to take your baby back for a checkup between two and four weeks of age and then again at two months.

During these visits, the baby will be weighed and measured and the results plotted on a standardized growth chart, which allows the health-care provider to track her progress over time. You will be asked how she is feeding, sleeping, and eliminating urine and stool. At the one- and two-month visits, specific be-havioral milestones such as smiling and head control will prob-ably be discussed. The baby will be examined from head to toe, so be sure to put her in an outfit that can be removed easily.

It is important that you bring up any problems or concerns you have, no matter how minor they seem. If you have a number of questions, write them down and present them at the beginning of the visit so the practitioner can see what's on your mind. Don't suddenly pull them out as a list of by-the-way items after everything else is done. If the examiner seems rushed and uneasy about taking time to deal with your concerns, find out how and when you can go over them. Some large practices have well-trained nurses or other health educators who can answer most of the questions you might have.

Your baby will most likely receive her first **hepatitis B** immunization either at birth or during the first two months of life. The second dose will be given one month after the first. At the two-month visit, it is customary for babies to receive their **DTaP (diphtheria/tetanus/pertussis), IPV (inactivated polio), hemophilus B,** and **pneumococcal** immunizations.

Many parents are anxious about the prospect of their tiny baby receiving these vaccines, and some have read literature suggesting that they are dangerous or ineffective. But the overwhelming evidence indicates that these shots do indeed drastically reduce the risk of these terrible diseases and that the odds of having a problem from any of the vaccines are far less than the odds of contracting the disease if no vaccine is given.

All the infections that vaccines guard us against can be very serious or even lethal. Some, such as diphtheria and polio, terrorized entire communities a century ago but have become extremely uncommon through widespread vaccination efforts. On the other hand, the bacteria that cause whooping cough and tetanus are still very prevalent, and quite ready, willing, and able to infect those who have not been adequately vaccinated. These illnesses can be prevented for a very modest amount of discomfort and cost and with an extremely low risk of any significant complications. Unfortunately, because

of concerns over the expense, risks, or appropriateness of vaccines, some parents neglect, avoid, or even actively oppose
immunization programs. This is unwise and places children
in needless peril. If you have any concerns over the safety or
effectiveness of any vaccine recommended for your child, be
sure to discuss them with her physician.

What about side effects of immunizations?
Of these routine immunizations, pertussis (the *P* in DTaP)
traditionally has caused the most side effects when given in the
original DPT format. Now most children are receiving the so-
called "acellular" form of pertussis (abbreviated *aP*), which
causes far fewer problems. Local soreness and fussiness after
the injection, if present, may be treated with a dose of
acetaminophen infant drops. These can be given at the time of
the immunization or shortly thereafter in order to relieve discomfort. For babies weighing less than twelve pounds, the appropriate amount is one-half a dropper (or 0.4 ml) of the
standard infant solution (which contains 80 mg per 0.8 ml).
For infants who are heavier than twelve pounds, a full dropper
(or 0.8 ml) may be used. Fewer than one in one hundred infants will develop a persistent cry (lasting longer than three
hours); about one in three hundred may get a high fever (ranging as high as 105°F); while about one in one thousand may
develop an unusual, high-pitched cry. *More severe neurologic
complications following the DTaP vaccine, such as a prolonged
seizure or change in consciousness, are extremely rare—and may
not be directly related to the vaccine at all.* All things considered,
these are reasonable risks to take in exchange for protection
against a very disruptive and potentially lethal illness.

If your baby is ill at the time of the visit, the vaccines will
usually be postponed, because it may be difficult to determine
afterwards whether a problem, especially a fever, has been
caused by the illness or by the vaccine. If your baby has only a

minor case of sniffles, the vaccines will usually be given. If you have any doubt or questions about vaccinations, be sure to get all your questions answered before any immunization is given to your baby.

What if the baby becomes ill?

Because newborns normally receive a healthy donation of Mom's antibodies through the umbilical cord blood supply prior to birth, they usually escape common illnesses such as colds and flu during the first several weeks, as long as they are well nourished and their environment is kept reasonably clean. Nursing infants have the added advantage of ingesting their mother's antibodies at every feeding.

This is indeed providential, because an illness in a baby younger than three months of age is a completely different situation from one in an older baby. For one thing, your new baby has very few ways to notify you that something is wrong. You will not have the luxury of language and specific complaints ("My ear hurts" or "I have a headache") to guide you. You won't have months or years of experience with this particular child to sense what is "normal" for her.

In addition, your baby's defense system is still under construction, and her ability to fight off microscopic invaders will not be fully operational for a number of months. As a result, a seemingly minor infection acquired during the first several weeks can turn into a major biological war.

Also—and this is the most unsettling reality of all—an illness can go sour much more rapidly in a newborn than in older children. If bacteria are on the move, they can spread like wildfire. If fluids are being lost through vomiting or diarrhea, dehydration can develop over several hours rather than days.

These warnings are not meant to generate undue anxiety but rather to encourage you to notify your baby's health-care provider if you think something is wrong, especially during

WHAT DO DTaP, IPV, HEMOPHILUS B, HEPATITIS B, AND PNEUMOCOCCAL VACCINES PREVENT?

Diphtheria is a serious bacterial infection that causes a thick membrane to form in the nose, throat, or airway. The membrane is attached to underlying tissues, so that attempting to remove it causes bleeding. Diphtheria bacteria within the membrane produce a toxin that can damage heart, liver, kidney, and nerve tissue. Paralysis and death may result. Because of widespread vaccinations, fewer than five cases occur in the U.S. each year.

Pertussis (whooping cough) causes severe coughing, often to the point of choking; it can last for months. It is particularly rough on infants and small children and can lead to pneumonia, seizures, and death. This disease is highly contagious and much more common than diphtheria. About four thousand cases are reported each year, half of which involve children less than a year old.

Tetanus results from a toxin produced by bacteria that enter the body through contaminated wounds. The toxin causes painful, spasmodic contractions of muscles (which gave rise to the colloquial term *lockjaw* for this disease) and can lead to death.

Polio is a viral infection that damages the central nervous system; it can cause mild or serious paralysis and results in death in 5 to 10 percent of the cases.

Hemophilus B is a type of bacteria that can cause, among other things, pneumonia and meningitis (an infection of the membranes that enclose the brain and spinal cord). Since the introduction of hemophilus B vaccines during the past decade, the number of cases of meningitis in young children caused by this bacteria has fallen dramatically.

Hepatitis B is an infection of the liver caused by a virus that is most commonly transmitted in three ways: from an infected mother to her infant, (later in life) through sexual contact with an infected person, or by exposure to infected blood. However, a large number of cases occur without a history of any of these events, which is one reason health officials recommend universal vaccination against this virus.

Fortunately, most people infected with hepatitis B recover without any long-term effects. In a small percentage of cases, however, the immediate illness can be severe enough to cause death. In others, prolonged active infection with the virus occurs, a process that can lead eventually to cirrhosis and cancer of the liver. While hepatitis B is not a common childhood disease, children are at a higher risk for developing long-term complications if they should become infected. Immunization of all children has been recommended as the most effective means to reduce the total number of cases of this disease over the next several years.

Pneumococcal infection is the leading cause of bacterial meningitis in the United States. The pneumococcus can also cause ear infections (an estimated five million each year), pneumonia, and sepsis—a serious illness in which large numbers of the bacteria are present in the bloodstream. Children under two years of age are at the greatest risk for significant infection. Unfortunately, many strains of pneumococcus have become resistant to antibiotics which were once effective in treating it. As a result, prevention of pneumococcal infection has become increasingly important, especially in young infants, who now routinely receive an immunization called the pneumococcal conjugate vaccine (or PCV) at ages two, four, six, and twelve to fifteen months.

the first three months of life. You can also reduce your new-born's risk of infection by keeping her out of crowded public places, preventing, if possible, direct contact with individuals who are ill with contagious infections, and minimizing group child-care situations, especially during the first few weeks after birth.

What are the signs that a baby might have a problem?
Some of the danger signals in infants are similar to those that will alert you to problems later in life. But in newborns, several of these signals are more critical and require a more immediate and detailed evaluation than in older babies and children. Here are some important newborn distress signals:

Fever. There will be many occasions in the coming months and years when your child will feel hot, and the thermometer will agree. In babies over three months of age, this may or may not be cause for alarm, depending on what else is going on. *Remember, in a baby under three months of age, a rectal temperature over 100.4°F should be considered cause for an immediate call to the doctor's office.*

(If your baby seems perfectly well, his temperature is slightly above 100.4°F, and there is a possibility that he was overdressed or in a hot environment, you can remove some clothing and try again in thirty to forty-five minutes. A temperature that is closer to normal will be reassuring—but you should run the story by your baby's physician anyway. Do not give the baby acetaminophen (Tylenol) or a tepid bath in this situation, because you need to know whether the fever will come down on its own. Besides, the fever itself is not dangerous. It is the possible causes of the fever that you need to worry about.)

If there is no doubt about the presence of fever, your baby needs to be evaluated right away, either by his own physician or at the emergency room. You may be surprised or even alarmed by the number of tests that may be requested after your baby is examined. The problem is that a newborn fever can indicate a serious bacterial infection that could involve the lungs, urinary tract, or the tissues that surround the brain and spinal cord (these tissues are called **meninges**). Bacteria could also be present in the bloodstream, in which case the baby is said to have **sepsis**.

It is not unusual for a doctor to recommend that a newborn with a fever undergo blood tests, an evaluation of the urine, and a lumbar puncture (or spinal tap), all of which obtain specimens to be cultured for bacteria. A chest X-ray may be ordered if there is any question about pneumonia. In addition, the baby may be admitted to the hospital for two or three days so antibiotics can be given intravenously (that is, through a vein) while the cultures are growing in the laboratory. If he is doing well and no bacteria are growing in the cultures, he will be sent home.

All of this may seem rather drastic in response to a simple fever, but babies in this age-group are more vulnerable to the spread of bacteria—especially into the bloodstream and meninges. If left untreated, the results could be disastrous.

Feeding poorly. Lack of interest in nursing, poor sucking, or failing to awaken for feeding well beyond the expected time could be an important indicator of a medical problem. If you contact a physician with a concern that your newborn is ill, the physician will want to know, among other things, how the baby appears to be feeding.

Vomiting. As will be discussed later in this chapter, you will need to distinguish between spitting up and vomiting, since the latter is much more significant in a newborn (see page 192).

Decreased activity or alertness. A baby who is listless—with eyes open but little spontaneous movement, an indifferent response to stimulation, or very floppy muscle tone—may be quite sick. Believe it or not, a vigorous protest by a baby during an examination is a reassuring finding. At this age, remaining quiet and disinterested while being poked and prodded by the doctor is not a sign of being a "good" patient but rather an indication of probable illness.

Nonstop crying. As will be described in the next chapter, many babies enter a "crying season" between two weeks and

TAKING AN ACCURATE TEMPERATURE

You cannot accurately judge your baby's temperature by placing your hand on her forehead or anywhere else. *Skin temperature strips are no better.* Furthermore, you cannot get an accurate reading using an oral thermometer in babies and small children because they can't cooperate in keeping the little bulb (whether mercury or electronic) under the tongue. Electronic ear thermometers will give you a ballpark number, but results may vary somewhat depending on your technique. Therefore, even in these days of slick and expensive electronic equipment, an old-fashioned, low-tech rectal mercury thermometer remains the standard when you need to know what's going on with a very young infant. (While mercury has been used in glass thermometers for decades, some now utilize a different silver-colored liquid that behaves the same way. We will use the term *mercury* to refer to the contents of all glass thermometers.)

You should get two or three of these at the drugstore, since they have a habit of breaking or disappearing just when you need one. A rectal thermometer has a short rounded mercury bulb at one end, while an oral thermometer has a longer straight bulb. If you're not experienced with a mercury thermometer, you may want to practice reading the temperature three months of age, without any specific medical cause. But you can't assume that prolonged, inconsolable crying is normal until the baby has been evaluated by his physician.

Abnormal movements. Unusual jerking of arms, legs, or head, especially if sustained for several seconds, may represent a seizure or other significant problem affecting the nervous system. Contact your baby's doctor immediately for further advice if you observe this type of activity.

before the moment of truth arrives. Hold the end opposite the mercury bulb between thumb and index finger and slowly rotate the thermometer back and forth. You should be able to see the squared-off end of the mercury column next to the temperature markers. When you read the result, be sure not to confuse numbers such as 100.2° (which lies just above 100°) with 102°, which is quite a bit higher.

Before taking the temperature, shake the thermometer until it reads below 98.6° by grasping the end opposite the bulb and snapping your wrist a few times. Make sure your fingers aren't slippery, and stay away from tables and counters.

You baby should be lying tummy-down on a bed or crib, or across your knees if he is very small. Keep one hand firmly in control of his lower back and don't try to take the temperature while he is actively squirming or resisting you. Lubricate the mercury tip of the thermometer with petroleum jelly and put a little around the baby's anus as well. Then gently insert the thermometer into the child's rectum about one inch. *Do not force the thermometer into the rectum.* Hold it for about three minutes, then remove it and read the temperature. Afterwards cleanse and rinse the bulb end, shake it down, and put it in its case—which should be labeled as a rectal, not oral, thermometer.

Unusual color. A pale or mottled color of the skin or bluish discoloration of the lips could indicate a change in circulation patterns.

HOME MEDICAL SUPPLIES FOR
BABY'S FIRST THREE MONTHS

rectal thermometers
bulb syringe for clearing nostrils
cotton swabs, cotton balls
acetaminophen infant drops
topical ointment for diaper rash
humidifier/vaporizer

COMMON MEDICAL PROBLEMS DURING
THE FIRST THREE MONTHS

Jaundice is a yellow-orange discoloration of skin caused by the buildup of a substance called **bilirubin** in the bloodstream. Bilirubin is a by-product of the breakdown of red blood cells, which normally circulate for about four months until they wear out. (New red cells are constantly produced within the bones in tissue called **marrow**). Removing and recycling the contents of red cells require the liver to process bilirubin, which before birth is largely managed through the mother's circulation. After birth, the newborn's liver takes a few days to gear up for this job, and the level of bilirubin in the bloodstream will increase by a modest amount. If a significant backlog of bilirubin develops, the baby's skin will take on a yellow orange hue, beginning with the head and gradually spreading toward the legs.[1]

Whether or not jaundice is significant will depend upon several factors, including the level of bilirubin, how soon and how fast it has risen, the suspected cause, and whether the baby was full-term or premature. In some instances, extremely high bilirubin levels can damage the central nervous system, especially in the premature infant. *Therefore, if you notice that your new baby's skin color is changing to pumpkin orange, or the white area of the eyes is turning yellow and/or your baby is feeding poorly, see your doctor.*

If there is any concern, the doctor will order blood tests to check the bilirubin level, and other studies may be done to look for underlying causes. Normally the jaundice will resolve on its own, although some healthy babies will carry a slight yellow-orange tint for weeks. Occasionally a little extra help is needed. This may involve five approaches, as directed by the baby's physician:

- Treat any underlying cause (such as an infection), if possible.
- Increase the baby's fluid intake by feeding him more often.
- Expose the baby to *indirect* sunlight—that is, undressed down to diapers in a room bright with sunlight *that does not directly shine on his sensitive skin.* Since indirect sunlight has only a modest effect on clearing bilirubin, don't use this approach unless you are sure that your baby won't become too hot or cold in the room you use.
- In some cases of jaundice, an enzyme found in mother's milk may interfere to a modest degree with the clearing of bilirubin. Occasionally your health-care provider may ask you to stop breast feeding briefly and use formula until the problem improves, after which nursing can resume. In such a case, it is important that you continue to express milk so your breasts will continue to produce it and will be ready when your baby is able to resume breast feeding. This should not be an occasion to stop nursing altogether.
- A treatment called **phototherapy** may be utilized if the bilirubin level needs to be treated more actively. Under

a physician's direction, the baby, wearing protective eyewear, lies under a special intense blue light like a sunbather at the beach. In addition, or as an alternative, a baby can lie on a thin plastic light source called a **Bili Blanket**. Whether carried out at a hospital or at home (using equipment provided by a home-health agency), phototherapy usually reduces bilirubin gradually within two or three days, if not sooner.

Colds and other respiratory infections are relatively uncommon in this age-group. The breathing patterns in a newborn baby, however, may cause you some concern. He will at times move air in and out noisily, with snorting and sniffing sounds emanating from his small nasal passages, even when they are completely dry. Some sneezing now and then isn't uncommon, but watery or thick drainage from one or both nostrils is definitely abnormal. A call to the doctor's office and usually an exam are in order when this "goop" appears in a baby under three months.

If your newborn has picked up a cold, you can gently suction the excess nasal drainage with a rubber-bulb syringe, since a clogged nose will cause some difficulty breathing while he is feeding. *Do not give any decongestant or cold preparations to a baby this young unless given very specific directions—not only what kind, but exactly how much—from your baby's physician.* (In general, experimental evidence has suggested that such medications are not terribly effective in babies and young children.)

Even when his nose is clear, your baby's breathing rate may be somewhat erratic, varying with his activity and excitement level. A typical rate is thirty to forty times per minute, often with brief pauses, sighs, and then a quick succession of breaths. If he is quiet and consistently breathing fifty or more times per minute, however, he may have an infection or another problem with his lungs or heart. Flaring of the nostrils, an inward sucking motion of the spaces between the ribs, and exaggerated movement of the abdomen with each breath suggest that he may be working harder than usual to breathe. An occasional cough probably doesn't signal a major problem, but frequent or prolonged bouts of coughing should be investigated, especially if there are any other signs of illness.

Infections of the middle ear (known as **otitis media**) may complicate a cold in any baby, including a newborn. There are, however, no specific signs of this important problem in a young baby. (At this age, movement of the hands around the side of the head are random, and your baby cannot deliberately point to or try to touch any area that is bothering him.) Furthermore, an ear infection can be much more serious in this age-group. If he is acting ill, irritable, running a fever, or all of these, he will need to have his ears checked by his doctor.

Some babies always seem to be overflowing with tears in one eye. This is caused by a narrowing of the duct near the inner corner of each eye, which acts like a drain for the tears that are produced constantly to keep the eye moist. Aside from causing a nonstop trail of tears down one side of the face, this narrowing can lead to a local infection, manifested by goopy, discolored drainage, crusting, and if more widespread, a generalized redness of the eye known as **conjunctivitis**. The crusting and drainage will need to be removed gently using moist cotton balls, which should be promptly thrown away after being used, since they may be contaminated with bacteria. In addition, the baby's health-care provider will probably prescribe antibiotic eye drops or ointment for a few days. He or she may also suggest that you gently massage the area between the inner corner of the eye and the nose to help displace and move any mucous plug that might have formed.

Usually the clogged tear duct will eventually open on its

own, but if it continues to be a problem after six months, talk to your baby's doctor, who may refer you to an ophthalmologist.

Spitting up breast milk or formula is not uncommon during the first weeks of life, and some babies return a little of their feedings for months, sometimes if they are not promptly burped. As long as he is otherwise doing well—gaining weight and making developmental progress—this can be considered a temporary annoyance that will correct itself. However, if a baby in this age-group begins vomiting, with stomach contents returning more forcefully, some prompt medical attention is in order.

If there is also a marked increase in the amount of stool (usually indicating that an infection in the intestinal tract has developed), the baby will need careful observation for signs of dehydration. These signs include poor feeding, a decrease in urine output (manifested by fewer wet diapers), sunken eyes, decreased tears or saliva, persistent fussiness or listlessness, and cool or mottled skin. A baby under three months of age with any of these problems should be evaluated immediately.

Projectile vomiting is an alarming event in which the stomach's contents fly an impressive distance. A young baby with this problem should be checked promptly. In a few cases forceful vomiting is caused by a thickening muscle in the portion of small intestine known as the pylorus, just past the stomach, which can begin to cause trouble after the second week of life. This condition, known as pyloric stenosis, has been traditionally considered a problem of firstborn males, but a baby of either gender or any birth-order position can be affected. In a young baby with forceful vomiting, a combination of an examination with an ultrasound or an X-ray study of the stomach will usually clarify the diagnosis. If pyloric stenosis is present, surgical correction is a must and should be carried out as soon as possible. The surgery is relatively simple, however, and is very well tolerated by the vast majority of infants.

Settling in at home and getting a good start with your baby's feeding are important accomplishments during the first few weeks of life. But there are other concerns to deal with and new learning curves to master as you and your baby become better acquainted. In the next chapter we will look at your baby's other important behaviors, especially sleeping and crying; a number of guidelines and ground rules for commonsense baby care; and some survival skills for new parents.

NOTES

1. Why jaundice progresses from the head downward rather than evenly over the entire body is unknown, but this peculiarity can give an examiner a rough idea of its severity.

CHAPTER 9

The First Three Months, Part Two
*Sleeping, Crying, and Other Newborn Pursuits
(. . . and Survival Skills for New Parents)*

From the moment you see, touch, and begin to live with your new baby, one basic reality will become abundantly clear: She can do nothing to meet her own needs. She can't feed herself, lift her head, change position, or scratch where she itches. She can—and will—let everyone know when she is unhappy, but she can't communicate exactly what is bothering her.

The fact that she is totally dependent on those who care for her may not sink in until your first day and night at home. Assuming that your baby was born in a hospital, it is likely that nurses and other health-care personnel provided some, if not most, of her care. Now you're on your own with this little person who needs you for everything. Don't feel strange if this thought creates a sense of mild anxiety or near panic. Almost every parent has felt the same sense of inadequacy.

For many young parents, a combination of grandparents, other relatives, and friends who are baby veterans is available to lend a hand, a few helpful hints, and a shoulder to lean on during these first weeks. Remember, however, that some of the advice you receive from others may not be medically accurate. Grandparents and other relatives may suggest—perhaps with considerable enthusiasm—approaches to baby care that differ from your own or even from your doctor's advice. Many of these are more a matter of style than substance, but if any differences of opinion seem significant, seek input from your baby's physician.

If you are isolated from your family or are a single parent, you may feel as if you're drowning in this new, nonstop responsibility. Most likely your discouragement won't last long, especially as you get used to the basic routines of baby care. *But don't be afraid to seek help if you feel that you are going under for the third time.* Your church, a local crisis pregnancy center, or even the social-services department of the nearest hospital should be able to provide both emotional and practical support.

Remember that your baby's need for total care has a time limit. Indeed, one of the most important tasks of your child's first two decades will be the gradual process of becoming completely independent of you. As she develops new skills, she will need and want you to do less and less for her—and she'll probably be quite vocal about telling you so. All too soon you will face the ultimate challenge of releasing her to live on her own. During those times of emerging independence, you will find yourself thinking back, perhaps misty-eyed, to the time when she needed you so much.

SPECIAL CONSIDERATIONS OF A NEWBORN'S TOTAL DEPENDENCE

Your baby's total dependence on you has a number of practical, as well as emotional, ramifications that should be kept in mind as you begin your first weeks of parenthood.

Controlling the head

Because a newborn's head is so large relative to his body size—more so than it will ever be in the future—and because his neck muscles are not strong enough to control it, his head must be constantly supported. Allowing it to flop freely in any direction could injure both his head and neck. Always pick him up with two hands, one of which should support and control the baby's head. Once you have picked him up, you can cradle him in one arm with his head resting in your hand.

Never pick him up quickly, especially if you don't have control of his head, and *never shake him for any reason, because this can cause brain damage.*

Temperature and clothing

A newborn is less capable of regulating his body temperature than he will be in just a few months. This doesn't mean that he should be bundled in arctic gear twenty-four hours a day or that your thermostat at home should be set at greenhouse levels. Keep his environment at a temperature that's comfortable for you, and dress him in about the same number of clothing layers that you would want for yourself, with a light receiving blanket added during the first few weeks. Typically this will involve a diaper and an infant T-shirt covered by a gown or sleeper set. If the weather is hot and you don't have air-conditioning, you can dispense with everything but the diaper and T-shirt. In cold weather, extra layers will be needed if you take him outside. Because he can lose a considerable amount of heat from the surface of his head, keep it covered when he is outside in chilly weather.

When dressing or undressing your young baby, be careful with his head and hands. Don't pull a shirt or sweater over his head in a way that drags the material forcefully past his skin, ears, and nose. Instead, use your hand to spread the shirt's neck wide open, and then maneuver it over his head so there's little if any pressure of the garment against his skin. Once his head is through, don't try to push his hands through the narrow opening of the sleeves. Instead—one sleeve at a time—reach through the opening, gently grasp his hand, and carefully pull the sleeve over it. When removing a top, reverse the procedure, pulling the garment over the hands first and then his head.

DIAPER DUTY

Before your child passes her final exam in Toilet Training 101, you can look forward to changing about five thousand diapers.

(Actually the number may seem more like about 43 trillion, especially if you have more than one baby in diapers at the same time.) Since your newborn will need to be changed eight to ten times a day, you'll have plenty of opportunities to practice this skill.

As discussed in chapter 2 (Developing a Birth Plan and Preparing the Nest), you'll need to decide whether your baby will spend most of her time in disposable or cloth diapers. You'll also need supplies to clean up dirty bottoms, either small washcloths that can be moistened with warm water or commercial baby wipes, which are convenient when you are away from home. Some babies' skin may be sensitive to fragrances or irritated by the alcohol contained in some wipes, but fragrance-free and alcohol-free varieties are also available. Baby powder isn't necessary and can be left out of the changing procedure altogether unless your baby's health-care provider recommends it for a moist rash. If you do need to use powder, shake a little into your hand and then apply it directly to the infant's skin. Don't shake out clouds of powder, which can be irritating if inhaled. And keep the powder can out of the reach of older babies and children.

You'll want to check your baby's diaper for moisture or stool every two or three hours when she's awake. You don't need to rouse a sleeping baby if you notice a wet diaper unless you are trying to calm down a rash. Urine alone is normally not irritating, although stool left in contact with skin can provoke a rash because of its acidity.

When it's time to change a diaper, gather all your supplies before you begin. This is particularly important if you are using a changing table. *Remember—you must not walk away from a baby lying on a table or, for that matter, on any open surface above the floor.* Unfasten the diaper while you gently grasp her feet by the ankles and pull them upward to expose the genital area. Use the diaper to remove the bulk of any stool that remains on the baby's skin and then use your washcloth or wipe to clean the skin. Be careful to cleanse the creases between legs and upper body, then lift up her ankles again to slide the new diaper under her bottom, and fasten it into place. A baby girl's bottom should be cleaned from front to back to avoid spreading bacteria from her rectal area to the vagina or urinary tract, and you don't need to wipe between the labia (the folds of skin that border the opening of the vagina) unless stool is present. If you are using diaper pins, keep your finger between the cloth and her skin. If the pin strays, you'll tolerate the point far better than your baby's sensitive abdomen will.

Changing diapers certainly isn't anyone's favorite activity, and the job shouldn't be left solely to Mom. Dad can and should learn to become adept at this task, along with any preadolescent or teenage children at home. Even if you're squeamish about cleaning up stool, avoid making a "yuck" face and groaning at every mess you find. As often as they occur during the day, diaper changes should be times when you communicate love and reassurance, not repulsion (even in fun). Some babies routinely put up a howl during these cleanup sessions, but with rare exception they eventually get used to the process. After two or three months, your baby may even coo at you during diaper changes.

BATHING YOUR BABY

Aside from daily cleansing of the diaper area, newborns and young babies don't need to be bathed more than two or three times a week. Before the umbilical remnant falls off, don't immerse your baby in water. Instead, give him a simple sponge bath, using a soft washcloth and a basin of warm water (comfortable to your touch) containing a small amount of a mild baby soap.

The remnant of your baby's umbilical cord may generate

some goopy material, and for the first several days the area around the umbilical stump should be kept clean and dry. Use a cotton swab moistened with rubbing alcohol to wipe away any moist debris that accumulates until the cord falls off. The remnant of the cord will shrivel and fall off within two or three weeks. You may notice small spots of blood at the umbilical site for a few days.

Occasionally, local bacteria will get a foothold at the stump site, generating pus, tenderness, and redness. Contact your baby's physician if this occurs or if there is any persistent swelling and moisture several days after the stump is gone. This area will normally be examined during the first few routine checkups, but be sure to bring it to the practitioner's attention if you don't like the way it looks.

DEALING WITH DIAPER RASH

Nearly every baby will develop diaper rash at some point. Causes can include:

- Prolonged exposure to urine or stool, especially after solid foods are started.
- Chemical or fragrance irritants in baby wipes, detergents used to wash diapers, or soaps used during bathing. Some babies will even react to the material used in a specific brand of disposable diaper.
- Infections with bacteria or, more commonly, yeast (candida). Yeast infections tend to cause a more intense irritation, often with small extensions or "satellites" around the edges of the rash.

Steps you can take to calm a diaper rash include:

- Change the diaper as soon as possible after it becomes wet or soiled. Once a rash develops, ongoing contact

If your baby was circumcised, he may have a small dressing wrapped around the area from which the foreskin was removed. The dressing will normally fall off within a day or two, and it does not need to be replaced. If a Plastibell was used for the circumcision, it will begin to separate after a couple of days. Don't try to pull it off; let it come loose by itself. A small dab of lubricating jelly applied to any moist or raw surfaces will prevent them from sticking to the diaper. Later on, you can use a soft, warm, moist washcloth to remove (gently) any debris that remains on the penis.

You can sponge-bathe your baby while he lies on any surface that is adequately padded. To keep him from losing body heat, cover him with towels, except for the area you are washing. Start with the head, using water only (no soap) around

with urine and stool can irritate it further. Super absorbent diapers, while more convenient, tend to be changed less frequently, which may unintentionally increase contact of urine with skin.

- Try to eliminate other types of irritants. Change to fragrance- and alcohol-free wipes. If you are washing your own cloth diapers, use soap rather than detergent (this will be marked on the label) and double-rinse. If using disposable diapers, try another brand.

- Let your baby's bottom air dry after it is cleaned. If you feel particularly adventurous, leave it open to the air for a while before putting on a new diaper.

- Ointments such as Desitin or A&D may have a soothing effect. If the rash is severe, your baby's physician may prescribe a mild cortisone cream for a few days. If yeast appears to be involved, an antifungal cream, either alone or in a blend with cortisone, will usually calm the rash within a few days.

the eyes and mouth. Then, using the washcloth dipped in soapy water, work your way down, saving the diaper area for last. Be sure to cleanse the skin creases of the neck, behind the ears, under the arms, in the groin, and beneath the scrotum in boys.

After the umbilical stump is dry, you can bathe your baby in a "bathinette" specifically designed for this purpose or even in the sink. As with the sponge bath, water should be comfortably warm but not hot (test with your elbow or wrist) and no more than a couple inches deep. Make sure you have all your supplies (washcloth, soap, shampoo, towel) ready before you undress your baby. If you have forgotten something you need or the phone rings, pick your baby up out of the water and take him with you. *Never leave a baby unattended in a bath, even with only one or two inches of water.*

If he has a dirty diaper at the time you undress him, clean the area as you normally would *before* he goes into the water. You may choose to give him a sponge bath just as you did before the umbilical cord remnant fell off and then rinse him off in the bathwater. If you plan to use shampoo (not necessary with every bath, especially if he isn't endowed with a lot of hair), be sure to control his head so the shampoo and water used to rinse it don't get in his eyes, nose, or mouth.

Your baby will have no interest in rubber ducks or other bath toys at this age. Some babies fuss when put into water, but usually the sensation of warmth and rubbing by a pair of loving hands will have a calming effect. At this age, long baths are neither necessary nor wise, since the effect of prolonged contact with water may dry out his skin and cause rashes. (This is also the reason he should not be bathed every day.) In a few months, as he comes to enjoy splashing and playing in water, baths can extend beyond the time it takes to be cleaned.

Because he can lose body heat so quickly when he's wet, be ready to wrap him in a towel as soon you bring him out of the water. This will also improve the stability of your hold on him. The last thing you want is to have a wet, wiggly baby slip out of your hands.

A NEWBORN'S SKIN

A new baby's skin is so sensitive that at times looking at her cross-eyed may seem to provoke a new rash. You will see spots and splotches come and go, especially in the first several weeks, but most don't need special treatment.

The characteristics of newborn skin and some common conditions including erythema toxicum, milia, and salmon patches were mentioned in chapter 6. In addition, during the first few weeks many babies develop pimples on the face, neck, and upper back, which in some cases look like acne. A full-blown eruption is sometimes referred to as **neonatal acne.** These pimples most likely are a response to some of mother's hormones acquired just before birth, and with rare exception they will resolve without treatment. If they become progressively worse, however, have them checked by your baby's health-care provider.

Another common skin problem in early infancy is **seborrheic dermatitis,** an inflammation of those areas of skin where the oil-producing sebaceous glands are most abundant: the scalp, behind the ears, and in the creases of the neck and armpits. The most striking form is **cradle cap,** a crusty, scaly, oily eruption of the scalp, which may persist for months. Fortunately, cradle cap is neither contagious nor uncomfortable, but you can help shorten its appearance with a few simple measures. Washing the hair with a gentle baby shampoo every two or three days, followed by gentle brushing, will remove much of the scaly material. Baby oil applied for a few minutes before shampooing may help soften more stubborn debris, but use it sparingly and be sure to wash all of it off. In more severe cases, your baby's doctor may recommend an antidandruff shampoo. A mild cortisone cream or lotion may also be prescribed, especially if there are patches of seborrhea on other parts of the body.

Another common rash appears on the chin and upper arms and is caused by excessive heat. **Heat rash** produces tiny red bumps rather than overt pimples and can usually be remedied by removing excess clothing.

A newborn's skin is easily dried out by excessive exposure to water, so if her skin seems dry or flaky, you may use a little baby lotion on the affected areas. Stay away from baby oil, which plugs pores and can actually provoke rashes. Keep your new baby completely out of direct sunlight because even very brief exposure can cause sunburn.

A Newborn's Behavior Patterns

As you settle into your routines with a new baby, you'll begin to notice patterns developing in a number of his behaviors. Although a newborn has only a few basic activities that occupy his first days and nights, he will carry them out in ways that are uniquely his. Mothers are often aware of differences between their children well before birth, as they feel the kicks and prods inside. The initial cry, the first waving of arms and legs, the attachment at the breast, and the willingness to cuddle will be some of the first strokes of a unique signature for this person you have brought into the world.

While every child is one of a kind, there are certain common threads and trends in behavior that have been observed in many newborns. Harvard pediatrician T. Berry Brazelton, M.D., who has studied and written extensively about newborn behavior, has described three basic types of babies, which he has dubbed "quiet," "active," and "average."

Quiet newborns sleep a lot—up to eighteen hours a day, even while nursing. They may sleep through the night very early and snooze through daytime feedings. They fuss or cry for about an hour each day and may communicate their needs quietly by sucking on their hands or wriggling in their cribs.

Active newborns behave quite differently. They sleep about twelve hours a day and spend half of what's left crying and fussing. They seem extremely sensitive to the environment, arouse easily, and may be slow to calm. When they're hungry, everyone will know about it. When it's time to nurse, they may clamp onto the breast or bottle frantically, gulping and swallowing air and then burping back a partial refund on whatever went down.

Average babies fall into the middle ground, sleeping fifteen hours or so each day, crying and fussing for about three hours a day. While more reactive to light and sound around them than quiet newborns are, they may calm themselves back to sleep if aroused. They'll let you know whenever they're hungry, but they usually settle fairly quickly when fed.

These are thumbnail sketches rather than detailed portraits, and no baby's behavior will fit precisely into one category or another. Furthermore, these characteristics are not necessarily previews of permanent coming attractions. During their first few days at home, many newborns go through a transition period that is marked either by seemingly endless sleeping or nonstop fussing. They may then shift gears after the first week, behaving quite differently as they adjust to their new surroundings. The newborn who is more active for the first weeks or longer may become much calmer later on, and vice versa.

What is most important for parents to know is that *these patterns are all inborn variations of behavior, not the result of child rearing techniques, the phase of the moon, or the virtues or sins of the parents.* Some newborn behaviors, however, may be altered if alcohol or drugs were used by the mother during pregnancy.

These characterizations of babies should not be taken as

value judgments. Because the quiet baby may not seem very demanding, it could be tempting to think of him as "sweet," "good-natured," or "mellow." On the other hand, the active baby might bring to mind a different vocabulary: "a handful," "high-strung," "a real pistol," or "exhausting." In fact, the weary parents who were not prepared for an active baby may find themselves bleary-eyed at 3 A.M., wondering if their child is still under warranty and whether it's too late to trade for another model.

Parents should not waste too many hours gloating over their angelette who sleeps peacefully all the time or reminiscing about the good old days before their baby kept them up for hours every night. The quiet baby may become lost in the shuffle unless parents deliberately take the time and effort to interact with him. Worse, his low-key nursing style could lead to an inadequate intake of calories and poor weight gain. If you have a quiet baby, you and the doctor will need to keep a close watch on his weight and possibly deliberately awaken him (at least during the day) to nurse at more frequent intervals. The active baby, on the other hand, for all of his intensity, will tend to be more social and interactive when he's not fussy. He may seem like a "taker" much of the time, especially during the first three months of life, but he will also give back quite a bit to those who hang in there with him.

"SLEEPING LIKE A BABY"

This timeworn phrase is reinforced whenever we behold a baby in deep, relaxed sleep. Wouldn't it be nice if we could sleep like that?

Well, not exactly.

During the first three months of life, a baby's sleeping patterns are quite different from those she will experience the rest of her life. A newborn sleeps anywhere from twelve to eighteen hours every day, but this is not unbroken slumber. Her small stomach capacity and her round-the-clock need for nutrients to fuel her rapid growth essentially guarantee that her life will consist of ongoing three- or four-hour cycles of feeding, wakefulness, and sleep. Like it or not, two or three feedings will be on the nighttime agenda for the first several weeks.

Furthermore, the patterns of brain activity during sleep are unique in a newborn. All of us experience cycles of two different types of sleep—rapid eye movement, or REM, and non-REM—throughout the night. During REM sleep, the brain is active with dreams, manifested by movements of the eyes and frequently other body parts as well. We may twitch, roll, or thrash, and we may be more easily awakened if the bed is cold, the bladder full, or the environment noisy. Non-REM sleep, during which little, if any, dreaming takes place, passes through phases of light, deep, and very deep sleep. There is less movement, deeper and slower breathing, and increasing relaxation of muscles when we pass through these stages in repeated cycles throughout the night. Adults spend about one-fourth of their sleep time in REM sleep and the rest in non-REM.

Babies also manifest these types of sleep but spend equal time in each, alternating about every thirty minutes. During non-REM, or quiet, sleep they will appear very relaxed, breathing regularly, and moving very little. During REM or active sleep, they seem to come to life, moving arms and legs, changing facial expressions, breathing less regularly, and perhaps making a variety of sounds. They may be experiencing their first dreams during these periods.

Adults and children older than about three months pass through the increasing depths of non-REM sleep before they enter a REM phase. *But newborns reverse this pattern*, starting with a period of REM sleep before moving into non-REM stages. As a result, the new baby who has just fallen asleep may be easily awakened for twenty minutes or more, until she moves into her non-REM phases.

This accounts for those character-building situations for some parents in which they feel they are dealing with a little time bomb with a short fuse. A fed, dry, and apparently tired baby fusses and resists but finally succumbs to sleep after prolonged cuddling and rocking. But when placed ever so gently into the cradle or crib, she suddenly startles and sounds off like a fire alarm. The cycle repeats over and over until everyone, baby included, is thoroughly exhausted and frustrated. The problem is that this baby isn't getting past her initial REM phase and happens to be one who is easily aroused out of it. If all else fails, the problem usually will resolve itself by the age of three months, when she shifts gears and enters non-REM sleep first.

Helping a new baby enter the slumber zone
For those parents who don't want to wait twelve weeks, there are two basic, but quite different, approaches to helping this baby—or, for that matter, any baby—fall asleep. Each approach has advocates who tend to view their ideas as vital to a happy, stable life for both parent and child, while seeing the other as producing troubled, insecure babies. In reality, both have something to offer, and neither will work for every baby-parent combination.

One method calls for parents to be intimately and directly involved in all phases of their baby's sleep. Proponents of this approach recommend that she be nursed, cuddled, rocked, and held continuously until she has fallen asleep for at least twenty minutes. She can then be put down in her customary sleeping place, which may be Mom and Dad's bed. The primary advantage of this approach is that it can help a baby navigate through drowsiness and REM sleep in the comfort and security of closeness to one or both parents. Those who favor this approach claim that a baby does best when she has more or less continuous contact with a warm body, having just exited from the inside of one. Those who challenge this approach argue that she may become so accustomed to being "manipulated" into sleep that she will not be able to fall asleep on her own for months or even years. Every bedtime or nap time will thus turn into a major project, and parents (or whoever is taking care of the baby) will be hostage to a prolonged routine of feeding and rocking well into the toddler years.

The other approach suggests that a baby can and should learn to "self-calm" and fall asleep on her own. Rather than nursing her to sleep, she can be fed thirty to sixty minutes before nap or bedtime and then put down before she is asleep. She may seem restless for fifteen or twenty minutes or even begin crying but will likely settle and fall asleep if left alone. Proponents of self-calming feel this approach frees Mom and Dad from hours of effort to settle their baby and allows the baby to become more flexible and independent, without her security being dependent on their immediate presence at all times. Critics argue that leaving her alone in a bassinet or crib represents cruel and unusual treatment at such a young age. Some even suggest that this repeated separation from parental closeness leads to sleep disorders (or worse) later in life.

You may be relieved to know that neither of these methods was carved in stone on Mount Sinai along with the Ten Commandments. You should tailor your approach to your baby's unique temperament and style and to your (and your family's) needs. Whatever you do will probably change over time as well. What works for your first baby may fail miserably for the second, and what helps this month may not the next. When dealing with newborns and very young infants, a fair amount of adjusting and pragmatism are not only wise but necessary. "Let's see if this works" is a much more useful approach than "We *have* to do it this way," except for a few ground rules dealing with safety.

Most babies give clues when they are ready to sleep—

yawning, droopy eyelids, fussiness—and you will want to become familiar with your child's particular signals. If she is giving you these cues, lay her down in a quiet, dimly lit setting and see if she will fall asleep. If she is clearly unhappy after fifteen or twenty minutes, check on her. Assuming that she is fed and dry, comfort her for a while and try again. If your baby is having problems settling herself, especially during the first few weeks of life, do not attempt to "train" her to do so by letting her cry for long periods of time. *During the first few months of life, it is unwise, for many reasons, to let a baby cry indefinitely without tending to her. Babies at this stage of life cannot be "spoiled" by adults who are very attentive to their needs.*

If you need to help your new baby transition into quiet sleep, any of these time-honored methods may help:

- Nursing (or a bottle, if using formula) may help induce sleep, especially at the end of the day. However,
  (a) Don't overfeed with formula or, worse, introduce solids such as cereal at this age in hopes of inducing a long snooze. A stomach that is too full will interfere with sleep as much as an empty one. Solids are inappropriate at this age and will not lengthen sleep.
  (b) Never put a baby to bed with a bottle propped in her mouth. Not only can this lead to a choking accident, but it also allows milk to flow into her eustachian tubes (which lead into the middle ears), increasing her risk of ear infections.
- Rocking gently while you cuddle your baby can calm both of you. If this works for your baby, relax and enjoy it. A comfortable rocking chair is a good investment, by the way, if one hasn't been handed down from earlier generations of your family.
- One alternative to the rocking chair is a cradle—again,

rocked smoothly and gently. Another alternative is a baby swing, but it must be one that is appropriately designed for this age-group.

- Many new babies settle more easily if they are swaddled—wrapped snugly in a light blanket.

- Quiet sounds such as the whirring of a small fan (not aimed toward the baby), a tape or CD recording of the ocean, or even small devices that generate monotonous "white noise" may help settle your baby and screen out other sounds in the home. For the musically inclined, there are several lovely anthologies of lullabies, quiet classical music, or gospel songs and hymns that might soothe a fussy baby.

- A gentle touch, pat, or massage may help settle a baby who is drowsy in your arms but squirmy in her bed.

- Many babies routinely fall asleep when they are continuously jostled during a car ride. Occasionally a frustrated parent who is dealing with a wakeful baby during the night may take her out for a 3 A.M. automobile trip—although this does not guarantee that she will stay asleep once the ride is over. Since staggering out into the night isn't much fun, especially in the dead of winter, some high-tech baby catalogues offer a device that attaches to a crib and simulates the motion of a car. Needless to say, both of these measures should be considered only as last-resort maneuvers for a very difficult sleeper.

All of the above, except for the white noise and the swaddling, involve ongoing parental activity to help settle a baby. In some situations, however, prolonged rocking, jostling, patting, and singing may be counterproductive, keeping a baby awake when she needs less stimulation in order to settle down. If a few weeks of heroic efforts to induce sleep don't seem to be working, it may be time to take another look at self-calming. Steps that may help the self-calming process when a baby has been put down but is not yet asleep include the following:

- Guide a baby's flailing hand toward her mouth. Many infants settle effectively by sucking on their hand or fingers.
- Identify a simple visual target for the baby's gaze such as a single-colored surface; a small, nonbreakable mirror in her crib; or a nearby window or night-light and place her in a position where she can see it. (Complex visual targets such as moving mobiles or busy patterns may not be as useful for settling during the earliest weeks, especially when a baby is very tired.)
- But make sure she is on her back before falling asleep.

What about sleeping through the night?

Newborns do not typically sleep in long stretches during the first several weeks of life, nor do they know the difference between day and night. By two months, however, they are capable of lasting for longer periods without a feeding. Most parents will go through the pulse-quickening experience of awakening at dawn and realizing that the baby didn't sound off in the middle of the night. "Is he okay?" is the first breathless concern, followed by both relief and quiet exultation: "He slept through the night!"

By three months of age, much to their parents' relief, a majority of babies have established a regular pattern of uninterrupted sleep for seven or eight hours each night. However, some will take longer to reach this milestone. A few actually drift in the wrong direction, sleeping peacefully through most of the day and then snapping wide-awake—often fidgeting and fussing—just when bleary-eyed parents are longing for some rest. If you have a baby who favors the wee hours, you will want to give him some gentle but definite nudges to use the night for sleeping:

- Make a specific effort to increase his awake time during the day. Don't let him fall asleep during or right after eating, but instead provide some gentle stimulation. Talk or sing to him, lock eyes, change his clothes, play with his hands and feet, rub his back, or let Grandma coo over him. Don't make loud noises to startle him, and do not under any circumstances shake him. (Sudden movements of a baby's head can cause physical damage to the brain.) Let him nap only after he has been awake for a while after nursing. This can also help prevent a baby from becoming dependent on a feeding to fall asleep.
- If your baby is sleeping for long periods during the day and fitfully at night, consider gently awakening him while he is in one of his active sleep phases when a nap has lasted more than three or four hours.
- By contrast, make nighttime interactions—especially those middle-of-the-night feedings—incredibly boring. Keep the lights low, the conversation minimal, and the diaper change (if needed) businesslike. This is not the time to party.
- Remember that babies frequently squirm, grunt, and even seem to awaken briefly during their REM sleep phases. Try to avoid intervening and interacting with him during these times, because you may unknowingly awaken your baby when he was just shifting gears into the next phase of sleep. This may require some adjusting of your sleeping arrangements.
- If your baby tends to awaken by the dawn's early light and you don't care to do likewise, try installing shades or blinds to block out the first rays of sunlight. Don't

assume that his rustling around in bed necessarily means he is waking up for good. Wait for a while before tending to him, because he may go back to sleep. Sometimes, however, he will wake up with the local roosters no matter what you do, at which point you may want to consider adjusting your schedule to follow the famous "early to bed, early to rise" proverb until a few more months pass.

Where should your baby sleep?
By the time your baby arrives home for the first night, you will have had to address a basic question: Will she sleep in her own room, in a cradle or bassinet next to your bed, or in your bed right next to you? There are advocates for each of these arrangements.

Those who espouse sleeping with your baby point out that this is widely practiced throughout the world and that it gives the newborn a sense of security and comfort she won't feel in a crib. Critics of shared sleeping raise concerns about parents accidentally rolling over and crushing the baby. While the risk of this is remote, recent research has suggested that the risk of sudden infant death syndrome (SIDS) may be higher in "shared sleep" situations, presumably because the parents' bedding materials are not the safest environment for a sleeping newborn. (See the sidebar entitled "Safe Sleep: Reducing the Risk of Sudden Infant Death Syndrome (SIDS)" for further information about safe sleeping surfaces for newborns.)[1]

Another very practical concern about sharing sleep with your newborn is the potential disruption of your own sleep, intimacy, and privacy. New babies don't quietly nod off to sleep at 10 P.M. and wake up calmly eight hours later. They also don't typically sleep silently during the few hours between feedings. As they pass through their REM sleep phases, they tend to move around and make all sorts of noises, often sounding as if they're waking up. All of this activity isn't easy to ignore, especially for new parents who tend to be tuned in and concerned, if not downright worried, about how their new arrival is doing. Unless you learn to screen out these distractions and respond only when she is truly awake and in need of your attention, you may find yourself woefully short on sleep and patience within a few days.

The other issue to consider is the effect on the mother and father's relationship. If Mom and Dad are equally enthused about having a new bedmate, great. But many young couples aren't prepared for the demands a new baby may place on them and especially on a mother who may have little energy left at the end of the day for maintaining her relationship with her husband. A father who feels that his wife's attention is already consumed by the baby's needs may begin to feel completely displaced if the baby is in his bed too.

Many parents prefer to have their baby sleep in another room but wonder whether they will hear her if she needs them. They need not worry. An infant who is truly awake, hungry, and crying during the night is difficult to ignore. And new parents, especially moms, are uniquely tuned in to their baby's nighttime vocalizing and will normally awaken at the first sounds of crying, even after sleeping through louder sounds such as the rumble of a passing truck.

The advantage of this arrangement is that parents will be less likely to be aroused repeatedly through the night by their baby's assorted movements and noises during sleep. They will also avoid intervening too quickly during a restless period, which can accidentally interrupt a baby's transition from active to quiet sleep. Having your baby sleep in another room may also increase her nighttime adaptability, allowing her to go to sleep in a variety of environments.

If you are truly concerned about hearing your baby when she first begins to cry, you can purchase an inexpensive

SAFE SLEEP: REDUCING THE RISK OF SUDDEN INFANT DEATH SYNDROME (SIDS)

Sudden infant death syndrome (SIDS), also called **crib death,** has been the subject of intense research for a number of years. While the exact cause is uncertain, SIDS involves a disturbance of breathing regulation during sleep. It is relatively rare, occurring in two or three out of every thousand newborns, most often between the first and sixth months, with a peak incidence between the second and third months. It is more common in the winter months, the reason of which remains unknown.

SIDS is more common in males with low birth weight and in premature infants of both sexes. Breast-fed babies, on the other hand, may have a reduced risk. In addition, some potential contributing factors to SIDS can be minimized by taking a few basic preventive measures:

- *Stay completely away from cigarettes during pregnancy, and don't allow anyone to smoke in your home after your baby is born.*
- *Lay your baby down on his back.* For decades, child-care guidebooks recommended that new babies sleep on their stomachs, based on the assumption that this would prevent them from choking on any material they might unexpectedly spit up. However, recent evidence suggests that this position might be a risk factor for SIDS. Therefore, it is now recommended that a newborn be positioned on his back to sleep. Exceptions to this guideline are made for premature infants, as well as for some infants with deformities of the face that might cause difficulty breathing when lying face up. In addition, your doctor may advise against the face

up position if your baby spits up excessively. If you have any question about sleeping position, check with your baby's doctor. Sometime after four months of age, your baby will begin rolling over on his own, at which point he will determine his own sleeping positions. By this age, fortunately, SIDS is extremely rare.

- Put your baby to sleep on a safe surface. Don't place pillows or any soft bedding material other than a fitted sheet under the baby. His head or face might become accidentally buried in the soft folds (especially if he happens to be face down), which could lead to suffocation. Sheepskin, down mattresses, and feather beds pose a similar risk. For similar reasons don't put your baby to sleep on a wavy waterbed or beanbag chair. Even on one of these plastic surfaces, a baby whose face shifts to the wrong position could suffocate.
- Don't overbundle your baby. Overcompensating for the cold of winter by turning up the thermostat and wrapping a baby in several layers of clothing should be avoided. If he looks or feels hot and sweaty, start peeling off layers until he appears more comfortable.

A few parents experience the terror of seeing their baby stop breathing, either momentarily or long enough to begin turning blue. It is obviously important in such cases to begin infant CPR and call 911 if he does not start breathing on his own (see Emergency Care, page 312). A careful evaluation by your doctor or at the emergency room is mandatory. It is also likely that this baby will be sent home with an **apnea monitor,** which will sound off if a breath is not taken after a specified number of seconds.

Parents who have suffered the loss of an infant for any reason must work through a profound grieving process. When

SIDS is the cause, they may also feel a great sense of guilt as well as great anxiety over the safety of their other children. It is important that they obtain support from family, church, and if available, a local support group for families who have dealt with such a loss.

electronic baby monitor, which will broadcast sounds from the baby's room into yours. However, you may find that you are hearing (and possibly being kept awake by) a lot of "false alarms" as your baby stirs and makes a variety of sounds without actually awakening. On the other hand, it would be unwise to leave your baby in a place where you would be totally unable to hear her and then rely on a monitor to be your electronic ears. If the monitor failed for some reason, your baby might lie uncomfortable, crying, and unattended for an extended period of time.

Many parents prefer to place their newborn in a cradle next to their bed. In order to get any sleep, however, they will have to filter out the baby's assorted nocturnal noises that do not need a response. Nevertheless, this arrangement may be useful with a newborn who has a difficult time settling during the night. If she is in another room, one or both parents may begin to feel like a yo-yo, circulating in and out of bed in response to repeated bouts of crying or fussing. These infants and their parents may have an easier time if they sleep in close proximity, so that Mom and Dad can offer nursing and comfort as often as needed without having to get up several times throughout the night.

As with the techniques you choose to help your baby settle down to sleep, you will need to determine which sleeping arrangements work best for your family and be flexible about the various possibilities. Moreover, it is important that parents keep their communications about this subject open with each other. If Mom is the one getting up to nurse a fussy baby and as a result spends more hours in the baby's room than in her own bed, Dad may need to assume a larger share of the nighttime duties. He could, for example, bring the baby to Mom for nursing and then return her to her crib when the feeding is done. Similarly, if Dad is feeling an increasing distance from Mom because of a baby in their bed, Mom may need to be willing to empty the nighttime nest of offspring.

One of the tricky issues for parents who share their bed with one or more children is deciding when and how to reclaim their bed for themselves. Most children are more than happy to sleep with Mom and Dad well into or beyond their toddler years, and making the transition to their own bed may be easier said than done. Parents who routinely allow one or more babies and children in bed with them for months or years should regularly take stock of the effect this custom is having on their marriage. Regaining sexual intimacy after the birth of a child normally requires some time and effort for both parents. It may be far more challenging if there are more than two bodies in the marriage bed.

CRYBABIES: WHAT HAPPENS WHEN THE TEARS WON'T STOP?

One of the greatest mental and emotional adjustments new parents must make is sorting out the meanings of, and their responses to, the new baby's crying. In most cases, crying is a clear signal that a stomach is empty or a diaper full, and the appropriate response will quiet it. Even in these routine circumstances, however, the newborn cry has distinct qualities—insistent, edgy, and downright irritating. Indeed, it can sound almost like an accusation—"I don't like the care you're giving me!"

If your new baby's cry gives you a twinge of discomfort

or even annoyance, don't panic; your response is quite normal. If you're a mother acutely short on sleep and sore in body (especially if you've had a cesarean delivery), with hormones shifting in all directions, you may find yourself harboring some troubling thoughts about your crying newborn. These feelings can enter the minds of even the most dedicated parents.

How should you feel about and deal with your baby's crying? First of all, it's important to understand the function of crying. Remember that a newborn baby is totally helpless and cannot do *anything* for himself other than suck on a breast or bottle given to him (or one or two of his own fingers that have accidentally found their way into his mouth). Unless someone meets his most basic needs on an ongoing basis, he will not survive. Crying is his only means—but a most effective one—of provoking a parent into action. It's *designed* to be annoying and irritating, to create all sorts of unpleasant feelings, especially among those closest to him. The responses that usually stop the crying—food, clean diapers and clothing, cuddling and cooing—are what keep him alive.

During these first three months of your baby's life, assume that when he cries, it's for a good reason. His crying is definitely *not* a deliberate effort to irritate you, manipulate you, or test parental limits. Therefore, it is appropriate to take action in response to your baby's crying, as opposed to ignoring it and hoping it will go away. *You cannot spoil a baby at this young age,* and for now it is far better to err on the side of giving too much attention than too little. He needs comfort, open arms, and ongoing love from those around him, even though he cannot express any signs of gratitude or even pleasure in response to all you give him. This is not the time for any misguided attempts to "train, mold, and discipline" your child. (In several months you will begin to have plenty of opportunities to carry out that important assignment.)

What is your baby trying to tell you when he cries? Most likely, one of these things:

- He's hungry and wants to be fed.
- He has a wet or dirty diaper.
- He's wet, hot, cold, or uncomfortable in some other way.
- He wants to be held.

At some point, usually between two weeks and three months, there will be at least one occasion when you suspect that *something has gone terribly wrong*. Just a day or so ago you could comfort your baby regularly and predictably. A feeding every few hours, dry diapers, and a little rocking and cooing would end crying fairly quickly. Now, however, he starts fussing late in the afternoon or early in the evening, and nothing works for an hour . . . or two . . . or three. Or he suddenly lets out an ear-piercing wail or screams for no apparent reason in the middle of the night. What's going on? You may never know for sure. But it may help if you understand that many babies cry like this now and then, some do it every day, and a few seem determined to set a world's record for the longest crying episode in history.

Dealing with colic

According to a long-standing definition, if your baby cries three hours a day three days a week for three weeks, and he's between two weeks and three months of age, he has **colic**. A simpler definition, without counting hours and days (and more to the point), is "a whole lot of crying that doesn't calm down with the normal measures, and the doctor says there's nothing really wrong with him." True colicky episodes tend to occur around the same time each day, usually in the late afternoon or evening, and are marked by intense activity on the baby's part, such as flailing about or pulling his knees to his chest. From all appearances, he acts like he's feeling a lot of discomfort—and undoubtedly he is.

The classic theories about the cause of colic have assumed that the baby's intestinal tract is at fault—that it goes into uncontrollable spasms, perhaps because of immaturity or a reaction to something in Mom's milk or the current formula. Other proposed explanations include a problem interacting with parents, often assuming that Mother is tense or highstrung, and as a result the baby is also. But changing feeding patterns or formulas may or may not help, and colicky babies may land in families that are intact or disjointed, relaxed or uptight. Basically, a universal cause for colic has yet to be determined.

If your baby begins having long stretches of crying, you will need to address two basic concerns:

1. Does he have a medical problem?
2. How is everyone—baby included—going to get through this?

The first question needs to be answered relatively quickly, because a medical illness can be a much more serious problem during the first three months of life than when the baby is older. Some indicators of a disturbance that might need a physician's care include:

- Any fever over 100.4°F taken with a rectal thermometer (see sidebar, page 186)
- Poor sucking at the breast or bottle
- Change in color from pink to pale or bluish (called **cyanosis**) during feeding or crying
- Overt vomiting, as opposed to spitting up. (When a baby spits up, the partially digested food burps into his mouth and dribbles down his chin and clothes. When he vomits, this material becomes airborne.)

- A marked increase in the amount and looseness of bowel movements
- Unusual jerking movements of the head, eyes, or other muscles that you don't recall seeing before

If any of these occur, you should contact your physician, and your baby should be checked—especially if he has a fever. If he is crying up a storm but seems okay otherwise, he should still have a medical evaluation, either as part of a routine checkup or at an appointment specifically for this purpose. The more specific information you can give the doctor, the better. When did the crying start? How long does it last? Does anything seem to set it off? Is it improved or worsened after a feeding? Are there any other symptoms?

Assuming your baby is doing well otherwise (gaining weight, arriving at his developmental milestones more or less on time, showing no apparent signs of medical illness), your primary tasks during his crying episodes are to be there for him and to make ongoing efforts to comfort him. *You are not a failure, and you should not give up if your measures do not succeed in stopping the crying.* Eventually each crying episode will end, and the crying season overall will come to a close, in nearly all cases by the third to fourth month of age.

So what do you do for a colicky baby, assuming that he is fed, dry, and not sick? You can try any or all of the following, once or many times. If a particular measure helps one time but doesn't the next, don't panic. You may get impressive results today with something that failed miserably last week.

Soothing movements. Gentle rocking or swaying in someone's arms is a time-honored baby comforter. Unfortunately, when a baby is wailing at full volume, you may unconsciously begin moving faster or more forcefully—but you should *avoid rapid, jerky movements,* which not only make the problem worse but may even injure the baby. Cradles and baby swings that support the body and head can also provide this type of movement.

Soothing sounds. Provide humming, gentle singing, white noise, or pleasant recorded music.

Soothing positions. Some colicky babies respond to being held tummy-down against your forearm like a football or across your thigh. Others seem to calm down while being carried close to Mom's or Dad's body in a baby sling. Swaddling in a light blanket and resting on one side or the other might help.

Soothing environments. Spending time in a quiet, dimly lit room can help calm a baby who may be in sensory overload at the end of the day. Turn down the TV and unplug the phone if you have to.

Soothing trips. A ride in the car or a stroller may provide the right mix of gentle movement and sound to soothe the crying.

Soothing touch. Gentle touching or stroking of the back, stomach, or head may help.

Soothing sucking. Nursing may seem to calm the crying, even if he just had a feeding. A pacifier may also work. If your baby doesn't seem satisfied by *any* of your feedings, you should check with his physician and possibly a lactation consultant as well. This is particularly important if he's not gaining adequate weight, because the problem may be that his hunger is never satisfied. If your colicky baby is formula-fed, you may at some point want to try a different brand or a different type of formula—for example, switching from cow's milk to soy-based formula. (Check with your baby's health-care provider on this.) Sometimes a change will bring about some noticeable improvement.

Self-soothing. Sometimes all the rocking, singing, touching, and pacifying maneuvers unwittingly overload the baby's capacity to handle stimulation. The self-soothing measures mentioned in the previous section on sleep (pages 210–211) may work wonders when everything else has failed.

What can you do for yourself while all of this is going on?

Keep reminding yourself that "this too will surely pass." You will deal with crying problems for only a short period of your child's life. Believe it or not, before you know it there will come a time when you'll wonder where all those baby years went.

If you find yourself reaching the end of your rope, *don't take it out on the baby.* Mounting frustration and anger are indications that you need a brief time-out. If that time arrives, don't allow yourself to become a martyr or a child abuser. Sounding off verbally at the baby will accomplish nothing, and *you must not carry out any physical act of anger*—picking him up or putting him down roughly, shaking him, hitting him, or anything else that inflicts pain or injury—no matter how upset you may feel. Instead, put him in his cradle or crib and *walk away* for fifteen or twenty minutes until you have a chance to collect your thoughts and calm down. It won't hurt him to cry by himself for that period of time, and you can then try comforting him again. He may have expended enough energy to become more responsive to calming efforts at this point. If necessary, call a friend or relative and get your frustration off your chest, or let someone else come look after your baby for a while (see sidebar, page 227).

If at all possible, husband and wife should pass the baton during a prolonged crying episode. Let Dad hold the baby while Mom takes a walk around the block and vice versa. Single moms—and for that matter, married ones—shouldn't be embarrassed to seek help from an experienced relative or friend. If Grandma wants to help you for a while during a rough evening, by all means let her do it. She may have a few tricks up her sleeve that aren't in any book.

Try to find some humor in all this to maintain your perspective. Pretend you are the next Erma Bombeck and jot down some of your observations. If you have one or more books that have made you laugh out loud, by all means keep them close at hand.

Try to maintain "self-preservation" activities as much as possible. A quiet time for reflection and prayer may have to occur during a feeding, but it will provide important perspective and strength. Having a world-class wailer is a humbling experience, and it is during these rough times that special intimacy with God often develops. The question to ask Him isn't "Why did You give me such a fussy baby?!" but "What do You want me to learn about myself and life in general through this experience?" You may be surprised at the answer.

Don't hesitate to ask well-wishers to come back at a later date if you are feeling overwhelmed. If your baby is fussy and you're running on empty with too little sleep, keep visitors to a minimum unless they're able and willing to roll up their sleeves and help you. Place a polite sign on the door asking not to be disturbed, and let the answering machine take care of incoming calls so you can get some extra rest. You'll have plenty of time to socialize in the coming months.

If you have "gone the distance," repeatedly trying every measure listed here (and perhaps a few others as well) without success, check back with your baby's doctor. Be prepared to give specific information—for example, how many hours the baby has been crying, not just "He won't stop!" Depending upon your situation and the baby's crying pattern, another medical evaluation may be in order.

MILESTONES AND MEMORIES

Even though nursing, sleeping, and crying may dominate the landscape during the first several weeks, you'll be happy to know that your baby will also be taking in all kinds of information and learning new ways to respond to it. Young babies

TO GRANDPARENTS AND OTHER PARENT SUPPORTERS: THE GIFT OF TIME

If you have experience as a parent, whether recently or in the more distant past, one of the greatest gifts you can offer a relative or friend with a fussy baby is a brief respite. This is particularly important for single moms, but even a married mother may have a husband who isn't much help when the baby is having full-throttle colic. And a baby who cries nonstop can wear out both Mom and Dad before much time has passed.

The sound of someone else's baby crying is not nearly as nerve-wracking as it is for the mother or father of the child. You may also be able to model some perspective, a reminder of the preciousness of this new life, by cooing and fussing over a baby who may not seem very lovable to her parents at this particular moment.

Take the initiative in asking a new parent how life with the new arrival is going, and in particular if there are any problems with fussing and crying. If you have time, energy, and child-rearing skills, offer to look after the baby for a while. You might suggest a specific time ("How about if I come over tomorrow or Wednesday night around six, so you can get out for a couple of hours?") rather than something vague ("Let me know if I can help you"), which may be more difficult to accept without sounding utterly desperate. Your offer to provide a time-out for a frazzled parent may be far more valuable than any baby-shower gift.

manifest six different levels of consciousness: quiet sleep, active sleep, drowsiness, quiet alertness, active alertness, and crying.

Quiet alertness occupies about 10 percent of your baby's time at first, but you will want to watch for these moments of calm attentiveness, during which you can begin to have some genuine interaction. Enjoy them, file them in your memory bank, and if you have time, you may want to jot your impressions in a personal journal. As the weeks pass, you will begin to notice that your baby is spending more time in calm and active alertness, during which you will see several wonderful developments in a variety of areas:

Vision. During the first few weeks, a baby focuses best on objects eight to fifteen inches from her face. You may find her staring intently at the fist at the end of her outstretched arm, which happens to be in her focusing range. She will prefer to study plain, high-contrast, black-and-white images such as stripes, checks, or spirals, or a simple drawing of a face. She may gaze intently into a small, unbreakable mirror attached to the inside of her crib. But her favorite subject to scrutinize will be the face of another person, about a foot away from hers. She will not respond directly to a smile for a few weeks, but a lot of smiles are what she should see.

Your baby will be able to follow an object with her eyes only momentarily at first. You can give her some practice at this ability by moving your face or a brightly colored object slowly from side to side across her field of vision. Around two months of age she will be able to coordinate her eye movements to stay locked on an interesting visual target that passes through a semicircle in front of her. She will also be interested in more complex shapes and patterns and will be able to hold her head steady enough to fixate on simple, high-contrast objects hung from a mobile over her crib. By three months of age her distant vision will be increased to the point that she will recognize you halfway across a room.

Responses to color also develop over the first several weeks. At first she will pay attention to objects with bright, strongly contrasting colors. Ironically, the soft colors that are so often used in decorating a baby's room won't be particularly interesting to her at first. It will take a few months before her color vision has matured enough to distinguish a full palette and varieties of shades.

From time to time all babies will briefly cross their eyes as they develop their tracking skills. But if she frequently appears to have crossed eyes as she approaches the age of six months, she should be checked by her physician and an ophthalmologist.[2]

Hearing. Newborns will vary in their sensitivity to sounds. Some infants seem capable of sleeping through a violent thunderstorm, while others appear to startle when a cat crosses the street a block away. If a young infant is placed in a very noisy environment, he may appear to "shut down," markedly reducing his activity level. This is a protective mechanism, an internal withdrawal from a situation that is overloading him. While you don't need to maintain a hushed silence around your newborn, you should try to keep the noise level around him at a comfortable level—no more than, for example, the intensity of pleasant conversation between two or three people. If you want to go to a ball game or a concert where the crowds and sounds are pumped up, leave the baby at home.

Within a few weeks, he will appear to pay attention to certain sounds, especially the voices of those who regularly care for him. By two months of age, he may begin to shift his eyes and head toward your voice. He may also show some movements and expressions indicating that he recognizes this familiar and comforting sound. As he continues toward three months of age, you will notice him starting to turn toward other interesting sounds, such as a tinkling bell. If the sound is repeated over and over, however, he will tune it out and stop responding to it.

Smell. A very young baby is capable of responding to a variety of smells and can distinguish the smell of his mother's breast from those of other nursing mothers by the end of the first week of life.

Touch. All of us are strongly affected by touch, but babies are particularly sensitive. They will startle in response to scratchy surfaces, rough handling, or sudden temperature changes—especially when their skin makes contact with something cold. Cuddling, caressing, and stroking may help calm a crying episode, but these shouldn't be used merely to stop tears. Touch is an important expression of love and will nourish her emotions before she can understand any words. It should be as routine a part of her day as her feedings.

These developments set the stage for your baby's first true **socializing**, which will probably begin just as you are starting to wonder whether all the nursing and diapers and nonstop caregiving are worth it. You may first notice a brief flicker of a grin after a feeding. Was that a smile or a gas pain? Maybe it was both or maybe neither, but it felt like a puff of fresh air on a hot day. Suddenly—at about the age of four to six weeks—it will be unmistakable: You will lock eyes with your baby, and a big grin will flash across her face. It will be an unforgettable moment, and the next time she smiles will be equally rewarding because you'll know that this milestone was for real.

Over the next month, you will catch smiles in response to your own grinning, cooing, talking, or singing to your baby. You may notice special enthusiastic body movements in response to familiar voices and the turning of eyes and head to seek them out. Even more pleasant are your first "conversations." At about two months your baby will begin to coo, often in response to your speaking to her in soft, soothing tones. At this age, she will not understand the words you speak, but the tone of your voice will communicate volumes.

Even at this young age, your baby may show some selectivity in her responses. Not everyone will necessarily receive the big grin and happy sounds. More often than not, it will go to the most familiar faces and voices. Your baby is already starting to sort out who is important in her life, and so whoever wants to be included in that category will need to log some time with her. This is particularly important for fathers, who may find it harder to interact with a squirmy two-month-old than an older child who likes to "wrestle" on the carpet or play catch. Mothers who are weighing decisions about work outside the home also need to ponder how much time the baby should spend with other caregivers.

Growth and movement. Babies lose and then regain several ounces (about a tenth of their birth weight) during the first ten days of life. From then on, you can anticipate a weight gain of about two-thirds to one ounce per day, or one to two pounds per month. Your baby will add between one and one and a half inches in height each month as well. These amounts will vary, of course, depending on your baby's feeding patterns and on genetics, which will affect whether this growing body will ultimately resemble a ballerina or a fullback. During each medical checkup, your baby's height, weight, and head circumference will be measured and then plotted on a growth chart. Tracking your baby's growth will be an important tool for her health-care provider to confirm how well she is doing.

During the first three months, you will see dramatic changes in your baby's movement patterns. At birth her arms and legs flail and jerk, her chin may twitch, and her hands may tremble. Many of her movements are reflexes, such as rooting, sucking, and grasping. In addition, you may see her do a "fencing" maneuver known as the **tonic neck reflex**: If her head is turned in one direction, you may see the arm on that side straighten and the other arm flex, as if she were about to enter a sword fight. In addition, if you gently hold her body upright, supporting her head, and then lower her gently until her feet touch a firm surface, she will begin stepping motions. This has nothing to do with how soon she will begin walking, and this so-called **stepping reflex** will be gone by the age of two months. However, she will kick her legs quite vigorously when awake and active while lying on her back or stomach.

Hand and arm movements will gradually become less jerky and almost appear purposeful. Between two and three months, she will begin to spend more time with her hands open rather than clenched and will bring them toward her mouth or in front of her face, where she may appear to study them. She still won't have the coordination to reach directly for something that interests her, although she will tightly grasp a small object placed in her hand. In fact, you may have to help her let it go.

At two months she will have developed enough control of her neck muscles to hold her head in one position while lying on her back. When lying on her stomach, she will be able to raise her head briefly, just long enough to turn it from one side to another. But her head control overall will not be secure until three to four months of age, so you must support her head whenever you hold or carry her.

OTHER PEOPLE IN YOUR BABY'S LIFE

Just as it is important for you to handle your newborn carefully and appropriately, any other children—whether belonging to family or to friends—will need to be supervised during their interactions with the baby. Toddlers and preschoolers who want to touch and caress the new baby must be shown how to do so gently, avoiding eyes, nose and mouth, and clearly told that they can only touch the baby while a grown-up is directly watching them. They should not be allowed to carry a new baby, play any of their physical games with the baby, or touch the baby with anything but their hands that have just been washed. If they have runny noses or are coughing, they'll need to wait until the illness is gone before getting near the baby.

If you see a child talking or acting in an aggressive way toward a new baby, immediately separate the two, find out what's going on, and make certain that the issue is settled before allowing any further contact. Small children, especially if they are upset (for whatever reason), are quite capable of injuring babies, whether or not they fully realize what they are doing. Toddlers and two-year-olds are particularly incapable of processing the moral and physical reasons they should not act aggressively toward a baby. Parents and other caregivers will thus need to remain constantly on guard to protect a young infant from a child in this age group—who herself was a baby not long ago.

The same rules about colds and acute illnesses apply to relatives and friends who may want to handle your baby. Because her immune system is not as competent as it will be in a few months, you should be careful to expose her to as little risk of infection as possible. This means that, at the risk of upsetting a well-meaning friend or relative, you may need to be firm about keeping your new baby away from anyone with an infection, especially one involving sneezing and coughing (which can easily spread contaminated droplets). Adults and older children will have a much easier time getting over their temporary disappointment than your newborn will have recovering from an acute infection. Your protective stance for the first three months of your baby's life should also include keeping her away from crowds in general and group nurseries in particular, unless it is absolutely necessary to do otherwise.

Don't hesitate to ask well-wishers to come back at a later date if you are feeling overwhelmed by all of your new responsibilities. If the baby is fussy and you're "running on empty" with too little sleep, keep visitors to a minimum, place a polite sign on the door asking not to be disturbed, and let the answering machine take care of incoming calls so that you can get some extra rest. You'll have plenty of time to socialize and show off your pride and joy in the coming months.

NOTES

1. Kemp, J. S. et al. Unsafe sleep practices and an analysis of bedsharing among infants dying suddenly and unexpectedly: Results of a four-year, population-based, death-scene investigation study of sudden infant death syndrome and related deaths. *Pediatrics.* Volume 100, No. 3 September 2000, p. e42 (electronic edition).

2. If the position of her eyes is constantly presenting two images instead of one to her brain, she will shut down the information arriving from one eye or the other, resulting in **amblyopia,** or "lazy eye."

CHAPTER 10

Caregivers

Who Will Care for Your Child While You Are Away?

> *Note—This material applies not only to caregiving issues you may be facing now, but also to decisions you will be making for many months and years to come.*

Even if you are the most dedicated and attentive parent(s) on earth, you cannot (and indeed should not) provide hands-on care for your child twenty-four hours a day, seven days a week, from the delivery room to the college dormitory. Many times during your child-rearing career you will need to release her to the temporary care of another person. Whether this involves an occasional time-out to run errands or a routine of several hours every workday, transferring responsibility for your child to someone else raises many questions:

- How do you choose a caregiver?
- Is it better for your child if the caregiver comes to your home, or is it okay to take her elsewhere (such as to another home or a day-care center)?
- How long is it appropriate for you to be away from your child?

Without question these are extremely important topics. Like many other concerns of parenting (such as discipline), there is no surefire formula that will apply to every family or even to one family through the development of all its children. What follows therefore are a few basic—but very important—overriding principles.

Child-care issues overall cluster around two major situations:

- Extended periods of child care on a regular basis, usually occurring when both parents (or a single parent) are employed outside the home.
- Short-term or episodic care, commonly referred to as baby-sitting, which is discussed at the end of this section (page 251).

The first of these concerns—and the question of whether the mother of one or more young children should be employed outside of the home—is by far the more complicated, emotional, and controversial of the two.

WORKING IN AND OUT OF THE HOME

Whether you are a young couple enthusiastically welcoming the first baby to your nest, a blended family, or a single mom or dad, you must deal with some of the following issues:

- How much income does the family need, and where will it come from?
- How will we divide labor in the home? Will one parent be the main income producer while the other's primary role is caring for children? Or will both parents share more equally in these tasks?
- How will bringing up one or more children mesh with one or both parents' work schedule, not to mention education and career plans?
- Is it wise for both mother and father to work outside the home? If this is done, who is going to take care of the child(ren)?
- How can a single mother or father best cope with the simultaneous demands of earning a living and rearing children?

Every family will have different circumstances that affect the answer to these questions:

- Age, abilities, and temperament of each child
- The state of the marital union or the absence of a marriage partner
- Educational background
- Job/professional skills
- Financial resources
- Relationships with immediate and extended family members
- Involvement with a church community
- Goals, plans, and dreams for the future

For some parents there will be many ways to approach these questions. For others, options are very limited and the answers will be defined by current circumstances. Most single parents, for example, have the daunting dual role of primary income provider and full-time parent. There is no standard solution that will work for every family or even for one family throughout its entire lifetime. But when thinking through these very important and often emotionally charged questions, it is important to keep some broad perspectives and reality checks in mind.

Faulty expectations, identity, and the "end of life" test
Much discontent over the question of balancing child rearing and career(s)—for both mothers and fathers—can arise from several powerful but faulty expectations:

The expectation that rearing one or more children won't require considerable effort or many changes in lifestyle. An infant cannot be fed and changed and then left to her own devices, nor can an older child be expected to grow up on her own. Not only must a child's basic health and safety be assured, but her intellectual and emotional development requires continuous monitoring and frequent interaction with adults who are deeply committed to her.

The expectation that a certain lifestyle is necessary for happiness. With rare exception, whatever standard of living young parents envision for themselves in the immediate or distant future will probably require more income than expected. Remember Murphy's Law of Money: Everything costs more than you expect—both to purchase and to maintain. The belief that a particular home or car, travel, and certain experiences are necessary for contentment in life can push the budgetary limits to the point that a second income becomes a necessity. But this could have the ultimate effect of trading irreplaceable interactions with one's own children for material goods that will eventually be worn out and discarded.

The expectation that mother can be Supermom, effortlessly managing a career, nurturing children, and experiencing extraordinary marital satisfaction—all with great style and finesse. TV commercials and magazine ads have helped create this fantasy, which more often than not leads to frustration, guilt, and, most of all, fatigue. There may be a few true Supermoms around, but the other 99 percent who are more earthbound usually realize that they must accept a number of compromises at home and/or work in order to survive.

An issue more often but not always for women: The expectation that being at home will result in the evaporation of one's intellect and ambition. Women have received this message from numerous voices, including popular media, friends and acquaintances who work outside the home, even insensitive husbands and family members who either don't understand or have forgotten what is involved in running a household and nurturing children. The decision to remain at home is often made at considerable sacrifice, and many women find themselves disadvantaged later when they try to reenter the outside marketplace after a few years' absence from it. However, to assume that staying home with the children will erode a woman's mental or professional powers is to subscribe to an extremely narrow view of life.

The rewards of participating significantly in a child's development cannot be measured. A parent who chooses to stay home is aware that her children will only be home for a season and that her impact on their intellect, development, and values will probably continue for decades. Rearing children is a career that requires a host of skills as well as insight, patience, and wisdom.

The world of work is changing to accommodate parents who have decided to spend more time with their children. An increasing number of options for working part-time or from a home office are making it possible for both moms and dads to be with their children more often and more consistently. Many women for whom an outside career or interest is important have created satisfying professional options for themselves from within the home setting. These are encouraging developments, both for women who want to pursue a career outside the home (whether now or in the future) and for women who are content to make home their career but who want to pursue artistic or community interests.

An issue more often but not always for men: The expectation that the career track defines identity and that all other concerns pale in comparison. Men are notorious for defining themselves in terms of their occupation and position. (How often do you hear a father answer the question "What do you do?" with "I'm Trevor and Amanda's dad"?) But the danger of this orientation is that the demands of a career and the "pursuit of excellence" at work can result in rampant absenteeism from home and mediocrity in parenting. Many fathers and mothers buy into the myth that a few minutes of time spent with one's children every day is just fine, as long as it's "quality time." But will a one-ounce steak be satisfying because it is "quality steak"? Or (perhaps more relevant for men) will sex every six months be adequate because it is "quality sex"?

Both mothers and fathers need to think very carefully about these issues. The truth is, *a true and lasting sense of worth, identity, and satisfaction comes ultimately from being present and accounted for in God's family and going about His business every day.* In the final analysis, these qualities are not derived from the initials after one's name, the title on one's door, the plaques on the walls, or the money in the bank. They do not come from being CEO of Universal Widget or having a home that is the envy of the neighborhood—or having kids who are perfect. Parents must beware of the "If only . . ." syndrome: "If only ____, then I'd be satisfied/content/happy." These are the longings of those who are perpetually restless and discontented, who never fill the gaping hole remaining in their lives, no matter how often they successfully accomplish last month's "If only . . ."

The "end of life" test. Parents who are making decisions about who will rear their children should ask themselves an important question: When you are staring down death's corridor, what in your life will really matter? Will you look back fondly at the hours spent at the office and pine over the fact that you weren't there longer? You may be the world's greatest Monopoly player—on the game table or in the real world—but eventually you will have to fold up the board, put the money back in the box, and put it in the closet. No one will remember for very long who won the game, but those who were at the table with you will long recall whether their time with you was pleasant or miserable.

More specifically, will your children arrive at your bedside and thank you for all the career goals you accomplished? They will probably remember most fondly and thank you for the times you spent with them—rocking them, listening to them, wrestling on the carpet, having lunch at their favorite restaurant, going fishing, walking on the beach, or helping them out of a jam. At that moment, what will matter most will be the people you care about, the lives you have touched, and the prospect of hearing, "Well done, my good and faithful servant."

Best and second best

These considerations are not intended to incite great pangs of guilt nor to say that careers launched from within or outside the home are somehow evil. They are, however, meant to raise serious questions about priorities, about what *really* matters, and to lay the foundation for the following observations.

While children are growing up, they should be cared for primarily by people who are *passionately and sacrificially committed to them.* In the vast majority of cases, the people who best fit this description are their own parents. However, grandparents, other relatives, or close friends may feel this way too.

People who are hired to take care of other people's children can and should be responsible, mature, kind, and attentive—but they will rarely be passionately and sacrificially committed to those children. Most paid caregivers are probably not going to develop a deep emotional bond or a relationship with a child that will last for years.

If at all possible, then, it is most desirable for children to spend the majority of their waking hours with one of their own parents or with someone else who has an equally intense commitment—especially during the first few years of life when children are dealing with basic issues of security and trust.

This will not always be possible for a variety of reasons. If it isn't and your child is going to spend a significant amount of time in the care of others, your energy should be expended not on guilt but on finding the best possible caregiver arrangements, a process that will be reviewed in the next section. As much as possible, continually seek ways to arrange schedules and time commitments that will maximize parental time with each child at home.

SEEKING A CAREGIVER

Assuming that your child is going to be spending time on a regular basis with a caregiver other than one of her parents, what options are available?

In-home care: the caregiver comes to your child
This person might be a relative such as a grandparent, a nanny that you hire for an extended period, or perhaps a college student or *au pair* from another country who provides care in exchange for room and board. There are several advantages of in-home care:

- Your child remains in a completely familiar environment—with access to his own crib or bed, toys, yard, etc.
- Assuming that the same person comes to your home regularly, there will be greater stability and consistency in your child's life.
- The caregiver's attention is focused specifically on your child(ren), rather than on a larger group.
- There is no exposure to contagious diseases from other children. If your child becomes ill, care does not have to be interrupted or rearranged.
- Convenience is maximized—there is no need to transport your child and the items she needs to another home or facility.

- Depending upon the caregiver's availability, there may be more flexibility in this arrangement; your home doesn't have "closing hours."

Disadvantages of in-home care are as follows:

- If you are hiring the caregiver, in-home care is likely to be more costly. In this case, the individual will in effect be your employee, so you will need to be aware of possible tax implications and even liability concerns. (For example, who pays the bills if the caregiver is injured in your home? Your homeowner's insurance may or may not cover such expenses.)
- What do you do if the caregiver is ill or can't come for some other reason? You will always need to have Plan B ready in case such a problem arises.

Family child care: your child stays in the caregiver's home
In this arrangement, an individual (or perhaps a couple) provides care in his or her home for a number of children who may be of similar or widely variable ages. (If the caregiver is a devoted relative who is responsible only for your child(ren), this situation may be essentially the equivalent of in-home care.) The advantages of family child care include:

- Your child remains in a home rather than a "facility" environment. If the family is someone you and your child already know, there will be some familiarity (and perhaps less separation anxiety).
- As with the in-home arrangement, having the same caregiver every day will provide consistency in your child's experiences.
- There are likely to be fewer children than in a day-care center, and thus less exposure to contagious diseases.
- Costs are sometimes less than for in-home care or a day-care facility.

- As with care in your own home, there is often more flexibility with hours.

Disadvantages of family child care include the following:

- There may be no licensing requirements for family caregivers in your state. In this case, you will need to rely more heavily on your own assessment of the caregiver and the home environment to determine if all is safe and sound. (Obviously, it is helpful if you know the family beforehand.)
- Plans may have to be rearranged (sometimes without warning) if the caregiver becomes ill, has an unexpected family problem, or simply goes on vacation.
- If the caregiver is responsible for several children, you will need to determine if she or he can give adequate attention to your child and not become overwhelmed.

Facility child care: your child stays at a day-care center operated by a church, university, or commercial entity
There are several advantages to this type of child care:

- These are normally licensed and thus accountable to regulations regarding the facility and the staff. These places may have extremely well-trained employees, age-appropriate learning programs, and physical resources (such as playground equipment) not available in homes.
- Facilities normally have predictable staffing and hours of operation. You will not need to make sudden adjustments because a caregiver is ill or unavailable.
- If care is provided by a church whose beliefs you share, your child might be exposed to songs, stories, and other input that build spiritual and moral values.

The disadvantages of facility child care include:

- Day-care centers sometimes have relatively large child-to-staff ratios so that individual attention for your child is in short supply.

- If the facility does not offer competitive wages, it might not attract well-trained or attentive staff. Staff turnover in some centers can be rapid, leading to unpredictable relationships between the children and their adult caregivers.

- Infections are spread much more easily among groups of children who are interacting at close range and handling the same toys. Both upper-respiratory infections (including middle-ear infection) and diarrhea are more frequent among children in day-care centers.

- While hours of operation are more predictable, they might not be very flexible. What happens if you are stuck in traffic or experience some other delay at the end of the day?

All things being equal, if care is provided on a regular, ongoing basis by someone other than a parent, the order of preference for choosing a caregiver would be as follows:

1. One or more relatives, either in your home or in theirs
2. A nonrelative in your home, such as a nanny or a live-in
3. Nonrelatives in a home setting
4. Large-group day care in a facility

This ranking is based on several key assumptions:

- A relative is more likely to be attached and attentive to your child than a nonrelative would be.
- A stable, predictable situation is more desirable than one in which there is constant change.
- If there are fewer children for each caregiver, your child is likely to receive more individual attention.
- Infections are less common among small numbers of

children than in large-group settings and even less
frequent in your own home.

As with so many other parenting concerns, there are always
exceptions to these guidelines. For example:

- A conscientious nonrelative is preferable to an
  irresponsible family member.
- A large day-care center that is well maintained and
  staffed by adults who love children is preferable to a
  home setting that is unsanitary and poorly supervised.
- A caregiver that you hire to stay in your home may not
  necessarily devote herself to your child's well-being
  while you are gone.

If you need, but do not yet have, child care available, ask some
trusted friends or coworkers for suggestions or referrals. Your
church might have references or a bulletin board listing caregivers in your community. Newspaper and yellow-page list-
ings are also possibilities, although with these you do not have
the advantage of a specific recommendation. Ultimately you
must survey the options available to you and then consider
carefully which might best meet your family's needs. In doing
so you will need to keep three factors in balance:

1. Is your child likely to thrive in this situation? How closely
   will the care duplicate (or at least resemble) the way *you*
   care for your child at home?
2. How well will the availability and location of the
   caregiver mesh with your own schedule and daily
   logistics?
3. Are the child-care arrangements affordable?

There are also specific considerations for infants and toddlers.
A baby's physical and intellectual development, as well as
emotional security, requires *ongoing* adult attention. Infants

need mental, emotional, and physical stimulation; they should not be left lying or sitting for hours in a crib or play-pen. They need to be changed when wet, comforted when crying, and played with when awake and comfortable. They should be hand-fed; propping a bottle in an infant's mouth creates a risk of choking and of ear infections. (If you are looking into a center that provides care for infants, check to see if there are a number of comfortable chairs in which adults can hold and feed babies.)

Mobile babies and toddlers need room to explore—safely. They can neither be confined to a small enclosure nor allowed to roam far and wide without supervision. Their attention can shift as rapidly as their mood, and they are not capable of playing cooperatively with other children.

In order to give adequate attention to the needs and development of infants and toddlers, there should be:

- at least one caregiver for every three children younger than two years of age. If at all possible each infant or toddler should have a main caregiver—that is, someone with whom she has an ongoing and consistent relationship.
- at least one caregiver for every four children between two and three years of age.
- at least one caregiver for every eight children between three and six years of age.

With these basic principles clearly in mind, you must also evaluate several aspects of any potential child-care arrangement, including short-term (baby-sitting) care:

The person or people involved (This is the most important.) *You should get to know those who are going to be responsible for your child's welfare.* Don't hesitate to request one or more interviews, and take the time to observe the caregiver's interactions with your own child as well as with other children.

- Does the caregiver appear comfortable, relaxed, and pleasant with children?
- How well does the caregiver interact with you?
- What prior experience does the caregiver have?
- Are references available?

If you are dealing with group care in a home or day-care center, ask the following questions about the staff before you make your decision:

- Who is in charge, and what are her or his credentials?
- What is the ratio of children to caregivers?
- If assistants are used, are they at least fourteen years old and properly supervised?
- Is everyone trained in child CPR?

The child-care setting (assuming it is not your own home)
Before choosing the best facility for your situation, look at the following:

- Is it clean, cheerful, and attractive to you and your child?
- Do tables, chairs, and other equipment appear to be in good repair?
- Are there any potential safety problems?
- Are electrical outlets covered?
- Are smoke detectors and fire extinguishers present?
- Are heating, air-conditioning, and overall ventilation adequate?
- Are cleaning supplies, medications, and other hazardous products inaccessible to children?
- Are appropriate toys available?
- Is the outdoor play area properly fenced and secured?
- Are enough mats, cots, cribs, or beds available for naps?
- Is there an area specifically designated for diaper changing? Is it cleaned after each use? Is it anywhere near where food is prepared?

- Are pets present? Are they child-friendly? Is your child allergic to animals?

Philosophy, policies, and programs (in day-care centers or group home care) Consider the following when choosing your facility:

- Are there written policies and procedures you can review?
- Is the basic worldview of the caregiver or facility compatible with yours?
- Will the values you teach at home be honored?
- Is there any spiritual input for older children?
- What is the caregiver's outlook on training and discipline?
- Are the disciplinary policies delineated and followed by all caregivers?
- Does there appear to be an appropriate balance between love and limits in dealing with behavior problems?
- What types of measures are used to maintain order?
- Is disciplinary spanking ever carried out, and if so, under what circumstances?
- Is disruptive or destructive behavior handled appropriately?
- If you observe a child's behavior being corrected, is it done with respect?
- Are children adequately supervised at all times?
- What kind of food is offered to children?
- Are activities planned and available for older children?
- Do these activities enhance learning and overall development?
- Are arts and crafts available?
- Is there excessive reliance on TV or other passive activities?

- Are there opportunities for physical exertion and outdoor play?
- What happens when a child is ill?
- Do children who are sick remain in contact with those who are not?
- Are the caregivers willing and able to give prescribed medications to infants and children?
- Are parents encouraged to drop in at any time to see how things are going? (*This is very important.* Be wary of any place where your access to your child or the facility is discouraged or restricted.)
- Is the caregiving situation appropriately secure?
- Are there clear policies regarding releasing children to adults who are not their parents?
- Can the facility prevent unauthorized individuals from entering?

RED FLAGS

While stable and nurturing child care is desirable, *safe* child care is an absolute necessity. Injuries resulting from adult carelessness, physical or sexual abuse, or assaults on a child's emotions are a parent's nightmare—and all are unacceptable in any setting. Unfortunately, signs of neglect or wrongdoing may not be especially obvious, and even if they are, it can be impossible to prove that the caregiver was at fault. Nevertheless, you will need to keep your eyes and ears wide open for any of these potential indicators of trouble:

- Does your child become unusually upset or fearful about being left with a particular caregiver?
- Does the caregiver appear impatient, irritable, or stressed?
- Has your child become more withdrawn or shown

    other signs of not being herself after spending time
    with a caregiver?
- Have you discovered unexplained bruises, welts,
  or other marks on your child's body?
- Has your child exhibited inappropriate language
  or sexual behavior?
- Do you feel uneasy whenever you leave your child with
  a particular caregiver?
- Are you discouraged from dropping in on the caregiver
  unannounced?
- If you have made an unexpected visit, have you found
  things in disarray, children improperly supervised or
  extremely upset?

If you observe one or more of these red flags, you should
strongly consider removing your child from that situation
until you can determine with greater certainty what is best in
the long run. You may need to speak candidly to the caregiver
about what you have observed and see if the response you receive is appropriate, evasive, or overtly hostile. If you believe
that your or someone else's child has been abused in a child-
care setting, you should contact your nearest child-protection
agency and explain your concerns. Even if you are not certain
whether abuse has actually taken place, it is their job to inves-
tigate more fully and take appropriate action if needed.

BABY-SITTERS

While it is vitally important to be diligent regarding the
choice of a long-term caregiver for your child, it is also important to be careful about your choice of baby-sitters, even
though the time your child spends in their care may be considerably shorter. During the first six months of your child's
life, it is best to leave her in the hands of experienced relatives
or other adults. As your child grows older, however, younger

baby-sitters can be utilized. Indeed, some of the best baby-sitters you may find will be students in high school or middle school. (Most states require that a baby-sitter be at least twelve years old if he or she is going to be unsupervised. Check your local statutes.) In many communities, hospitals or other organizations offer short courses (including CPR training) for baby-sitters, and those who have completed such a program could be excellent candidates for you to consider.

It is best to build a roster of trustworthy baby-sitters before you actually need one. Ask other mothers of young children whom they recommend and why. Responsibility, experience, and good rapport with young children are important qualities to seek. You might find some excellent sitters and have a chance to see them in action in the church nursery or Sunday school.

Once you have potential candidates, it is helpful to spend time with each one in your home. If possible, have him or her watch your child while you do some other work at home. This will give you a chance to observe how the sitter interacts with your child; it will also allow your child time to become familiar with the baby-sitter, thus reducing separation anxiety (if the child is old enough to manifest it) when you leave.

When you leave your child with a sitter, always leave the address and phone number of the location(s) where you can be reached, along with the number of your doctor, the local hospital, and another relative or friend who will be home in case you can't be reached. You might want to invest in a cell phone or pager to allow you more geographical flexibility.

Let the baby-sitter know when you expect to be home and what you expect to happen while you're gone—including feeding, bathing, and bedtime routines. If a child needs medication, make sure the baby-sitter knows exactly how much and when to give it. The sitter should also know any other family rules, such as those applying to TV or video watching, as well as any reliable ways to comfort your child when you leave. The baby-sitter should allow no visitors into your home unless you have made prior arrangements. If it helps you feel comfortable, check in with the sitter by phone after you've been gone awhile to find out how things are going.

Make sure that your pay rate is clear from the start. Ask a friend what the going rate is for each age-group and don't hesitate to offer more for the best sitter on your list. If you would like the sitter to clean up dishes or straighten up elsewhere in the home, offer to pay a little extra.

If your child is old enough to understand, tell her that you are leaving and you will be back. Don't sneak out when she isn't looking, and don't be pulled into a long, emotional parting scene. Your child will survive and, with rare exception, will calm down shortly after you leave. Enjoy the night out!

A FINAL NOTE: WHO WILL PROVIDE CARE IF YOU ARE GONE . . . FOR GOOD?

Planning for a disaster is never enjoyable. But an accident during even the most routine errand might unexpectedly leave your child(ren) without one or both parents. If such a tragedy were to take place, who would care for your children, and how would their material needs be met?

All parents must consider this possibility, carefully decide whom they would want to care for their children—along with a number of other financial, practical, and spiritual considerations—and then express their desires in a legally binding document. The specific steps involved in the preparation of a will or a living trust are beyond the scope of this book and should be reviewed with an attorney who is well versed in estate planning.

What matters most is that parents not succumb to the notion that "it can't happen to me/us" but instead take the proper measures to provide for their children should the unthinkable happen.

Emergency Care

TABLE OF CONTENTS

IF YOU DIAL 911 . . .

- Tell the dispatcher that you have a medical emergency, and then state briefly what has happened (including the age of your baby), where you are, and the number from which you are calling.
- *Stay on the line* so you can answer any questions the dispatcher might ask. He or she may also give you specific instructions for emergency care prior to the arrival of emergency personnel. Do not hang up until the dispatcher indicates it is time to do so. (He or she should hang up first.)
- If it is nighttime, turn on your outside lights— especially those that illuminate your address.
- If possible, have someone stand outside to direct the emergency personnel to the victim.

THE MEDICINE CABINET

- appropriate thermometer for infants. Know how to read it.
- petroleum jelly (Vaseline)
- antiseptic wipes
- Band-Aids and gauze pads with adhesive tape
- Steri-strips or butterfly closures
- antibacterial ointment
- elastic (Ace) bandages: 2-inch width
- acetaminophen drops or liquid (Tylenol and other brands)
- ibuprofen liquid (Children's Advil, Motrin, and others)
- instant cold packs (small plastic bags that become cold when squeezed to mix the chemicals inside them)
- tweezers

FIRST AID KIT

EMERGENCY

Prepare a first aid kit for each car and a smaller version for hiking or biking. Include the following items:

- antiseptic wipes for cleaning cuts
- antibacterial ointment
- Band-Aids
- gauze pads and adhesive tape
- infant sunblock
- instant cold pack
- elastic bandage—2-inch width
- acetaminophen (Tylenol) or ibuprofen (Children's Advil, Motrin, or others)
- tweezers
- Steri-strips or butterfly closures
- money for a phone call

Emergencies
(listed alphabetically)

Important: For the convenience of new parents, this section includes material encompassing the first year of your baby's life. This advice is intended solely to assist you in providing immediate care for your baby while you are contacting his or her physician or another qualified professional (such as your local emergency department, or, if necessary, the 911 emergency response line). All of the problems discussed in this section should be discussed with—and in most cases evaluated by—a health-care provider who cares for infants. *This is especially important if your baby is younger than three months of age.*

ALLERGIC REACTIONS

GENERALIZED ALLERGIC REACTIONS
Generalized allergic reactions can vary greatly in severity, from mild itching to life-threatening anaphylaxis, and may occur in response to:

- medications
- foods
- substances called **contrast materials** that are injected into the body during certain X-ray procedures
- insect stings

SYMPTOMS   *of mild reactions*
- rash—typically scattered widely over the body. Raised, itchy welts called **hives** are a common manifestation of a generalized allergic reaction.
- in more severe reactions, coughing,

E M E R G E N C Y

wheezing, and/or swelling of the face, tongue, or throat may occur

SYMPTOMS   *of anaphylaxis (anaphylactic shock)*

In the more severe, life-threatening reaction known as anaphylaxis, these symptoms may develop very rapidly and be very intense. In addition to the above, the following may occur:

- difficulty swallowing or breathing
- nausea/vomiting
- abdominal cramps
- sudden drop in blood pressure, manifested by pale, clammy skin; altered consciousness or unconsciousness; and rapid, weak pulse

Anaphylaxis may lead to cardiac arrest and death if not treated promptly.

TREATMENT   *for mild or moderate reactions*

- Your baby's physician may recommend an antihistamine to relieve itching and help diminish the reaction. He or she will advise you regarding the specific medication and dose.
- If you think the reaction involves a medication, discuss with your baby's physician (or the physician on call if he or she is not available) whether that medication should be discontinued, and if so whether another can or should be substituted for it.
- When a drug reaction (of any kind—see

E M E R G E N C Y

below) has occurred, remind your baby's doctor during the next office visit to ensure that the information about the reaction is recorded on the permanent medical record. You should also keep your own list of any such reactions so that you can provide it if needed in an emergency or after office hours.

♦ If coughing, wheezing, or swelling of the face or tongue are occurring, call your baby's physician immediately or go to the nearest emergency room.

TREATMENT   *for severe reactions (those involving rapid swelling of face/throat/tongue or difficulty breathing)*

♦ Call 911.
♦ If the baby has been bitten, stung, or has ingested a substance, any of which have caused severe reactions in the past, call 911, even before symptoms are evident.
♦ Try to keep yourself and your baby calm.
♦ Check the ABCs—airway, breathing, and circulation. If necessary, begin CPR (see page 312).
♦ If the episode follows a bee sting, remove the stinger. Scrape it off with a credit card or other flat object—*do not use tweezers, since this may squeeze more venom into the skin.*
♦ Lay the infant down on a flat surface, cover him with a blanket or a coat, and elevate his feet (to help maintain his blood pressure).

- DO NOT elevate the head if there is a breathing problem; this may aggravate a blockage of the airway.
- If your baby has had an anaphylactic reaction, talk to his doctor about obtaining emergency treatment kits containing an injection of epinephrine (for example, EpiPen or Ana-Kit) that can partially or completely reverse the reaction. These should be available at home, in the car, and in the gear taken on camping trips or other outings.
- A child who has had an anaphylactic reaction should wear a medical ID tag with this information, especially if he may need an emergency injection of epinephrine.

A child can have an allergic reaction to a substance that has never caused problems before, even with many prior contacts. If a reaction occurs, every reasonable effort should be made to prevent contact with that substance in the future because reactions that were initially mild can become more severe with further exposure.

ALLERGIC REACTION OR DRUG SIDE EFFECT?
Some children (and adults) experience side effects from over-the-counter (OTC) or prescription medications. Examples of common side effects are drowsiness with many antihistamines, nausea and/or diarrhea from certain antibiotics, and dry mouth from some forms of antidepressants. These reactions can vary considerably from person to person, and over time they can also change in a given individual using the same

drug. Usually the potential side effects of a medication are listed on the label of an OTC drug. For prescription drugs, the physician will often review possible side effects, or the effects will be noted by the pharmacist when the prescription is filled.

Side effects are not the same as allergic reactions, which involve a specific response of the immune system. Distinguishing between side effects and allergic reactions is important: if a true allergic reaction has occurred, repeated doses of the same or a related drug might cause a more serious reaction in the future. By contrast, side effects may or may not occur if the drug is taken in the future. Sometimes a symptom that might seem like a drug reaction actually has no relationship to the medication, and the timing of its appearance is purely coincidental. Deciding whether or not a drug has caused a particular problem and whether it may be safely taken in the future can often be difficult and should be discussed with your child's physician.

BITES AND STINGS

ANIMAL BITES

TREATMENT — If your baby has been bitten by any animal, wild or domestic, do the following:

- Clean the wound at once with water and mild soap.
- If the wound is severe—with large tears or perforations—handle it as you would any large wound (see Wounds and Wound Care).
- Contact your baby's doctor as soon as possible.

CONCERNS ABOUT RABIES

The major concern after the bite wound is treated is whether or not the baby will need specific treatment to prevent rabies (a viral infection that is nearly always fatal). If the wild animal has been caught, it will be killed and its brain examined microscopically for evidence of this disease. While awaiting the results of this examination—or more commonly, if the animal is not captured and its brain cannot be evaluated—a decision must be made whether or not to begin a rabies vaccination series. This will depend to a large degree on the type of animal involved and the circumstances of the bite.

In most parts of the United States, bites from wild rodents such as squirrels, rats, chipmunks, mice, and rabbits usually will not be treated with rabies vaccination. However, your baby's doctor may consult the local public-health authority for specific advice. On the other hand, skunks, raccoons, opossums, bats, and all wild carnivores should always be considered potentially rabid (rabies carrying) and should never be touched, even in a park or other setting where they are accustomed to receiving food from human hands. A bite from one of these animals—especially if the animal was not provoked or defending itself—is more likely to raise concerns about rabies.

Bites from domestic animals (dogs, cats, etc.) are more common but rarely cause rabies. If someone is bitten by a domestic animal, treat the wound as described above. The animal will usually be available for observation, and public-health officials may quarantine it for ten to fourteen days. If the animal appears normal at the end of the quarantine, no rabies vaccination is required. But if the animal becomes ill, it will be promptly sacrificed and its brain examined microscopically for rabies. Rabies treatment and vaccination should be started as soon as a quarantined animal is found to be ill, and not delayed while awaiting results of the brain examination.

When purchased from pet stores, **mice, rats, gerbils,** and **hamsters** are not known to transmit rabies.

Wild animals that have been raised as pets—such as raccoons, skunks, foxes, wolves, ferrets, and small wildcats can carry rabies even if they have appeared healthy in captivity for long periods. This is particularly true of skunks, which have had rabies virus isolated from their saliva even when born in captivity.

PREVENTING DOG BITES

- Before you get a dog, consider the breed and gender. Female dogs and neutered males are less likely to bite than non-neutered males. Some breeds of dogs are more aggressive than others.
- Don't leave infants unattended with a dog.
- Obedience training for dogs—which should not involve harsh physical punishment—is a worthwhile investment.
- When walking your dog, observe local leash laws. Do not let your dog approach an infant or child it does not know.

HUMAN BITES

These bites commonly become infected because they are likely to be heavily contaminated by bacteria, which are abundant in saliva.

TREATMENT
- Clean the wound at once with water and mild soap.
- If the wound is actively bleeding, apply steady pressure with clean gauze or washcloth.
- Keep covered with a sterile bandage, or at

least a clean cloth, until the wound is
examined by a medical professional.

◆ Because of the risk of infection, any
human bite that breaks the skin should
be evaluated by your baby's physician or
other qualified professional. Antibiotics
are usually prescribed for all but the most
minor wounds.

BEE AND WASP STINGS

Honeybees almost always leave the stinger (with attached
venom sac) in the skin. This should be removed as quickly
as possible by scraping the skin at the stinger base with a
credit card or other flat object. Do not grasp the venom sac
with fingers or tweezers because this will inject the venom
remaining in the sac into the skin. (Wasp stingers are
smooth and do not remain in the skin.)

SYMPTOMS   *of response to venom*

◆ pain, redness, and swelling at the sting site
◆ itching, sometimes intense, 12 to 24 hours
later

TREATMENT   ◆ Apply a cool, moistened washcloth to the
affected area.
◆ Call your baby's physician for further
advice.

SYMPTOMS   *of hypersensitivity reaction*

◆ significant swelling, usually beginning one
or two days after the sting and spreading
past one or more neighboring joints
◆ mild itchiness
◆ usually very mild pain, or no pain at all

EMERGENCY

TREATMENT
- After evaluating the reaction, your baby's physician may recommend an antihistamine (to relieve itching) and/or prescribe a brief course of oral cortisone to help diminish the reaction. He or she will advise you regarding the specific medication(s) and dose.
- Antibiotics are rarely necessary.

SYMPTOMS *of multiple stings*

A toxic reaction may occur when a person is stung multiple times, often 10 or more.
- moderate swelling
- vomiting
- diarrhea

TREATMENT Go to an emergency facility immediately or call 911. Severe symptoms can develop quickly, and the emergency room is better equipped to treat a serious reaction to bee or wasp venom.

SYMPTOMS *of life-threatening or anaphylactic reaction*

This reaction affects the entire body and can result from one or multiple stings. Initial symptoms occur shortly after the sting. For symptoms and treatment, see *Anaphylaxis*, page 260.

PREVENTION

If your baby has a severe reaction to an insect sting, talk to his doctor about obtaining emergency treatment kits containing an injection of epinephrine (for example, EpiPen or Ana-Kit) that can partially or completely reverse a similar reaction in the future. These should be available at home, in the car, and in gear taken on camping trips or other outings. The child should wear a medical ID tag indicating that he is at risk for this type of reaction, especially if he may need an emergency injection of epinephrine.

SPIDER BITES

In the continental United States and Canada only the bites of brown recluse and black widow spiders inject venom that can cause serious problems. However, any spider bite can cause significant swelling.

BROWN RECLUSE

SYMPTOMS   Often the brown recluse bite is at first painless or causes only a brief stinging. Several hours later pain begins around the site and can become severe. The involved area often has a "red, white, and blue" appearance: a wide area of reddened skin, within which is a smaller patch of white-appearing skin, and finally a central bluish discoloration around the fang marks. The central (blue) area usually forms an ulcer that may take weeks or months to heal and occasionally requires skin grafting. This procedure is generally done about two months after the bite because the graft may slough off if applied to the poisoned area too early. Other possible symptoms of brown recluse bites include fever, skin rash, nausea or vomiting, joint pain, and bloody urine.

TREATMENT   Treatment will depend on the response of the skin where the bite occurred, as well as the presence of other symptoms. You should contact your baby's physician if you believe she has been bitten by a brown recluse spider, or if you notice the symptoms described above.

PREVENTION

Brown recluse spiders prefer warm, dry, and abandoned locations—for example, vacant buildings, woodpiles or sheds, or seldom-used closets. The spider is brown with a violin-shaped marking on its back. Active primarily at night, they usually bite when trapped in clothing or shoes. Be careful when delving into closets and other spaces that have been undisturbed, and shake out clothes and shoes that have been stored awhile or that are kept in areas where brown recluse spiders have been seen.

BLACK WIDOW

SYMPTOMS   A black widow bite is generally unnoticed at first but then becomes painful—often severely so—within 15 minutes to 4 hours. Pain will usually reach a peak in 2 or 3 hours, but it can last up to 48 hours. Associated muscle spasm, which may be very severe, contributes to the pain. Usually only two tiny red spots are visible at the bite site, or no local reaction may be seen at all.

TREATMENT   Treatment will depend on the infant's response to the bite. You should contact your baby's doctor's immediately if you believe she has been bitten by a black widow spider, or if you notice the symptoms described above. An antivenin is available, but it is generally reserved for severe cases, which are more commonly seen in infants and young children.

PREVENTION
The black widow is a shy, coal black spider with a red or yellow hourglass marking on the underside of the abdomen. Only the female spider bites. She builds a chaotic, irregular-shaped web that is easy to recognize when compared to the highly symmetrical webs of other spiders. The black widow is found throughout the United States, preferring warm, dry environments, both indoors and out.

TARANTULAS
These spiders bite only when handled roughly, and thus the likelihood of a newborn or young infant accidentally being bitten by one is extremely remote. Tarantula bites can be painless or can cause a deep, throbbing discomfort that generally stops after an hour. Usually the only treatment needed is pain relief, although most of the discomfort usually subsides before the medication takes effect. Nevertheless, in the unlikely event of a bite involving a young infant, contact your baby's physician or a local emergency department.

TICK BITES
Because ticks cannot fly or jump, they are normally picked up when humans brush against shrubs, grasses, or animals that harbor them. As a result, tick bites in young infants are very uncommon. While insignificant in and of themselves, some ticks transmit infections that can be serious, including Lyme disease and Rocky Mountain spotted fever. Generally, most tick-borne diseases are transmitted only after the tick has remained attached to the skin for many hours. For example, transmission of Lyme disease is unusual if the tick has been attached less than 24 to 48 hours.

In the unlikely event that you find a tick attached to your baby's skin, contact his physician or a local emergency department to discuss removing it, as well as any recommended follow up. If you cannot get medical care immediately and need to remove the tick yourself, proceed as follows:

> Ticks must be removed *gently* and *completely*. Do not squeeze, crush, or squash ticks that are on your child's body. Instead, use a pair of tweezers to pull the tick off with a gentle, outward motion. Do not twist while pulling, because this may cause the head to break off and remain within the skin. If you don't have tweezers, use your fingertip—covered with tissue or a latex glove if available—and some thread. Place the thread around the tick and pull gently. If the head remains under the skin, use a sterilized needle to remove it as you would a splinter or sliver.
>
> Applying rubbing alcohol, fingernail polish, or petroleum jelly to the tick is not likely to cause it to release its grip. Once the tick is removed, wash the area thoroughly with soap and water.

BLEEDING

Bleeding can arise from two sources:

- veins, which carry a slow and steady supply of blood back to the heart, or
- arteries, which carry blood under higher pressure from the heart to the rest of the body

An arterial injury is potentially more serious because blood escaping under pressure may be lost in large amounts in relatively little time. The amount of blood directly visible is not necessarily a reliable sign of the severity of an injury and may not reflect how much blood a person has lost. For example, some serious injuries do not bleed heavily or may bleed internally. Some minor wounds, such as scalp lacerations, may appear to bleed profusely, but in fact the amount of blood lost is relatively insignificant.

TREATMENT

- If time permits, wash your hands before tending a wound. This will help prevent infecting the wound with any bacteria on your hands.
- If there is severe external bleeding or evidence of major trauma, CALL 911.
- Try to keep the infant (and yourself) calm.
- Remove any loose debris from the wound.
- Apply direct pressure to the wound using a sterile dressing or a clean cloth unless there is an eye injury, skull fracture, or an embedded object. In these cases do not apply direct pressure.
- If an arm or a leg is bleeding, elevate it above the level of the heart unless movement causes increased pain or you suspect the arm or leg is fractured.
- If direct pressure has stopped the bleeding but it starts again, reapply pressure.
- If you must free your hands, apply a pressure bandage (see page 274).
- If the wound is large enough to make direct pressure ineffective or if direct pressure has not stopped the bleeding after 15 minutes, pressure-point bleeding control may be necessary (see page 274).

- If there is no indication of neck, head, or back injury and the bleeding is severe, take steps to prevent shock (a severe drop in blood pressure). Signs of shock include bluish color of the fingernails or lips, clammy skin, pale skin color, weakness, and decreasing alertness. If one or more of these occur, be sure that someone has called 911. Lay the baby flat, and if possible elevate the feet. Cover the baby with a blanket or coat.
- DO NOT move a baby who may have an injury to the head, neck, or back.
- DO NOT attempt to clean a large wound because this could aggravate bleeding that would otherwise slow down.
- DO NOT probe, explore, or pull any embedded object out of a wound. This also may increase bleeding.
- DO NOT apply ice directly to a wound.
- DO NOT use a tourniquet.
- DO NOT remove a dressing that becomes soaked with blood or attempt to peek at the wound to see if bleeding has stopped. These actions can disturb the wound surface and may actually increase bleeding. If necessary, add more dressings.

Even when bleeding is controlled, many wounds require medical attention, including:

- gaping wounds
- animal or human bites
- wounds located directly over joints
- wounds associated with a broken bone,

loss of muscular function, or loss of sensation

TREATMENT   *applying a pressure bandage*

If you need to free your hands to move the baby or attend to other injuries (whether or not the bleeding has stopped), a pressure bandage can be applied. This holds the dressings in place while maintaining direct pressure on the wound.

1. Apply a dressing of sterile gauze to the wound or clean cloth if gauze is not available. Wrap long strips of cloth or a long bandage around the area where the wound is located to hold the dressing in place.
2. Cut or split the end of the bandage or cloth into two strips and tie these together to secure the bandage in place. The knot should be tied directly over the wound.
3. Make sure the pressure dressing is not too tight! It should be tight enough to maintain pressure on the wound, but not so tight that it prevents the tissue beyond the wound (that is, more distant from the heart) from receiving the blood it needs. If the area beyond the dressing is throb-bing with pain and/or becoming blue and cold, the bandage should be loosened.

TREATMENT   *pressure-point bleeding control*

Important: If you need to use this technique, be sure that someone has called 911 and medical help is on the way.

This technique is used to control bleeding from an extremity (an arm or leg) only when other methods have not worked. First try using direct pressure combined with elevation of the extremity. Pressure-point bleeding control is a last resort because areas of the body that are not bleeding will also have their blood flow reduced.

Each arm or leg has a major artery supplying it. When bleeding cannot be controlled by other means, pressure on that specific artery can reduce blood flow. When this approach is accompanied by direct pressure to the wound and (if possible) elevation of the injured area, bleeding can usually be controlled.

When the bleeding is coming from the leg, the pressure point is over the **femoral artery**. If there are no suspected injuries to the head, neck, or spine and the baby can be moved, place her on her back. Locate the femoral artery at the point where the leg and the groin meet, a little toward the groin side. Use four fingers to feel for a pulse. Once the pulse has been located, apply firm pressure with the heel of the hand to compress the artery against the underlying bone.

When the bleeding is coming from the arm, the pressure point is over the **brachial artery**. This can be found at the middle of the inner aspect of the arm, just underneath the biceps muscle on the top of the arm. After you have found the pulse, use four fingers along the path of the artery to apply pressure and compress the artery against the underlying bone.

Remember: Elevation of the limb and direct pressure on the wound should be continued along with pressure-point bleeding control. When performed correctly, this technique will stop or significantly reduce major bleeding.

BLEEDING WITHOUT A VISIBLE WOUND

Symptoms   Bleeding can occur without visible wounds. Bleeding can be significant in these situations:

- Blood in the stool. This can be bright red, which indicates bleeding from a source at or near the anal opening, or a deep purplish black, which usually is more characteristic of blood lost from the upper intestinal tract.
- Any vaginal bleeding.
- Blood in the urine. This may be bright red, which usually occurs with bleeding from the bladder or urethra (the tube through which urine exits the body) or a darker (tea) color, which suggests an origin within the kidney. Blood in the urine should be fully investigated by your child's doctor.
- Vomited blood. This may arise from bleeding within the stomach or esophagus (the passage between the throat and stomach). An acute illness such as gastroenteritis (stomach flu) may produce

blood-tinged vomited material but not
blood itself. Any vomiting of bright red
material should prompt an immediate call
to your baby's physician.

TREATMENT | Any of the above situations calls for medical
evaluation or consultation.

BONE AND JOINT INJURIES

FRACTURES AND DISLOCATIONS

A fracture (or broken bone) occurs when enough force is
applied to a bone to disrupt its structure and break it.

A dislocation occurs when the bones on either side of a
joint move out of their normal alignment with one another.
Either of the bones involved in a dislocation may also be
fractured.

SYMPTOMS | One or more of the following may indicate
that a fracture or dislocation has taken
place:
  ◆ swelling
  ◆ deformity
  ◆ moderate to severe pain
  ◆ localized tenderness
  ◆ poor function or movement of the
    involved area

TREATMENT | ◆ Avoid putting pressure or weight on the
    affected area.
  ◆ Gently splint the affected area to reduce
    pain and prevent further damage. Splints
    should be applied across at least one joint
    above and below the suspected fracture.

Elbows should be supported on a pillow, and suspected arm or shoulder injuries should be placed in a sling while the infant is taken to the emergency room. A leg may be splinted by carefully binding it to the other leg with a towel placed between them. Toes and fingers usually do not require splinting but should be protected until they're examined by a doctor.

- If the neck appears to be involved, the baby should not be moved without a backboard and neck brace, which will normally be provided by an emergency transport team.
- Don't try to set or realign fractures or dislocations. Significant additional injury can occur through inappropriate movement of an injured limb.
- If possible, cover any open wounds to try to prevent further contamination.
- Take your baby to his physician or the nearest emergency room for treatment.

OPEN FRACTURES

With this type of injury one end of a fractured bone is protruding through the skin.

TREATMENT   Cover the wound (using a sterile dressing, if available) and take the baby to an emergency facility immediately. Don't give the baby anything to eat or drink, because surgery will likely be required.

BURNS

The most widely used classification system for burns categorizes them according to size and depth. Since first aid treatment depends on a burn's severity, it is important to check the center of the wound. This is usually where the burn will be deepest, and its appearance will give an indication of the type of treatment the burn needs.

Important: *Any* burn involving a baby—especially a newborn—should be immediately discussed with (and will nearly always need to be evaluated by) a physician or other qualified health-care provider.

WHAT NOT TO DO FOR A BURN

- Do not open blisters. When sealed, they normally provide excellent protection for the underlying skin. However, in some situations a physician may rupture and remove the covering of a blister using a sterile technique, especially if infection is evident.
- Do not attempt to remove clothing that is stuck to a burn because this could peel away the skin.
- Do not use butter, antiseptic creams, or any other folk remedies on burns. These items may significantly slow the healing process and can actually cause or contribute to infection.

FIRST-DEGREE (SUPERFICIAL) BURNS

These burns are the most common and the least severe. They can be caused by sun exposure or brief contact of skin with hot water or a hot surface such as the burner on a stove.

Symptoms	• bright redness of the affected area, but no blisters
	• mild swelling

- minor pain—because first-degree burns irritate nerve endings

TREATMENT
- Hold the affected area under cold running water for several minutes.
- Do not use ice, which might reduce the local blood supply.
- To soothe the pain, use a nonprescription pain reliever for infants.

SECOND-DEGREE (PARTIAL-THICKNESS) BURNS

These are generally caused by contact with hot liquid and occasionally by sunburn.

SYMPTOMS
Second-degree burns are characterized by blisters that form because the burn penetrates more deeply into the skin, causing body fluids to be released.

TREATMENT
- Immediately submerge the burned area in cold water.
- Keep cold water in contact with the burn for at least five minutes or until medical help is given.
- If the burn covers a very small area, treat it the same as a first-degree burn, but call your baby's doctor for further advice.
- If the burn is more widespread, apply cool, wet cloths to the affected areas and see a doctor immediately. A sizable burn will require medical follow-up, including regular dressing changes, topical medication if appropriate, adequate pain relief, and possibly antibiotics.

- ◆ Extensive partial-thickness burns can be serious or even fatal and may require specialized medical care. Very often this is carried out at a regional burn center.

THIRD-DEGREE (FULL-THICKNESS) BURNS

These are the most serious and, if extensive, can be fatal. All skin layers are destroyed, and the surface will usually appear charred or white. Paradoxically, full-thickness burns do not hurt as much as the others because the nerve endings in the skin are no longer functioning.

TREATMENT Do not attempt to treat this type of burn; call for medical attention immediately.

Burns of varying size and depth can occur in the following ways:

THERMAL BURNS

Scalds, the most common thermal burns, are usually caused by contact with hot water. Exposing skin to water at 140°F for three seconds or 156°F for one second will result in a scald. (Coffee is usually about 180°F when freshly brewed.) Immersion burns (such as occur in a hot bathtub) involve longer contact and usually burn a wider area. Because grease or hot oil is around 400°F and may not run off of skin as quickly as water does, it tends to cause deeper burns.

Flame or **flash burns** are the next most common thermal burns, and these result from fires or explosions. It is important to remove the baby immediately from the heat source and take off burning or smoldering clothing. An infant with flash burns should be observed for wheezing or difficulty in breathing.

Contact burns are often deep and are caused by touching hot surfaces such as curling irons, stoves, hot coals, etc.

TREATMENT Treatment for any thermal burn includes
immediate application of cool water,
which will decrease pain and may reduce
the extent of skin damage. Do not apply
sprays, creams, or butter to this (or any
other) type of burn.

ELECTRICAL BURNS
See Also Electric Shock.

TREATMENT ♦ Separate the baby from the electrical
source. Do not touch the child until it
is certain that he is no longer in contact
with the source of electricity.
♦ Check for a pulse and administer CPR
if necessary.
♦ Because of the possibility of internal
damage, a baby who has sustained an
electrical burn should see a physician
even if it does not appear he is in
immediate discomfort.

CHEMICAL BURNS
Chemical burns are commonly caused by household
cleansers and solvents. Alkali burns tend to be more serious
than acid burns.

TREATMENT ♦ Carefully remove contaminated clothing.
♦ Flush thoroughly with water for at least
10 minutes.
♦ Call your baby's physician or take the
baby to the nearest emergency facility.

CARBON MONOXIDE POISONING

Carbon monoxide poisoning is likely to occur

- wherever there is fire or smoke, especially in enclosed places
- in poorly ventilated rooms that are heated by wood-burning stoves or kerosene-type space heaters
- in closed garages where gasoline engines are running
- in cars that have faulty exhaust systems

You would be wise to buy and install one or more carbon monoxide detectors in your home. They are relatively inexpensive, and their early warning of the presence of this deadly but odorless gas may save the life of your infant or your entire family.

SYMPTOMS	Early signs of carbon monoxide poisoning include

- headache (which could be signaled by crying or irritability)
- mild difficulty breathing

Signs of more severe poisoning are

- nausea/vomiting
- reddening of the skin
- sleepiness
- unusual behavior
- loss of consciousness

Carbon monoxide poisoning should be strongly suspected if several individuals in the same house develop these symptoms simultaneously.

TREATMENT	• Move everyone to fresh air immediately.

- If someone is unconscious, begin rescue breathing or CPR if necessary (see page 312).
- Whether there is one or many victims, seek medical evaluation as quickly as possible. If no one can drive or a victim is unconscious, call 911 for emergency treatment and transportation.
- After each person has received treatment, contact the local gas company or fire department so they can check for carbon monoxide in the home.
- The primary treatment for carbon monoxide poisoning is 100 percent oxygen given by mask for several hours.

CHOKING

See also **Cardiopulmonary Resuscitation (CPR) and Choking Emergencies, page 312.**

1. Determine if the baby is choking.
   - If there is forceful coughing or the baby can cry, do not interfere.
   - If she is unable to cry, cough, or breathe or if she is coughing very weakly, have someone call 911 and take immediate action (step 2 and following).

2. Position the baby face down on your forearm.
   - Support the baby's head and jaw as you turn her face down.
   - Position her so that her head is lower than her chest.

3. Give 5 back blows.
   - Use the heel of your free hand.
   - Strike forcefully between her shoulder blades.

4. Turn the baby onto her back.
   - Support the baby's head and jaw as you roll her over.
   - Rest her back on your thigh.

5. Give 5 thrusts to the chest.
   - Place 2 fingers in the center of her breastbone (just below the level of the nipples).
   - Thrust downward quickly about $\frac{1}{3}$ to $\frac{1}{2}$ the depth of the chest.

6. Repeat steps 2 through 5.
   - Turn the baby face down.
   - Give 5 back blows.
   - Turn the baby on her back.
   - Give 5 chest thrusts.

7. Repeat this sequence until the baby begins to cough or breathe, or until she coughs up the object.

If the baby is unconscious:

8. Have someone call 911 for help, if this has not been done already.

9. Roll the baby onto her back.
   - Support her head and neck, keeping them in a straight line with her back.
   - Lay the baby on a firm surface.

10. Clear any material from the baby's mouth.
    - Use the fingers and thumb of one hand to grasp and lift the baby's lower jaw and tongue.
    - Use the little finger of your other hand to sweep the object or food out.
      (a) Be careful not to push any object or food farther down.

E
M
E
R
G
E
N
C
Y

11. Check to see if she is breathing.
    ◆ Gently tilt her head back and lift her chin to open
      the airway.
    ◆ Put your head near the infant's mouth and nose.
    ◆ For 3 to 5 seconds, look, listen, and feel for
      breathing.
      (a) Is the chest rising?
      (b) Can you hear breathing sounds?
      (c) Can you feel air moving against your face?

12. If you can't see, hear, or feel the infant breathing, you
    must immediately begin breathing for her (rescue
    breathing).
    ◆ With your lips make a tight seal around the baby's
      nose and mouth.
    ◆ Give 2 slow breaths.
      (a) Breathe into the infant for about 1 to 1½
          seconds, watching for the chest to rise.
      (b) Pause to let the air flow out, and then give
          another breath.

If the breaths will not go in:

13. Tilt the head farther back, lift the chin, and try to
    ventilate again.

If the breaths still will not go in, the airway is probably blocked.

14. Repeat the sequence of back blows and chest thrusts
    until the baby is breathing on her own or you are able
    to inflate her lungs.
    ◆ Turn the baby face down.
    ◆ Give 4 back blows.
    ◆ Turn the baby on her back.
    ◆ Give 4 chest thrusts.
    ◆ Check the mouth for any object or food. If you see

> an object, remove it. DO NOT perform a blind
> finger sweep.
> ♦ Tilt the head back.
> ♦ Attempt to give a breath. If the chest does not rise,
>   then re-tilt the head and attempt ventilation again.
> ♦ Continue this cycle until the object is expelled or
>   advanced care arrives.

15. Once you are getting air into the victim, check for
    breathing and pulse. (See CPR, page 312.)
    ♦ If she is not breathing, begin rescue breathing.
      (See CPR, page 312.)
    ♦ If she does not have a pulse, begin CPR. (See CPR,
      page 312.)

PREVENTION
♦ Keep small, hard objects away from your baby. This
  includes hard candy, nuts, popcorn, hot dogs, chewing
  gum, and hard fruits and vegetables.
♦ Remove small toys or hanging mobiles from the crib
  before the baby is able to reach them.
♦ Use only unbreakable toys that have no sharp edges
  or small parts that can come loose.
♦ Do not allow electrical or hanging cords within reach
  of a crib.
♦ Do not allow an infant to wear a necklace.
♦ Keep plastic bags and balloons out of reach of all
  children. A popped or deflated balloon in a baby's
  mouth, if inhaled, could easily obstruct his airway.

SWALLOWED OBJECTS

It is not uncommon for children to swallow nonfood
objects, either deliberately or accidentally. Toddlers, who are
prone to place small items into the mouth, are at particular
risk for this type of accident. Fortunately, once the object

passes through the esophagus (the tube that carries food from the throat to the stomach), it will usually progress through the rest of the intestinal tract without difficulty. As this occurs, the child will not show any signs of distress, except in rare cases where an odd-shaped (and usually pointed) object such as a toothpick becomes stuck or perforates the bowel.

TREATMENT   An X-ray may be done to try to confirm the object's location (although not all objects will be visible on an X-ray), and the child's stools may be examined for the next few days until the object passes. If it is not found after 4 to 7 days, a second X-ray may be performed. (If the object is metallic, some emergency facilities use a metal detector to track its progress.) Seek immediate medical attention if abdominal pain develops before the object has passed out of the child's body.

SYMPTOMS   *of object lodged in esophagus*

A small percentage of swallowed objects become lodged in the esophagus. When this occurs, a mild pain will usually develop in the chest below the sternum (breastbone), along with increased salivation caused by the inability to swallow.

TREATMENT   ◆ DO NOT attempt to force the object into the stomach by giving fluids or food.
◆ In most cases the object will pass into the stomach within 10 minutes. But if pain or difficulty in swallowing persists, the child will need emergency medical attention.

EMERGENCY

An X-ray of the chest/abdomen will usually disclose the location of the object. A specialist may be consulted and an **endoscopy** done. In this procedure a narrow, flexible fiber-optic device, known as an endoscope, is passed into the sedated child's esophagus in an attempt to dislodge or remove the foreign body.

TREATMENT *for swallowing small batteries*

If a child swallows a small "button battery"—the small, round battery used in watches, hearing aids, and other electronic devices—see a doctor immediately. A button battery that does not pass through the esophagus must be removed (usually using an endoscope) because it can cause a serious local erosion or even a perforation within a matter of hours.

DROWNING

TREATMENT
- Prolonged lack of oxygen from being submerged under water leads to cardiac arrest, so it is important that rescue breathing or CPR (either mouth-to-mouth or mouth-to-nose ventilation) be started immediately—even in the water if necessary.
- Call 911 for medical assistance and a quick transfer to the nearest emergency center.
- If you know what happened prior to the accident, tell the rescue workers,

> particularly if head and neck injuries are
> likely.
> ♦ Keep the infant warm, especially if he was
>   in cold water. Wrap him in towels or a
>   blanket until medical personnel arrive.

PREVENTION

Studies show that 70 percent of drowning accidents could
be avoided if self-closing, self-latching doors were installed
in homes and on gates in the fences around pools. Sturdy,
childproof pool covers and alarms on doors leading to the
pool area—or even an alarm that sounds when someone
enters the water—are also appropriate safety measures. Parents need to teach their children the importance of swimming only when supervised and the necessity of life jackets
when boating. Older children and adolescents should be
warned explicitly of the risks of alcohol and/or drug consumption while swimming or boating.

When young children are around water, they must always be supervised by an adult. Parents and teens should
strongly consider becoming certified in CPR. Poolside tele-
phones are helpful because they allow adults to answer the
phone while continuing supervision. They also can speed
the process of calling for help if an accident occurs.

RATES OF SURVIVAL

The chances of surviving submersion are not significantly
affected by the type of water (salt, fresh, or pool water with
chemicals). How long a child can survive without oxygen
depends on many other factors, including age, previous
health, the water temperature, and the speed and effectiveness of the rescue effort. Children under age five have an
advantage because of a nerve reflex that causes the heart to
slow down and blood to be diverted to the brain and heart.
Younger children usually survive if submersion lasts less

than 3 minutes and may survive a submersion lasting up to 10 minutes if the water temperature is 50° to 60°F (10° to 15°C). In general, cold water temperatures improve survival chances.

EAR PAIN AND INJURY

A blow to the side of the head that results in significant swelling or bleeding from the outer ear, bleeding from the ear canal, or loss of hearing should be evaluated by a physician as soon as possible. Ear pain that is not associated with trauma usually arises from infection of the ear canal or middle ear and will also need medical assessment.

REMOVING OBJECTS FROM THE EAR

Occasionally a small object (such as a bead, a small bean, or an insect) may find its way into your infant's ear. While the sensations experienced by the child can be annoying, these situations do not pose a threat to hearing, and you should try to remain calm.

TREATMENT   It may be possible to remove the object/insect at home by following these steps:

- If an insect has entered the ear canal, put a few drops of oil (mineral, baby, or vegetable) or peroxide in the ear canal.
- If you can see the object or insect in the ear, carefully remove it with tweezers—but only if it is clearly visible at the opening of the ear canal.
- If you cannot see the object clearly or if it is deeper within the ear canal, tilt your child's head to the side of the injured ear.

- ◆ If this doesn't work, leave the infant
  alone. Attempting to remove the object
  may damage the ear. Seek medical
  attention as soon as possible.

ELECTRIC SHOCK

Most electric-shock incidents involving young children
occur in the home through contact with electrical outlets,
cords, or appliances. Crawling babies and toddlers are particularly at risk of shock from biting electrical cords or
inserting objects into electrical sockets. Most of these shocks
cause minor injuries or burns unless the child is in water
when the electrical contact is made.

PREVENTION

- ◆ Cover all electrical outlets with safety plugs before
  your infant is able to crawl or walk.
- ◆ Unplug bathroom and other small appliances when
  they are not in use.
- ◆ Keep electrical cords out of children's reach.

EYE INJURIES

In general, any direct injury to an infant's eye—cut or puncture, a blow with an object or fist, or debris in the eye—
should receive immediate medical attention.

TREATMENT   ◆ Until it is seen by a doctor, keep the eye
              closed. This is a natural response to eye
              injury and helps reduce discomfort.
            ◆ If the eye has been penetrated or cut
              open, take the infant directly to the
              emergency room. If there is fluid oozing

from the eye, transfer your baby lying flat on his back so additional fluid will not escape.

♦ Hold a simple shield, such as a paper cup, over the eye to protect it—but don't exert any pressure on the eye.

CHEMICALS IN THE EYE

TREATMENT   Take prompt action whenever any chemical has splashed into the eye. Although many materials will cause only minor irritation, some can result in serious injury or blindness if not attended to immediately.

Start immediate and continued flushing with lukewarm water. A gentle flow of water should run into the affected eye(s). Carefully pour water from a glass or pitcher into the eye(s) with the infant lying down. If only one eye is involved, hold the baby on her side with the affected eye down so none of the chemical can accidentally flow into the other eye. You will probably need to have another adult hold the eye open while you pour the water. Use the following formula guidelines to determine how long to irrigate the eye:

♦ alkaline materials: 20 minutes
♦ acids: 10 minutes
♦ less reactive chemicals: 5 minutes

After the eye(s) has been irrigated, seek medical attention as soon as possible.

Alkaline materials can penetrate deeply and cause serious damage. Examples of alkaline materials are drain cleaners, oven cleaners, and bleach. Look for these words on product labels:

- lye
- sodium hydroxide
- potassium hydroxide
- ammonia
- calcium oxide
- trisodium phosphate
- wood ash

Acids tend to cause more localized tissue damage but can still cause significant injury. Examples of acids are automobile battery fluid, toilet bowl cleaners, and swimming pool acid. Look for these words on product labels:

- sulfuric acid
- hydrochloric acid
- phosphoric acid
- hydrofluoric acid
- oxalic acid

Less dangerous chemicals should be washed out of the eye also. Most of these materials will cause only mild redness, stinging, and temporary swelling involving the conjunctiva (the thin, clear tissue lining the white surface of the eyeball and inner surfaces of the eyelid). Irrigation will lessen the irritation and probably prevent the child from rubbing the eye and aggravating the soreness. Examples of less dangerous chemicals include food, alcohol, and household soaps.

HEAD AND NECK INJURIES

Head injuries during infancy usually are the result of house-hold accidents such as falls (rolling off of a changing table or sofa, for example) or a blow from a flying or falling object (a toy carelessly tossed by an older child, perhaps, or a book pulled off the shelf by an inquisitive crawling/cruising infant). Fortunately, most bumps on the head do not cause significant damage, although many result in a lump or "goose egg," which may alarm parents when it appears soon after the accident. This localized collection of blood, called a *hematoma*, is not unusual because of the abundant blood supply in the scalp. The lump will gradually decrease in size over the next few days, although local discoloration may persist for weeks.

TREATMENT
- Typically he will cry for a few minutes after bumping his head. He will need comforting; a cold pack gently applied to the point of impact may help reduce local swelling.
- If he continues to cry or fuss after 10 or 15 minutes, acetaminophen (Tylenol) in a dose appropriate for his size may help. If you have not already done so, you should contact his physician at this point. (See below.)
- You will need to watch his progress over the next 24 to 48 hours because in very rare instances a blow to the head results in bleeding within the skull. This compli-cation is commonly associated with increasing irritability, vomiting, and/or (most important) difficulty arousing the

E
M
E
R
G
E
N
C
Y

infant. Your baby's physician may direct
you to observe his daytime behavior for
possible signs of trouble (see below), and/
or to awaken him when you go to bed and
once again three or four hours later. You
will need to be sure that he can be fully
awakened, that he has normal strength
and movement of arms and legs, and that
he interacts normally with you.

SYMPTOMS   *of more serious injury*

While bumps on the head do not always
need medical attention, you should contact
your child's doctor when this occurs in any
infant younger than twelve months of age.
It is particularly important to do so if one
or more of the following occur:

◆ There is loss of consciousness, even if it
  lasts only a few seconds. An infant who
  remains unconscious for more than a
  few minutes after a head injury should
  be taken immediately to the nearest
  emergency department. If there is any
  possibility of a neck injury, he should
  not be moved until he has been properly
  immobilized using a backboard and
  neck brace provided by an emergency
  transport team.
◆ The infant becomes increasingly difficult
  to arouse.
◆ Crying continues for more than 10
  minutes after the injury.
◆ The baby displays ongoing irritability.

- The infant vomits during the 48 hours after the accident.
- A seizure occurs.
- There is a cut on the head (or elsewhere) that may require suturing.
- Clear or bloody fluid is draining from the nose or ears.
- You have any questions or concerns about the injury or your infant's behavior.

TREATMENT *for more severe head or neck injury*

If your baby appears to have had a more severe head or neck injury, keep him as still as possible, especially his head and neck. Check for loss of consciousness by calling his name or tapping his chest. If he has lost consciousness, check his breathing and pulse as well. If they are absent, start rescue breathing or CPR immediately (see page 312).

If the baby was not unconscious for more than a few seconds and doesn't seem to be in distress, it is probably all right to let him move. However, if you are concerned that he might have hurt his neck, do not move him. A neck injury that might not be immediately apparent could lead to paralysis if he is improperly moved. Call 911 and have medical personnel evaluate and transport him to the hospital using appropriate immobilization techniques.

EMERGENCY

LOSS OF CONSCIOUSNESS

See also **Head and Neck Injuries.**

Loss of consciousness in infants and children may have a
number of causes, including direct trauma to the head, seizures, severe allergic reactions, and accidental or intentional
drug ingestion. **Even if it is brief and appears to resolve
completely, any loss of consciousness in an infant should
be evaluated by a physician.**

TREATMENT   Check breathing and pulse. If they are
              absent, start rescue breathing or CPR
              immediately (see page 312). Any apparent
              loss of consciousness can be confirmed by
              calling the infant's name, gently shaking
              him (unless there is concern about head
              or neck injury), or tapping his chest. An
              unconscious child will not respond.
                  Whenever an infant has lost conscious-
              ness, it is important to consider the possibil-
              ity of a head injury. If there is any evidence
              that this has occurred (for example, bleeding
              or visible swelling), keep the head and neck
              immobilized and call 911 for transport to
              an emergency facility.

NOSEBLEEDS

TREATMENT   Nosebleeds are unusual during infancy.
              If your baby has a nosebleed, follow these
              steps:
                  ◆ Hold the baby over a sink with his head
                    slightly forward to prevent the blood
                    from running down the throat.

- ◆ Apply gentle pressure, pinching the nose near the opening of the nostrils (not high on the bridge of the nose) for five minutes or more.
- ◆ After five minutes slowly remove your fingers. If the nose continues to bleed, repeat for 10 more minutes.
- ◆ If the nose continues to bleed, contact your physician or proceed to the nearest emergency department. Even if you have succeeded in stopping the bleeding, your baby's physician should be notified so that appropriate follow-up can be arranged.

OVEREXPOSURE TO HEAT OR COLD

HYPOTHERMIA

Hypothermia, or low body temperature, results from prolonged unprotected exposure to a cold environment. Immersion in cold water causes much greater loss of body heat than exposure to air the same temperature and thus can cause hypothermia within minutes. (Wearing wet clothes in a cold environment also increases heat loss and the likelihood of hypothermia.) Infants are especially prone to hypothermia.

Our physiological functions, metabolism, and central nervous system can function only within a very narrow temperature range. As the body loses heat, several internal responses attempt to maintain the internal or core temperature as close to 98.6°F (37°C) as possible. Blood flow is diverted to the upper body to preserve heat within the brain, heart, lungs, and other vital organs. The hands, feet, arms, and legs become cold first, but our limbs are designed to tolerate this decrease in temperature fairly well. Shivering (rapid involuntary contractions of muscles) generates heat to preserve core body temperature.

Symptoms	◆ numbness and/or weakness
	◆ lethargy
	◆ sleepiness
	◆ loss of coordination
	◆ inappropriate behavior

Treatment	◆ Move infant to a warm area. If this is not possible, shelter him from the wind, change any wet clothing, and put him in a sleeping bag if one is available. An adult lying in the same sleeping bag may provide additional heat. Give him something warm to drink, if he is able to drink and it is available.
	◆ If symptoms persist, if there is any loss of consciousness, or if there has been an immersion in near-freezing water, take the victim to the nearest emergency room immediately.

FROSTBITE

This freezing injury to skin occurs most often in windy or wet conditions. It typically affects areas of the body that are exposed or have a limited blood supply, such as the nose, ears, fingers, and toes. Frostbitten fingers or toes are usually flushed. If the frostbite is severe, the affected skin will become hard, white or mottled, and numb.

Treatment	As soon as you recognize any change in local skin color (especially in a vulnerable area) after being outdoors, take the following steps:

◆ Bring the baby in from the cold as quickly as possible and remove any wet clothing.

◆ "Thaw" out the frostbitten part of the body by immersing it in warm (but not hot) water or applying warm moist compresses to it. (Use a bathtub if multiple areas are involved.) Do not use a heat lamp or electric heater, which might overheat and actually burn frostbitten skin.

◆ Numbness will usually disappear, and the normal skin color will return within a half hour. Pain may be felt as the affected areas rewarm; acetaminophen may be given if needed.

◆ Keep the rest of your child's body comfortable with blankets or other warm clothing.

◆ Do not massage or rub snow on frostbitten areas of the body—this can cause damage to local tissue.

◆ If skin color and sensation are not normal within 20 to 30 minutes or if blisters develop in the frostbitten areas, seek medical attention.

PREVENTION

The primary means of preventing hypothermia or frostbite is to dress your baby appropriately for cold weather. Additional helps include the following:

◆ Because a significant amount of heat is lost from the surface of the head and because ears and fingers are particularly vulnerable to frostbite, make sure your baby's head and ears are covered and that she has mittens on whenever she's outdoors in cold weather.

302 No Fear Guide for First Time Parents

♦ Multiple layers of clothing help prevent loss of body heat. Since wet clothing significantly increases heat loss, the outermost layer should be waterproof.

HYPERTHERMIA

Hyperthermia is an increase in the internal or core body temperature resulting from circumstances such as strenuous exercise or exposure to high environmental temperatures. During infancy, the latter situation—for example, an infant left in a hot, enclosed car—is the most common scenario for hyperthermia. The body responds to this heat stress with mechanisms designed to maintain core temperature close to 98.6°F (37°C). The respiratory rate will increase (which causes heat to be lost from the lungs), and sweat will evaporate from the skin (which helps the body cool).

If the environmental temperature is higher than body temperature, the only way heat can be lost from the body is through evaporation. In high humidity conditions sweat does not readily evaporate, thus slowing the cooling process even more. Dehydration increases the risk of hyperthermia, as do certain medications that may reduce the body's ability to sweat.

Hyperthermia can take the following forms.

HEATSTROKE

This is the most severe form of hyperthermia, arising from extremes of temperature and (in older children) very strenuous exercise. The body temperature often climbs above 105°F, sometimes with an absence of sweating.

SYMPTOMS	♦ confusion ♦ impaired coordination ♦ loss of consciousness

TREATMENT   Heatstroke is a medical emergency that
            should be treated immediately.

            ◆ Remove the infant's clothing.
            ◆ Move him to a cooler environment.
            ◆ Blow air on him with a fan while spraying
              him with a mist of water.
            ◆ Give him liquids. (If the baby cannot take
              enough liquid by mouth, he will need
              intravenous fluids.)
            ◆ Apply cold packs to the groin or the
              armpits.
            ◆ Transport to an emergency department
              or call 911 for assistance.

HEAT EXHAUSTION

Milder than heatstroke; the body temperature may or may
not be elevated.

SYMPTOMS   ◆ nausea
            ◆ vomiting
            ◆ fatigue/listlessness
            ◆ headache (in a baby, manifested by crying
              and irritability)

TREATMENT   Heat exhaustion can progress to heatstroke
            if not treated properly, but symptoms
            should resolve within one hour with proper
            treatment. Follow the same treatment as
            given above for heatstroke (including
            medical attention).

POISONING

SYMPTOMS   Indications that your child has swallowed
a toxic substance (or an overdose of
medication) could include the following:

- sudden illness for no apparent reason
- unusual behavior
- unusual liquids, stains, or powder on the
  skin, clothing, or around the mouth
- weakness, stupor, confusion, or coma
- a change in the normal size of the pupils
- rapid heart rate
- fever, headache (in a baby, manifested
  by crying and irritability)
- rash or changes in skin color (blue,
  flushed, or pale)
- coughing or difficulty breathing—with or
  without increased noise during breathing
- nausea, vomiting, diarrhea or abdominal
  pain or cramping (manifested by crying)
- twitching muscles
- excessive saliva
- loss of appetite
- abnormal breath odor

TREATMENT   • Check the ABCs—airway, breathing, and
circulation—and begin rescue breathing
or CPR if necessary (see page 312). If
CPR has been initiated, have someone
call 911. (If you are alone, call 911 after
you have carried out CPR for approximately one minute.)
- If CPR is not needed, call your baby's
  physician, the nearest emergency room,

or a local poison-control center. If you can't find a number for a poison-control center, call 1-212-POISONS.

♦ If the baby is having seizures, protect him from injury (see *Seizures,* page 306).

♦ If the infant vomits, try to protect the airway. Position him so that whatever is vomited will exit away from the mouth and not accidentally be inhaled into the airway. If necessary, gently remove any remaining material from his mouth.

♦ If the exposure was a skin contamination, remove all contaminated clothing and wash skin, hair, and nails.

♦ If he has been exposed to fumes, remove him from the area in which the fumes are present.

♦ If the material went into the eye, irrigate it thoroughly with tap water (see *Chemicals in the Eye,* page 293).

♦ Take the substance and its container with you to the doctor's office or emergency room and be prepared to answer some questions: Where was the baby? What and how much was ingested? When did symptoms (if any) begin? Did symptoms begin gradually or abruptly? What treatment was done at home and when?

♦ DO NOT wait for dramatic signs of illness before seeking medical assistance.

♦ DO NOT give anything as an antidote or attempt to neutralize a poison unless you have been told to do so by a physician or poison-control center.

EMERGENCY

- DO NOT attempt to give the baby anything by mouth if he is unconscious.
- DO NOT induce vomiting unless directed to do so by a physician or a poison-control center.
- DO NOT rely on the label of a medication or other substance to tell you whether or not it is potentially hazardous.

SEIZURES

A seizure is a sudden abnormal surge of electrical activity in the brain.

SYMPTOMS

These vary according to the type of seizure. A seizure may manifest as one or more subtle lapses in consciousness; twitching or jerking of one or more arms or legs; eye-rolling or other sudden eye movements; or a full-blown convulsion, with generalized and uncontrolled shaking of the entire body.

TREATMENT

If your child is having a generalized seizure,

- Gently lay him on a soft surface such as a bed or carpet, away from any hard objects. Position the head to the side so that any saliva (or any material that comes up if he vomits) can drain from the mouth.
- If his mouth is empty, don't put a finger, stick, or spoon in it because this may cause him to vomit. If he has anything in his mouth, gently remove it with your finger. Do not try to pour a liquid into his mouth.

- ◆ Since he cannot swallow his tongue, don't try to grab it with your fingers.
- ◆ Don't restrain the infant.
- ◆ Do not immerse him in a tub of water, even if he has a fever.
- ◆ If you can, time the seizure's length and carefully observe your child's movements during the episode.
- ◆ If the seizure lasts for more than five minutes, call 911 for emergency medical assistance. Even if the seizure ends before help arrives, allow the paramedics to assess your child.
- ◆ If the seizure ends within five minutes, call your child's physician immediately for further advice.

If your baby manifests abnormal movements which might represent a seizure, it is important to contact her physician immediately for further advice. *This is particularly important if your infant is younger than three months of age.*

Because it may be difficult to distinguish a seizure from other behaviors in infants and young children such as a shuddering episode or a breath-holding spell, it is very important to pay close attention (as distracted or upset as you may be) so that you can describe to the doctor what happened in as much detail as possible. Did the episode begin gradually or suddenly? Was the whole body, or only a limited area (such as a twitching arm or leg) involved? How long did it last? Did the baby seem to lose consciousness? If so, how quickly did he return to normal? Was he ill at the time, or was there any injury (such as a blow to the head) prior to the episode? The medical evaluation which follows will depend on a number of factors, including the history of the episode, the infant's age, and his appearance on physical examination. Do not be alarmed if your baby's physician recommends a number of tests in order to determine what might have occurred—especially if he is younger than three months of age.

WOUNDS AND WOUND CARE

BRUISES AND HEMATOMAS

Bruises (also called contusions) usually form a bluish discoloration at the site of the injury and fade from blue to green to yellow over one to two weeks.

A hematoma (goose egg) is a collection of blood and swelling in the skin or just underneath it. Depending upon its size and location, this swelling will go down in one to ten days.

TREATMENT   Normally no specific treatment is necessary. However, if a baby is irritable or unwilling to move an arm or leg that is bruised, call her physician for further evaluation. It is also important to contact her doctor if she develops bruises for no apparent reason, or if you notice bruises that appeared while she was in someone else's care.

ABRASIONS

Abrasions (or scrapes) are broad areas of superficial skin damage; they seldom result in any deep underlying damage and rarely leave a significant scar. They heal quickly and usually do not become infected. While they are not unusual among toddlers and older children as they fall while running and playing, abrasions would not be expected during infancy unless the baby was accidentally dropped or rolled off of a surface such as a changing table. Therefore, depending on the circumstances, an infant with a scrape may need to be checked for other injuries.

TREATMENT
- Cleanse the wound gently with warm soapy water to remove any dirt and debris. A painless antiseptic such as hydrogen peroxide can help cleanse an abrasion.
- Apply an antibiotic ointment such as a neomycin-polysporin mixture (Neosporin) or one prescribed by your baby's physician. Cover with a nonstick wound dressing to keep it clean.
- Change the dressing once or twice daily until the wound is no longer moist and sensitive.
- Depending on the circumstances, an infant with a scrape may need to be checked by his physician for other injuries.

LACERATIONS

A laceration can range from a minimal break in the skin surface, requiring only a brief cleansing and a day or two of a simple dressing, to a long, gaping wound requiring extensive repair. A deep laceration may damage tendons, nerves, joints, or other underlying tissues. It may also contain dirt or other foreign material that can lead to infection. Because of these potential complications, most wounds deeper or wider than 1 or 2 mm should be examined by a physician to determine appropriate treatment.

TREATMENT   First aid for lacerations that might require sutures (stitches) includes the following:

- Apply steady pressure with clean gauze or washcloth to stop bleeding.
- Keep the area clean.
- Rinse with clean water if available.
- Keep covered with a sterile bandage, or at least a clean cloth, until the wound can be examined by a medical professional.
- A laceration should be closed within 24 hours. The sooner the wound is treated, the less likely it will become infected. If a laceration is not sutured, the consequences are usually not serious, but healing could take longer and the resulting scar is likely to be wider or more prominent.
- Sometimes lacerations are deep enough to involve injury to a nerve or tendon. For this reason, any laceration that looks deep at all should be examined and cleaned by your child's physician or another medical professional.

WHEN SUTURES ARE NOT USED

With some contaminated lacerations or certain types of animal or human bites, the physician may not use sutures because closing the wound could increase the risk of infection. In such cases the wound will be left open, but it will gradually heal as the body's repair processes close the defect.

CONCERNS ABOUT TETANUS

Any laceration, puncture, bite, abrasion, or burn should prompt a review of a child's tetanus immunization status. Tetanus is a potential threat following any wound, but it is a greater concern following punctures or contaminated wounds. If a child is on schedule for his or her immunizations or is fully immunized, no tetanus update will be needed. Otherwise a tetanus booster should be given.

SIGNS OF INFECTION

Signs and symptoms of infection include local pain, swelling, and redness, which may spread over a large area around the wound. There may also be fever. Inflammation of local lymph channels may form a red streak that extends away from the wound. Some bacteria cause the production of discolored drainage (or pus). If a wound appears to be developing an infection, show it to a physician. Mild heat on the affected area, rest, elevation of the affected area (if an arm or leg), and antibiotics will most likely be recommended.

THE IMPORTANCE OF FOLLOW-UP

Be sure to obtain specific wound-care instructions before leaving the office or emergency facility. In general, if sutures or sterile strips have been used, the wound should be kept dry for a few days. This will mean that the child should not go swimming or soak the wounds while bathing. In some cases, the physician may instruct you to clean the wound and apply fresh dressings. He or she should also tell you when the strips or bandages should be removed. A follow-up appointment is usually required when stitches need to be removed.

Cardiopulmonary Resuscitation (CPR) and Choking Emergencies

It is highly recommended that parents take a Red Cross class in first aid and cardiopulmonary resuscitation (CPR), and then take a refresher class every two years. For those who have completed this training, the following material is a review of the basic steps for assisting a choking victim and for performing CPR.

CARDIOPULMONARY RESUSCITATION (CPR): NEWBORN TO ONE YEAR

1. Check to see if the baby is conscious.
   - Tap his shoulder, or give his body a gentle shake.
   - Do not shake his head and neck.

2. If there is no response, shout for help.
   - As soon as someone is available, have him or her call 911.

3. Roll the baby onto his back if he is not in that position already.
   - Support his head and neck, keeping them in a straight line with his back.
   - Lay the baby on a firm surface.

4. Check to see if he is breathing.
   - Gently tilt his head back and lift his chin to open the airway.
   - Put your head near the infant's mouth and nose.
   - For 3 to 5 seconds, look, listen, and feel for breathing.

(a) Is the chest rising?
(b) Can you hear breathing sounds?
(c) Can you feel air moving against your face?

5. If you can't see, hear, or feel the infant breathing, you must immediately begin breathing for him (rescue breathing).
   - With your lips make a tight seal around the baby's nose and mouth.
   - Give 2 slow breaths.
   (a) Breathe into the infant for about 1 to 1½ seconds, watching for the chest to rise.
   (b) Pause to let the air flow out, and then give another breath.

6. Check his pulse.
   - With one hand, keep the baby's head tilted back.
   - With your other hand, check for a pulse.
   (a) Feel for 5 seconds on the inside of the baby's upper arm, between the elbow and shoulder. Also listen for a heartbeat by placing your ear next to the baby's chest.
   - If you feel a pulse but he is not breathing:
   (a) Give one breath every 3 seconds.
   (b) Recheck the pulse every 20 breaths (about once per minute).
   (c) Continue breathing for the infant until
     —he begins to breathe without help, or
     —another rescuer takes over, or
     —you do not feel a pulse.

7. If there is no pulse or heartbeat, begin CPR.

Have someone call 911 for help, if this has not been done already.

8. Position your fingers on the baby's chest.
   - With one hand, keep the baby's head tilted back.
   - Place the index finger of your other hand on the center of the breastbone, just below the level of the nipples.
   - Place your next 2 fingers (the middle and ring fingers) right next to your index finger (slightly farther down the baby's breastbone). Then lift your index finger.

9. Compress the baby's chest using your 2 fingers.
   - Push the breastbone straight down to 1 inch.
   - Give 5 compressions over about 3 seconds.

10. After you have given 5 compressions, give 1 full breath.
    - With your lips make a tight seal around the baby's nose and mouth.
    - Give 1 full breath for 1 to 1 1/2 seconds.
    - Check the pulse.

If there is no pulse:

11. Repeat the cycle of 5 compressions and 1 breath for 10 cycles.
    - After 10 cycles (about 1 minute), check for a pulse.
    - If there is no pulse, continue CPR.
    - If a pulse is present, check for breathing.
      (a) Carry out rescue breathing if the baby is not breathing.
    - Continue CPR or rescue breathing until
      (a) the baby is breathing and has a pulse, or
      (b) another rescuer takes over.

CHOKING EMERGENCIES: NEWBORN TO ONE YEAR

1. Determine if the baby is choking.
   - If there is forceful coughing or the baby can cry, do not interfere.
   - If he is unable to cry, cough, or breathe or if he is coughing very weakly, have someone call 911 and take immediate action (step 2 and following).

2. Position the baby face down on your forearm.
   - Support the baby's head and jaw as you turn his face down.
   - Position him so that his head is lower than his chest.

3. Give 5 back blows.
   - Use the heel of your free hand.
   - Strike forcefully between his shoulder blades.

4. Turn the baby onto his back.
   - Support the baby's head and jaw as you roll him over.
   - Rest his back on your thigh.

5. Give 5 thrusts to the chest.
   - Place 2 fingers in the center of his breastbone (just below the level of the nipples).
   - Thrust downward quickly about $\frac{1}{3}$ to $\frac{1}{2}$ the depth of the chest.

6. Repeat steps 2 through 5.
   - Turn the baby face down.
   - Give 5 back blows.
   - Turn the baby on his back.
   - Give 5 chest thrusts.

7. Repeat this sequence until the baby begins to cough or breathe, or until he coughs up the object.

If the baby is unconscious:

8. Have someone call 911 for help, if this has not been done already.

9. Roll the baby onto his back.
   - Support his head and neck, keeping them in a straight line with his back.
   - Lay the baby on a firm surface.

10. Clear any material from the baby's mouth.
    - Use the fingers and thumb of one hand to grasp and lift the baby's lower jaw and tongue.
    - Use the little finger of your other hand to sweep the object or food out.
      (a) **Be careful not to push any object or food farther down.**

11. Check to see if he is breathing.
    - Gently tilt his head back and lift his chin to open the airway.
    - Put your head near the infant's mouth and nose.
    - For 3 to 5 seconds, look, listen, and feel for breathing.
      (a) Is the chest rising?
      (b) Can you hear breathing sounds?
      (c) Can you feel air moving against your face?

12. If you can't see, hear, or feel the infant breathing, you must immediately begin breathing for him (rescue breathing).
    - With your lips make a tight seal around the baby's nose and mouth.
    - Give 2 slow breaths.
      (a) Breathe into the infant for about 1 to $1\frac{1}{2}$ seconds, watching for the chest to rise.

(b) Pause to let the air flow out, and then give
another breath.

If the breaths will not go in:

13. Tilt the head farther back, lift the chin, and try again.

If the breaths still will not go in, the airway is probably blocked.

14. Repeat the sequence of back blows and chest thrusts
until the baby is breathing on his own or you are able
to inflate his lungs.
 • Turn the baby face down.
 • Give 5 back blows.
 • Turn the baby on his back.
 • Give 5 chest thrusts.
 • Check the mouth for any object or food. If you see
an object, remove it. DO NOT perform a blind
finger sweep.
 • Tilt the head back.
 • Attempt to give a breath. If the chest does not rise,
re-tilt the head and attempt ventilation again.
 • Continue this cycle until the object is expelled or
advanced care arrives.

15. Once you are getting air into the victim, check for
breathing and pulse. (See CPR, page 312.)
 • If he is not breathing, begin rescue breathing.
(See CPR, page 312.)
 • If he does not have a pulse, begin CPR. (See CPR,
page 312.)

Safety—Indoors and Out

HOME SAFETY: INDOORS

- Never step away when your baby is on a high surface such as a changing table or countertop.
- Keep the sides of a baby's crib raised.
- If an infant seat is used outside the car, place it on the floor.
- Avoid infant walkers.
- Install safety gates (not accordion-style) to guard stairways.
- Lock doors to dangerous areas such as the basement and garage.
- Check the stability of drawers, tall furniture, and lamps before a baby becomes mobile.
- Remove tablecloths that might be within the reach of a toddler.
- Make sure any windows above the first floor of a multistory house are closed or have screens or guards that cannot be pushed out.
- Don't underestimate the climbing ability of a toddler.
- Remove or pad low furniture with sharp corners, such as coffee tables, in your child's living area.
- Place safety latches on all drawers and cupboards that are off-limits.
- Move anything dangerous—cleaning products; plumbing, gardening, painting, refinishing, and agricultural chemicals and supplies; knives or other sharp utensils; and medicines—to high cabinets that are latched.
- Make knives off-limits to a child until he is old enough to learn (and demonstrate) how to use them correctly.

- Put covers on unused electrical outlets.
- Keep electrical cords out of the reach of children.
- Remove all poisonous plants from the home.
- Put the number of the nearest poison center on all phones. Call if a baby puts something in his mouth that might be poisonous.
- Buy syrup of ipecac, but use only if directed to do so.
- Purchase all medicines in containers with safety caps.
- Do not transfer toxic substances to bottles, glasses, or jars, especially if those containers originally contained familiar liquids for drinking (such as juice).
- When leaving your baby with a sitter, leave emergency phone numbers, a permission slip for emergency care, and insurance information. (Or designate whom the sitter should call.) Make certain the sitter knows the address and phone number of your home, in case she needs to provide this information to emergency personnel.

FIRE AND BURN PREVENTION

- Never eat, drink, or carry anything hot near or while holding a baby or a small child.
- Don't cook when holding your baby. Use a playpen, high chair, or crib as a safety area for infants while you are preparing food.
- Get into the habit of using the rear burners on your stove, and keeping the pan handles out of reach.
- Check formula, food, and drink temperatures carefully.
- Keep hot appliances and cords out of the reach of children.
- Install and maintain smoke detectors in accordance

with fire regulations in your area. If they are not wired directly into your home's electrical system, check smoke detectors monthly and replace batteries annually.

- Provide nonflammable barriers around heating surfaces and fireplaces.
- Have your heating system checked annually.
- If there are one or more tobacco smokers in the family, they should not be allowed to smoke inside the home.
- Keep matches and lighters out of the reach of children.
- Have a working fire extinguisher near the kitchen, but out of reach of children.

SMOKE DETECTORS

Residential fires kill about 5,000 people every year in the United States, and the majority of these fatalities result not from burn injuries but from inhalation of smoke and toxic gases. Death usually occurs at night, when the victim is sleeping. Properly installed and maintained home smoke detectors could prevent many of these deaths.

Smoke detectors are considered the best and least expensive early-warning systems because they can alert people in a home *before* the fire ignites, *before* the concentration of smoke reaches a dangerous level, or *before* a fire becomes extremely intense. The risk of dying from a fire-related incident is twice as high in a home without functioning smoke detectors as in a home with them.

Smoke detectors can be wired directly into a home's electrical system, or they may be battery powered, in which case fresh batteries should be installed at least once a year. Each smoke detector should be tested regularly in accordance with the manufacturer's recommendations to ensure it is operating properly.

At least one detector should be installed on each floor of a multistory home, preferably near a bedroom so that sleeping residents will be given early warning in the event of a fire. Local fire regulations and/or building codes may specify that more smoke detectors must be installed for a particular home's floor plan.

WATER AND TUB SAFETY

- Turn down your water heater to 120°F or less.
- Make sure that an adult—not another child—bathes a baby.
- Remain in the room during every second of a child's bath. Have everything you'll need available at the tub before you start.
- Install strips with a roughened surface or lay a rubber mat in the bathtub to prevent slips and falls.
- Provide a barrier around any pool or spa. This should consist of a tall, hard-to-climb fence (which can be locked) extending around all four sides of a pool or an approved pool or spa cover.
- Do not leave buckets filled with water in any area where a toddler might play.
- Never take the baby into fast-moving water such as a creek, river, or canal.
- Never leave your child unsupervised when he is in, on, or around water.
- Keep rescue equipment at the waterside, and take CPR training.

FIREARMS

- Any guns kept in the home should be unloaded and

locked up, with ammunition locked in a separate location.

♦ Keeping a handgun for protection is dangerous to your family.

♦ Non-gunpowder firearms (BB or pellet guns) should not be considered toys and are not recommended for children.

HOME SAFETY: OUTDOORS

♦ Before your baby becomes mobile, take an infant's-level survey of any area he might reach. Once he becomes a skilled crawler, he'll be able to move quite quickly while your attention is diverted.

♦ If you have a swimming pool, make sure that a childproof fence surrounds it. (Some states require this safety barrier by law.) If your yard contains a spa, it should be securely covered when not in use.

♦ Check the lawn for mushrooms—if you are not absolutely certain that they are nontoxic, get rid of them because anything a young child finds will likely go straight into his mouth.

♦ Make sure that potentially hazardous items such as garden tools, insecticides, or fertilizer are not accessible to children.

♦ Don't forget to apply sunscreen with a sun protection factor (SPF) rating of 15 or more if your family is going to be outdoors for any length of time, especially between the hours of 10 A.M. and 3 P.M.—even on a hazy or overcast day. This is particularly important at higher altitudes or around lakes and seashores where the sun's ultraviolet light (which provokes the burn) can reflect off of water and sand. Special caution is needed for infants, because *a baby's skin can become*

sunburned *after as little as 15 minutes of direct exposure.*
Sunscreens containing PABA shouldn't be used on a
baby's skin before six months of age. If you take your
baby outdoors for any length of time, keep him in the
shade or use an umbrella, and make sure that her skin
is covered with appropriate clothing (including a hat
or bonnet) if some sun exposure is unavoidable.

WEATHER SAFETY
- Dress your child appropriately for the outing,
  allowing for adjustments if the weather changes.
- Carry rain gear in your car.
- Apply sunblock (SPF 15 to 45, depending on skin
  type) before you and your baby go outside.
- Take and use hats and sunglasses.

MOTOR VEHICLE SAFETY

SEAT BELTS AND CAR SEATS
Over the last 20 years, widespread use of seat belts has led to
a steady reduction in traffic fatalities. Proper use of seat belts
and car seats decreases the risk of serious injury or death by
as much as 50 percent. But in the United States, the leading
cause of death in people under age thirty-five continues to
be motor-vehicle-related injuries. Most of these individuals
were not properly restrained by seat belts or car seats.

SAFETY ON THE ROAD
- Parents and children should wear their seat belts.
  *Do not start the car until everyone is secured in an
  infant or child seat or properly belted.*
- *Never hold a child in your lap when you are riding
  in a car.*

EMERGENCY

- A child under twelve should never be placed in the front seat of an automobile with a passenger-side air bag because deployment of the bag can cause fatal injuries in a young passenger—even during a minor accident.
- For children under 40 pounds (18 kg), use a car safety seat approved for your child's age and weight in accordance with the manufacturer's directions. (Make sure you have a safety seat for your infant's first important ride home from the hospital.) *The seat should be secured in the rear seat of the vehicle.* For an infant who weighs less than 20 pounds (9 kg), the seat should face backwards. Buy or rent the next size up as your child grows larger.
- Toddlers 40 to 60 pounds should be properly secured in a booster seat.
- When the child reaches 60 pounds, lap and shoulder belts should be used. The lap belt should be low and tight across the pelvis, not the abdomen. The shoulder harness should be placed snugly over the collarbone and breastbone, not the shoulder.
- Never leave your child unattended in a car.
- Never transport a child in a cargo area that is not properly equipped to carry passengers (specifically, the back of a station wagon, van, or pickup truck).

Index